PRIVACY, LAW, AND PUBLIC POLICY

PRIVACY, LAW, AND PUBLIC POLICY

David M. O'Brien

Foreword by
C. Herman Pritchett

PRAEGER

PRAEGER SPECIAL STUDIES • PRAEGER SCIENTIFIC

Library of Congress Cataloging in Publication Data

O'Brien, David M
  Privacy, law, and public policy.

  Bibliography: p.
  Includes indexes.
  1. Privacy, Right of--United States. 2. Public
policy (Law)--United States. 3. Freedom of infor-
mation--United States. I. Title.
KF1262.025   342'.73'085   79-14131

ISBN 0-03-050406-6

Published in 1979 by Praeger Publishers
A Division of Holt, Rinehart and Winston/CBS, Inc.
383 Madison Avenue, New York, New York 10017 U.S.A.

9 038 987654321

Printed in the United States of America

FOR
MY PARENTS

Foreword by
C. Herman Pritchett

Privacy is a confusing and complicated idea. It is a primary value of an open society, and it is still possible, several centuries later, to quicken the pulse by quoting William Pitt's stirring peroration denying to the king of England the right to cross the threshold of the "ruined tenement" of the poorest subject in his kingdom. The English common law protected against eavesdropping as well as trespassing and other violations of property rights. Abuse of general search warrants, or writs of assistance, by English authorities in the American colonies led to adoption of the Fourth Amendment subjecting searches and seizures to warrant requirements, while the Fifth Amendment ban on self-incrimination stemmed from an even deeper conception of individual integrity.

A famous 1886 decision of the Supreme Court, Boyd v. United States, initiated a broad interpretation of the Fourth and Fifth Amendments in the context of criminal prosecutions. But in 1890 an influential Harvard Law Review article by Samuel Warren and Louis D. Brandeis freed the privacy concept from its propertied and criminal procedure history and defined it as a broader "right to be let alone." Not until 75 years later did the Supreme Court translate this right into constitutional terms. Then, in Griswold v. Connecticut (1965), Justice Douglas, in a classic exercise of judicial activism, found a right to privacy in the "penumbras" of the First, Third, Fourth, Fifth, and Ninth Amendments, while two of his colleagues located it more simply in the due process clause of the Fourteenth Amendment.

The threat to privacy in the Griswold case was criminal prosecution for use of contraceptives, but there were other contemporaneous invocations of the right to privacy, particularly against collection of personal information in computers and data banks that make complete life histories available to anyone with access to a computer terminal. The resulting pressures led most of the states as well as Congress to pass legislation protecting privacy in very broad terms. For example, the people of California adopted the following constitutional amendment in 1974, the same year that Congress passed a federal Privacy Act:

> All people are by nature free and independent, and have certain inalienable rights, among which are those of enjoying and defending life and liberty; acquiring, possessing, and protecting property; and pursuing and obtaining safety, and happiness, and privacy.

But it soon became obvious that the privacy issue had not been thought through, and that privacy is one of those good things that it is possible to have too much of. Oregon, for example, passed a privacy law forbidding disclosure of arrests, indictments, convictions, sentences, and prison releases. Immediately, arrested individuals began piling up in jails because officials could not tell relatives and friends that they had been arrested and needed bail. Within four days the Oregon legislature repealed the statute. The U.S. Embassy in Moscow thought that the federal privacy law forbade release of the name of a U.S. citizen who died in a fall from a Moscow hotel. The California Supreme Court reversed the conviction of a drug peddler because a telephone lineman who had legally overheard the crime being planned was forbidden by the state privacy act from telling anyone about it.

One of the principal responsibilities of the Supreme Court, particularly since 1965, has been to establish the constitutional basis for privacy claims and the necessary limits of those claims. The Court's decisions have attracted an extraordinary amount of interest, not only in law reviews and scholarly journals but in public prints and the media. What David O'Brien's noteworthy study contributes to this ongoing dialogue is, first of all, an informed and exhaustive analysis of these decisions. In four tightly packed and closely reasoned chapters, he presents the privacy doctrines that the Court has drawn from the First, Fourth, Fifth, and Ninth Amendments. It is of necessity a complex story, from the pioneering defense of privacy in Boyd to the retrenchments of the Burger Court.

Many others have done this kind of analysis, though few with O'Brien's sharpness and grasp. But constitutional analysis is not his sole, and perhaps not even his major, contribution. His real goal is to straighten out our thinking about privacy, and in a brilliant introductory chapter he examines the different conceptions of privacy. He finds shortcomings in the prevailing understandings that lead him to propose an alternative definition of privacy "as an existential condition of limited access to an individual's experiences and engagements." It is important, he asserts, to distinguish between privacy and the right to privacy. For, he says, "not every intrusion upon or disclosure of personal affairs gives rise to a primary interest of sufficient weight to warrant legal safeguards." Moreover, too much emphasis on the legal right to privacy narrows the focus of privacy definitions and neglects nonlegal safeguards of privacy.

In his concluding chapters O'Brien turns to assessments and policy recommendations, particularly on the subject of informational privacy. Partly because of recent unhelpful Supreme Court decisions, an imbalance has developed between individuals and record-keeping institutions. The impact of computer technology on citizens' lives continually increases. The conflict between personal privacy and the public's right to know sharpens. The Freedom of Information Act, passed in 1966, had to be countered by the Privacy Act of 1974, which the book discusses at length. The goals of the two acts are at least to some degree irreconcilable, but the author invents a model of information flow to illuminate, if not to reconcile, the conflict between privacy and access.

Privacy claims are increasingly the subject of litigation, legislation, and political concern. The author of this book has made a masterful contribution toward an understanding of privacy as a political ideal and a practical problem.

Preface

We are discussing no trivial matter, but how men ought
to live.

> Plato
> The Republic, Book 1

In the twentieth century, individual privacy has emerged as a
complex political ideal with wide symbolic appeal. Public opinion
nevertheless diverges widely over the meaning of privacy and its importance to political life. There exists little agreement as to a constitutional right of privacy and the extent to which law and public policies should promote and safeguard individuals' privacy interests. Indeed, the political ideal of privacy often appears evanescent, almost
always renders discussions of its legal protection controversial, and
at times leads into paradox.

No small part of the difficulties in safeguarding privacy arises
because of inadequate conceptualization of its nature and legal protection. For example, all too frequently the concept of privacy is collapsed with those of freedom, liberty, and rights; hence, the distinction between the concept of privacy itself and the right of privacy remains obscure. Politically, it matters a great deal whether privacy
is understood in terms of only those claims that have been recognized
as legally enforceable, or whether privacy is comprehended as a fundamentally nonlegal concept, which may or may not be accorded legal
status. Blurring the concept of privacy with that of a right of privacy
unduly circumscribes legal recognition of privacy claims and narrows
discussions of the extent to which public policies should protect individuals' privacy interests. Without a theory of privacy independent
from, albeit interrelated with, a theory of rights, it is difficult—if not
impossible—to dispel the paradox of justifying a political ideal and a
right of privacy on the basis of a written Constitution that does not expressly guarantee personal privacy.

This book undertakes an analysis of the contours, as defined by
constitutional law and public policy, of the political ideal of privacy.
Part I, Privacy as a Political Value, examines competing conceptuali-
zations of privacy and the right of privacy in order to clarify the political ideal of privacy.

Part II, Privacy and the Constitution, focuses on the political
ideal of privacy embedded within the legal parchment of the Constitution and Bill of Rights and elaborated within the practice of rights in

the United States by judicially enforced claims to protected privacy. While the developing constitutional law of privacy is placed within a historical perspective, principal attention is given to judicial construction of constitutionally protected privacy and application of the Bill of Rights. More specifically, Chapters 2 and 3 examine constitutional interpretation establishing Fourth Amendment- and Fifth Amendment-protected privacy. Chapter 4 explores the developing constitutional claims of privacy with regard to First Amendment freedoms. Chapter 5 concludes the discussion of constitutionally protected privacy by examining judicial reliance on the Ninth and Fourteenth Amendments in validating privacy claims and fashioning a constitutional right of privacy.

Part III, Privacy and Public Policy, discusses personal privacy as an issue of contemporary public policy. Privacy emerged in the 1970s as an issue of public policy partly because of the impact of information technology on government operations and partly because of the failure of constitutional interpretation to conceptualize adequately, and hence protect, interests in personal information collected, maintained, and utilized by the government. Chapter 6 assesses the development of and prospects for public policies designed to secure and safeguard privacy interests in our information-oriented society. Chapter 7 concludes with a reconsideration of the political ideal of privacy and the contours of protected privacy as shaped by constitutional law and public policy.

Because privacy so intimately and inwardly touches individuals' lives, hopefully this study will contribute to our understanding of privacy and the role of law and public policy in safeguarding individuals' privacy interests. While the book aims at a systematic discussion of the conceptual, constitutional, and public policy issues of personal privacy, it does not aim at an exhaustive coverage of the field. The book does not treat adequately three important dimensions: privacy, law, and public policy. My analysis of privacy shows that in crucial respects social conditions promote and maintain individual privacy, yet the nature of and extent to which nonlegal safeguards ensure personal privacy remain largely unexplored. Discussion of the legal recognition and protection of privacy, moreover, is confined to the area of constitutional law and, consequently, neglects significant developments in state law. Similarly, my treatment of privacy-protecting policies emphasizes federal legislation—principally, the Privacy Act of 1974—at the cost of treating only tangentially policies designed to safeguard particular kinds of privacy interests—interests, for example, in student, criminal, or health records—and neglecting related developments in state legislation and the private sector. Although these areas are important and require further research, they presuppose a discussion of the nature of privacy and of the right of privacy as recognized in constitutional law and basic federal policy.

For whatever may be useful in my study, I remain indebted to my teachers, C. Herman Pritchett, John E. Moore, and Gordon E. Baker. I am also obligated to Professors Stanley V. Anderson and Herbert Fingarette for their encouragement and critical comments that proved invaluable. A National Endowment for the Humanities grant permitted me to attend a summer seminar and rework portions of my analysis, for which I am grateful to the National Endowment for the Humanities and to Professor Loren Beth, sponsor of the seminar. Finally, portions of Chapters 1, 2, and 3 previously appeared in the Administrative Law Review, the New England Law Review, and the Notre Dame Lawyer, respectively, and, although in each case changes have been made, I appreciate permission to use sections here. While I am deeply indebted to my friends at the University of California, Santa Barbara, I must inevitably assume responsibility for this book.

Contents

PART I

PRIVACY AS A
POLITICAL VALUE

1

Privacy as a Concept
and a Political Ideal

Privacy is a special kind of independence, which can be
understood as an attempt to secure autonomy in at least
a few personal and spiritual concerns, if necessary in defiance of all the pressures of modern society. It is an attempt, that is to say, to do more than maintain a posture
of self-respecting independence toward other men; it seeks
to erect an unbreachable wall of dignity and reserve against
the entire world.

> Clinton Rossiter
> "The Free Man in the Free Society,"
> The Essentials of Freedom

Recent legislative and judicial recognition of the significance of
individual privacy and a right to personal privacy are understandable
from several perspectives: historical changes and advanced technology, notably in computerization, in the last 30 years; recent acknowledgment of the psychological and sociological need for individuals to
maintain minimal conditions of privacy for self-development; and the
U.S. heritage of limited government and ideological commitment to individualism in the United States. Indeed, the growing controversy over
privacy safeguards appears in the broadest political perspective as
nothing less than a concern for freedom from governmental intrusion
into citizens' lives.

Our nation's current preoccupation with privacy protection, however, is both unique and paradoxical: unique among the nations of the
world in terms of the number of judicial decisions and legislation relating to personal privacy, and paradoxical because, even though the
Constitution does not guarantee a right of privacy, the Supreme Court
in 1965 constitutionally denominated a right of privacy as "a fundamen-

3

tally personal right emanating from the totality of the Constitutional scheme under which we live."[1] Actually, the legal right of privacy was born out of the dicta and dissent of more than a century of judicial opinion. Prior judicial policies had afforded privacy interests considerable albeit inconsistent protection. Claims of personal privacy had been recognized under the Fourth Amendment's protection against unreasonable searches and seizures and the Fifth Amendment's privilege against self-incrimination. Also, the Supreme Court legitimated privacy interests under the First Amendment in the contexts of freedom of belief, speech, and association, as well as those of freedom from governmental surveillance and public intrusions by the media and possession of obscenity and pornography in one's own home. Individual justices on several occasions also have acknowledged protection of privacy interests under the guarantees of the Third, Ninth, and Fourteenth Amendments. The legal right of privacy therefore emerged as the product of incremental judicial decision making, and the concept of privacy became a salient political issue in the United States.

Nevertheless, the privacy interests that have been protected are so wide-ranging as to suggest that constitutional law and even the concept of privacy itself have no principle, no core meaning; consequently, for many scholars, lawyers, and administrators, protection of privacy appears random, ad hoc, and unprincipled.

No small part of the problems of securing privacy safeguards lies with conceptualizing the nature of privacy. Often conceptual approaches merely consist of lengthy enumerations of privacy-invading conduct or unitary definitions that are imprecise, or too broad, or too narrow.

Conceptual approaches to privacy—though sometimes offered as competing rationales for privacy protection—also cohere in a fundamentally legalistic orientation. To the extent that these approaches cohere they constitute a paradigmatic framework for analyzing privacy. Specifically, four assumptions are made about the concept:

1. Privacy denotes the seclusion or withdrawal of an individual from public affairs.
2. Privacy is voluntary; it is, therefore, basically an aspect of individual freedom and control over personal engagements.
3. Privacy is equated with a right.
4. Privacy is valued for either its intrinsic worth or its instrumental value, but rarely are both of these values considered simultaneously.

These four assumptions are examined in the next two sections; then in the third section, an analysis of privacy based on a different set of presuppositions is offered. The fourth and fifth sections discuss the implications of the two analyses of privacy with regard to a right of privacy and the political ideal of privacy.

SOME DEFINITIONS OF PRIVACY

Initial Analysis by Warren and Brandeis

The assumption that privacy denotes an individual's seclusion or withdrawal from public affairs has been shared by both early proponents of privacy protection and some contemporary psychologists and sociologists. In 1888, noting for the first time "a right to be let alone," Judge Thomas M. Cooley planted the seed for the legal profession's interest in privacy.[2] Two years later Samuel Warren and Louis Brandeis cultivated the notion with the initial analysis of the concept of privacy.[3] Anticipating judicial "recognition of new rights," they argued inductively that common law protected against invasions of privacy, albeit parasitically, in the areas of contract and industrial property. They believed that the expansion of property rights constituted a "recognition of man's spiritual nature." "The principle which protects personal writings and all other personal productions, not against theft and physical appropriation but against publication in any form, is in reality not the principle of private property, but that of an inviolate personality."[4]

The significance of the Warren and Brandeis article resided "not so much in the power of its argument as in the social status it gave to the tort."[5] In fact, what has been particularly unusual about tort invasions in the United States is that Warren's and Brandeis's acknowledgment of privacy interests preceded and led to the development of the tort. As a matter of legal history, the Warren and Brandeis argument was contrived. The concept of privacy as a legal entity was unheard of in the seventeenth century, and eighteenth and nineteenth century case law established no precedents for their argument. In both U.S. and English law a property right was essential to any remedy for unauthorized intrusions upon or invasions of private affairs. Protection of privacy interests was mentioned only in dicta and judicial philosophy, never as precedent.[6]

From an analytical perspective, the Warren and Brandeis interpretation of privacy as a "right to be let alone" that protects man's "inviolate personality" is unsatisfying. Their definition is too imprecise for judicial construction and principled application, let alone incorporation into public policy. Yet, other scholars in the United States, following jurists in the Continental tradition, shared their impulses for a broad unitary definition by including privacy interests in a "right of personality."[7] Today, many psychologists and sociologists are also inclined to similarly broad definitions—of which the following are illustrative:

> A person's feeling that others should be excluded from something which is of concern to him, and also recognition that others have a right to do this.[8]
>
> A value to be oneself: relief from the pressures of the presence of others.[9]
>
> An outcome of a person's wish to withhold from others certain knowledge as to his past and present experience and action and his intention for the future; a desire to be an enigma to others or to control others' perceptions and beliefs about the self.[10]

Such definitions have two common features: the equation of privacy with withdrawal, or the desire to be withdrawn, from public affairs and the assumption that privacy is voluntary and essentially involves individual self-control.

Frederick Davis's Criticisms

The imprecision inherent in such broad unitary definitions convinced some scholars that privacy was too vague, too subjective, to permit its incorporation into either public law or public policies. Frederick Davis suggested that the right of privacy has little more utility for judicial, and, by implication, administrative decision making than the "pursuit of happiness." He argued that "the concept of a right to privacy was never required in the first place, and . . . its whole history is an illustration of how well-meaning academicians can upset the normal development of laws by pushing too hard."[11] For Davis, and other scholars, the concept of privacy has utility only in a psychosociological sense but should not be afforded independent legal recognition. Arguably, psychological and social interests in privacy could be protected by more "elementary interests": principally, infliction of mental suffering and expropriation of personality or some proprietary interest. Hence, for Davis, "privacy is an interest or condition which derives from and is automatically secured by the protection of more recognizable rights."[12]

This approach is extreme inasmuch as it constitutes an absolute denial of a legal right and assumes that interests in privacy are not intrinsic but merely derivative from and instrumental to other individual rights. Yet, like other proponents of privacy protection, Davis assumes that recognition of privacy interests is tantamount to legitimating a right to privacy. That assumption, however, prejudges and confuses the whole issue of privacy protection, which involves determining the degree to which law and public policies should extend protection for privacy interests.

Judicial and legislative recognition of privacy interests do not determine what privacy is. Rather, they only declare in what contexts and under what circumstances privacy will be afforded legal protection. Early proponents of privacy protection mistakenly assumed that privacy is isomorphic with a right of privacy. As Louis Lusky has pointed out, however, conceptual clarity requires that we "distinguish the use of a term connoting the underlying human value that is the object of our concern [that is, privacy] and [defer] judgment as to whether, how, and to what extent it should be afforded legal protection."[13]

The conceptual muddle surrounding the concept of privacy was reflected in judicial policies extending protection to privacy interests. Although 12 states (plus Alaska and the District of Columbia) recognized legitimate privacy interests between 1890 and 1941, and the number of states increased to 18 in 1956 and to 31 by 1960, the common law of privacy was "still a haystack in a hurricane."[14]

William Prosser's Classification

In 1960 William Prosser reexamined the concept and law of privacy only to conclude that there was no independent privacy interest—hence, no right of privacy per se. Prosser found only a complex of four interests and torts: "The law of privacy comprises four distinct kinds of invasions of four distinct interests of the plaintiff, which are tied together by the common name, but otherwise have almost nothing in common except that each represents an interference with the right of the plaintiff . . . 'to be let alone.'"[15]

The four interests and torts Prosser found were described as follows:

1. Intrusions upon the plaintiff's seclusion or solitude, or into his private affairs. Protected here is the interest in freedom from mental distress. It has been used chiefly to fill in the gaps left by trespass, nuisance, the intentional infliction of mental distress, and whatever remedies there may be for the invasions of constitutional rights.

2. Public disclosure of embarrassing private facts about the plaintiff.

3. <u>Publicity that places the plaintiff in a false light</u>. The public disclosure and false-light torts protect interests in reputation and mental distress; both, however, overlap with the law of defamation.

4. <u>Appropriation for the defendant's advantage of the plaintiff's name or likeness</u>. Unlike the other three interests protected, here the interest is not mental but a proprietary one—an interest in the exclusive use of the plaintiff's name and likeness.

Prosser's classification of privacy torts was widely accepted, and his analysis also seemed to confirm some jurists' worst suspicions that the right of privacy was more "subjective even than 'liberty' and 'justice,' [and] the 'privacy' ideal overlaps both, and even turns back to create internal contradictions."[16]

Prosser's reexamination and classification of privacy interests rekindled controversy over the theoretical and legal foundations of privacy. If Prosser's analysis was correct, then Warren and Brandeis were wrong. Instead of a single interest, there were four interests represented by four torts, none of which bore a distinctive interest in privacy. Prosser's reexamination, therefore, presented proponents of privacy protection with a paradox: either there is no single privacy interest and privacy is inherently ambiguous, or privacy can be adequately protected by other interests in which case protection of privacy per se is redundant.

Edward Bloustein's Answer to Dean Prosser

Edward Bloustein endeavored to resolve the paradox by developing a general theory of individual privacy, which he also hoped would reconcile divergent trends in case law. By reanalyzing Prosser's classification, Bloustein attempted to show that the principle of "inviolate personality" was still the fundamental interest in privacy cases. "The injury is to our individuality, to our dignity as individuals, and the legal remedy represents a social vindication of the human spirit thus threatened rather than a recompense for the loss suffered."[17] Like Warren and Brandeis, Bloustein assumed that privacy interests have an intrinsic value, and for this reason they involve more than mere protection of instrumental values, such as protection of property, reputation, and mental suffering.

The significance of Bloustein's analysis is threefold. First, he correctly points out that if privacy should be respected for its intrinsic worth rather than for its instrumental value, then it becomes irrelevant whether, for example, public disclosures of personal information are true or have economic value. Second, if the social interest in privacy has an intrinsic worth, then privacy must be given

greater weight in policies than the simple legitimation accorded interests having only derivative or instrumental values. Third, it is only
with an encompassing principle of privacy that one can reconcile the
constitutional law of privacy—that is, reconcile privacy cases such
as those of contraception and abortion with those dealing with the privacy of association, possession of pornography, and unreasonable intrusions upon and disclosures of private engagements. Likewise, a
unifying principle of privacy compensates for another major weakness
in Prosser's analysis, namely, the impossibility of reconciling privacy in tort and nontort contexts, since the fundamental interests in
each context diverge. Whereas the constitutional right of privacy protects the "sanctity of a man's home and the privacies of life,"[18] tort
protection extends to the interests in economic security, reputation,
and mental stability. Bloustein's analysis, then, correctly criticizes
Prosser for acknowledging a concept of privacy while failing to articulate the underlying interest in privacy applicable to tort and nontort
contexts.

Although Bloustein's critique usefully emphasizes that Prosser's
reexamination cannot be accepted unconditionally, his definition, like
that of Warren and Brandeis, remains imprecise. The problem with
Bloustein's analysis, however, is not that his "explanation is so wide
as to be meaningless"[19] but that he does not define and analyze privacy itself. Rather, his approach consists of a broad characterization
of the reason privacy is of value at all—namely, that privacy is associated with human freedom and dignity.

PRIVACY AS CONTROL OVER
PERSONAL INFORMATION

Initial approaches to the concept of privacy did not find wide acceptance, owing to their lack of precision and their failure to analyze
the concept of privacy systematically. It was assumed that privacy
interests are defined in the course of their legal recognition. Consequently, instead of providing a definitional analysis of privacy per se,
commentators characterized only those interests associated with privacy in law. Furthermore, characterizations of the values underlying
privacy protection diverged as a result of two normative orientations:
some commentators assumed that privacy was important for its intrinsic worth; others acknowledged only its instrumental value.

The conceptual muddle surrounding early definitional approaches
stems from a failure to distinguish the concept of privacy from that
of a right to privacy, that is, to recognize the difference between privacy and its legal protection.

Privacy and the Bewitchment of Language

Hyman Gross attributed the conceptual confusion to "the bewitch-ment of our intelligence by means of language."[20] He believed that it could be dispelled by demonstrating that definitional approaches to privacy are ambiguous because uses of the word privacy vary in both law and ordinary language. Gross argued the word privacy used col-loquially has two senses: a strong and a weak. In the strong sense of privacy, privacy has no synonym. Here privacy refers to either intrusions in which transgressors become acquainted with private mat-ters or disclosures in which transgressors acquaint others with some-thing private although known to him. The interest in privacy, there-fore, lies in the freedom from either intrusions upon or disclosures of private facts, rather than in freedom to be let alone or to withdraw. Gross argued that privacy in the strong sense is the only permissible usage in law. By contrast, privacy in a weak sense is used as a synonym for other terms. These are principally mental repose, phy-sical solitude, physical exclusiveness, and personal autonomy. In-juries to privacy in the weak sense are met with legal remedies for wrongs (such as trespass or nuisance) other than an offense to privacy.

By distinguishing the strong from the weak sense of privacy, Gross attempts to resolve the paradox of privacy presented by the conflicting positions of Prosser and Bloustein. Gross states that Prosser's thesis that privacy "may be reduced without remainder to one of several other interests protected in other areas of the law of torts . . . [derives from] a conceptual fault regarding privacy." On the other hand, Bloustein's focus on freedom from intrusions upon or disclosures of personal affairs indicated "why [privacy] is important enough to merit legal protection, but not what it is."[21]

Unfortunately, Gross himself does not escape ambiguity when discussing his own definition: "Privacy is the condition of human life in which acquaintance with a person or with affairs of his life which are personal to him is limited."[22] His definition does have the prin-cipal advantage of distinguishing between the concept of privacy and that of a right to privacy. As Gross points out:

> A legal right of privacy exists to the extent that such legal interest may be (not could be) accorded protection by legal procedures. But privacy in these contexts does not exist because of such legal recognition. It exists—like secrecy, security, or tranquility—by virtue of habits of life appro-priate to its existence.[23]

Yet, Gross encounters problems when discussing what makes certain conduct offensive to privacy. Privacy is lost, he argues, "when the limits one has set on acquaintance with his personal affairs are not respected."[24] There are two kinds of limits: restrictions on what is known about oneself and restrictions on who may know what. Privacy is surrendered when one gives it up, or lost when some party intrudes into one's affairs. Hence, until an individual loses control over what is known and by whom, privacy remains uncompromised.

Gross errs when he asserts that privacy is essentially voluntary and that it involves control over personal information about oneself. Unfortunately, this is a commonly held assumption.

Privacy and Control
over Personal Information

Charles Fried proposed that privacy provides "the rational context for a number of our most significant ends, such as love, trust, and friendship, respect and self-respect."[25] Like Gross, Fried views privacy as a context for other intrinsic ends. But unlike Gross, Bloustein, and Warren and Brandeis, Fried argues that the normative import attached to privacy derives from its utility, its instrumental value. Privacy is "a necessary element of those ends [love, respect, and trust], it draws its significance from them. And yet since privacy is only an element of those ends, not the whole value, we have not felt inclined to attribute privacy ultimate significance."[26] Privacy provides a rational context for human ends because privacy is chosen. Consequently, privacy should be respected and legally recognized since intrusions upon or disclosures of personal engagements constitute deprivations of individual liberty. Accordingly, Fried offers the following definition:

> Privacy is not simply an absence of information about us in the minds of others; rather it is the control we have over information about ourselves. . . . The person who enjoys privacy is able to grant or deny access to others. . . . Privacy, thus is control over knowledge about oneself. But it is not simply control over the quantity of information abroad; there are modulations in the quality of knowledge as well.[27]

Fried's definition, "control over access to information about oneself," appears to contradict his analysis of privacy as a condition of life. His definition, like Gross's, actually suffers two further defects: first, his definition is too narrow and, second, it presupposes that privacy primarily involves control.

The same two defects not only appear in the definitions offered by Fried and Gross but are symptomatic of most contemporary psychological approaches to privacy. For example, psychologists have defined privacy as follows:

> The essence of privacy is no more, and certainly no less, than the freedom of the individual to pick and choose for himself the time and circumstances under which and most importantly, the extent to which, his attitudes, beliefs, behavior, and opinions are to be shared with or withheld from others.[28]

> Obtaining freedom of choice or options to achieve goals, control over what, how, and to whom a person communicates information about the self.[29]

> Selective control of access to the self or to one's group.[30]

The picture that these psychologists present of privacy is one of a dynamic process of interpersonal relations allowing for varying degrees of access to an individual. From a psychologist's point of view, Irwin Altman suggests that the key elements for understanding privacy are the following:

> (1) Privacy is a dialectic process involving both a closing off of the self and an opening of the self to others. (2) Privacy is an interpersonal boundary control process, or a series of events involving regulation and control of social interaction or "permeability" of the self to others. This boundary control process aids in the placing and management of social interaction. (3) Privacy is a non-monotonic process, with a region above and below which interaction amount and quality are unsatisfactory. (4) Privacy involves various social units, or different combinations of persons and groups. (5) A distinction is made between subjectively desired or momentary ideal levels of privacy (desired privacy) and actual outcomes (achieved privacy). (6) Privacy is an input and output process, or a combination of incoming social stimulation from others and outgoing interaction from the self to others.[31]

Such a psychological perspective also informs the approaches advanced by Arthur Miller, Alan Westin, and Richard Parker, who, respectively, offer these definitions of privacy:

> The individual's ability to control the circulation of information relating to him.[32]

The claim of individuals, groups, or institutions to determine for themselves when, how, and to what extent information about them is communicated to others. . . . The
right of an individual to decide what information about himself should be communicated to others and under what circumstances. Viewed in terms of the relation of the individual to social participation, privacy is the voluntary and
temporary withdrawal of a person from the general society
through physical or psychological means, either in a state
of solitude or small-group intimacy or, when among larger
groups, in a condition of anonymity or reserve. [33]

Privacy is control over whom and by whom the various
parts of us can be sensed by others . . . [more specifically,] control over who can see us, hear us, touch us, smell
us, and taste us, in sum, control over who can sense us,
is the core of the concept of privacy. It is control over the
sort of information found in dossiers and data banks. [34]

One finds, then, agreement on a fundamental perspective and a
definitional approach to privacy as "control over personal information." This approach has been appealing for a number of reasons:
it embraces a broad range of privacy interests; it appears appropriate
and applicable to the problems associated with personal information
held by government agencies; and, finally, it lends itself to normative
arguments for legislating privacy safeguards.

Problems with the Prevailing Approach to Privacy

The prevailing approach to privacy nevertheless is inadequate
because, first, its definitions are at once too broad and too narrow
and, second, it assumes fallaciously that privacy is solely voluntary
and fundamentally involves control over personal information.
Defining privacy as "control over personal information" is both
too nonrestrictive and too restrictive. Certainly, as Richard Parker
notes, "Not every loss or gain of control over information about ourselves is a loss or gain of privacy." [35] Taken literally this definition
leads to absurdities, for individual privacy would be invaded "or at
least affected somehow," as Louis Lusky points out, "if my neighbor
tells my second neighbor (without my consent) that I am a vegetarian,
or that I am suffering from spring fever, or that I like oysters." [36]
By merely observing a person enter a room one gains some information about that person, but does that observation constitute an invasion
of privacy? In certain situations, as when a private "eye" or photog-
rapher tracks an individual, that person's privacy may be invaded,

but in such instances there is no communication or disclosure of personal information.

Besides these problems, difficulties also arise because such definitions are too narrow. A related problem, particularly with respect to Fried's, Westin's, and Miller's definitions, lies in ignoring the range of privacy interests already recognized in constitutional law but that are not connected with personal information. Many privacy interests that have been constitutionally recognized involve neither dissemination nor acquisition of personal information. Examples range from cases involving music on public buses, loudspeakers on public streets, and door-to-door salesmen to decisions on the use of contraceptives and the permissibility of abortions. In all of these instances, the interests in privacy have nothing to do with disclosures of personal information but rather with an individual's freedom to engage in private activities.

Regarding privacy as control over personal information renders all derivative definitions inadequate, because they oversimplify the problems of information control. No distinction is drawn between two radically different kinds of personal information disclosures. There are situations in which the disclosure of personal information, even if true, should not be permitted because of decency or commercial exploitation. On the other hand, there are situations, such as those involving computerized personal information, in which the information disclosed may be so incomplete as to be misleading, if not false. Indeed, conceiving of privacy as simply control over personal information deceptively suggests that personal information consists of discrete particles of information, but such is not the case. The main problem with computerized personal data arises precisely because the oversimplification of such records leads to inaccuracies and misrepresentations.

The other fundamental problem with such definitions of privacy is the emphasis placed on individual control or voluntary deprivation. Defining privacy as "control over access" or "the claim of individuals to control the circulation of information" excludes a number of privacy situations while confusing privacy as a condition with a right or claim to privacy. Roland Garrett makes the latter point:

> If privacy is voluntary, one who possesses privacy has the
> power to decide whether he will retain or abandon it. Pri-
> vacy has accordingly been defined as control over access
> to oneself; as, for example, control over knowledge about
> oneself. However, there is a logical error in the reason-
> ing that evidently underlies this definition. Even if privacy
> does involve or presuppose control over access to oneself,
> it need not be identical with such control. A person may

retain control over access to all (as with an exhibitionist). The mere fact that granting access to all is voluntary does not imply that the individual is still in a condition of privacy. On the contrary, the result is a voluntary abandonment of privacy.[37]

Privacy is not identical with control over access to oneself, because not all privacy is chosen. Some privacy is accidental, compulsory, or even involuntary. Privacy refers to a condition of life and, as such, has no necessary connection with control over personal information.

Hence, like the early definitional approaches to the concept of privacy, recent attempts to formulate a theoretical framework for approaching privacy have been inadequate and inaccurate. All these approaches rely on four fallacious assumptions: (1) privacy denotes primarily the seclusion or withdrawal of an individual from public affairs, (2) privacy entails a right because (3) privacy presumably is essentially voluntary, and, (4) privacy is meaningful by virtue of either its intrinsic worth or its instrumental value.

The immediate consequence of the ambiguity surrounding definitional approaches to privacy is that legislation purporting to protect privacy will be subject to varying interpretations and difficult to implement. Without a critical conceptual analysis of the concept of privacy the constitutional law of privacy will continue to appear unprincipled and disparate, and, more important, public policies relating to privacy protection will be difficult to formulate, let alone implement.

AN ALTERNATIVE ANALYSIS OF PRIVACY

The critique of definitional approaches to privacy revealed logical fallacies and the failure to account for various kinds of privacy interests and litigation. As a logical and practical matter, privacy seems to differ significantly from the right of privacy. A person may have a large degree of privacy without having chosen it, let alone having had a right to choose it; rights of privacy are products of social structure, conventions, and legal policy. Moreover, a right of privacy does not necessarily include claims to choose where, when, and how one will have privacy. Therefore, in order to elucidate the legal boundaries of privacy, an alternative analysis of privacy must construct a framework that does not confuse privacy and the right of privacy.

Privacy as an Existential Condition

Privacy is a condition and as such it may be forgone, forfeited, or invaded. A right of privacy includes the notions of control and voluntariness in denoting individuals' claims of entitlement to the recognition of their interests in privacy. H. J. McCloskey emphasizes the difference between privacy and a right of privacy by pointing out that privacy contrasts with publicity; whereas negative liberty (freedom from) and positive liberty (freedom to) oppose the notions of coercion, interference, and the lack of some facilities or opportunities, all of which imply the denial of a right or claim to do or forbear from doing something.[38] Privacy is a condition about which claims may be made as to individuals' freedom from unwanted intrusions upon or disclosures of their affairs as well as their freedom to limit and define for themselves their engagements with others.

Accordingly, privacy may be understood as fundamentally denoting an existential condition of limited access to an individual's life experiences and engagements. This definition is similar to that of Roland Garrett, who stated: "Privacy is a limitation on the access of one or more entities to an entity that possesses experience."[39] Yet, the new definition differs from his in two substantial respects. First, it emphasizes that privacy is a matter of individuals' lives—of their life experiences and engagements or relationships with others. Garrett's definition is so broad as to apply not only to individuals but also to groups and organizations; for this reason it confuses privacy and secrecy. Privacy is a condition in which individuals may find themselves, as well as create. Groups and organizations may conduct business in private, with secrecy or confidentiality. The danger of such a broad definition lies with its implication that if individuals have rights to privacy then, ipso facto, so do groups and organizations. Groups, organizations, and governmental institutions have power and may be granted privileges; but individuals alone have rights.

Second, the author's definition differs from Garrett's in emphasizing that privacy is a condition of limited access, not a limitation on access per se. To suggest that privacy is a limitation on access implies that someone or something is limiting access, and, consequently, one returns to the problems of defining privacy as control over access to oneself.

Because it focuses on a condition in which access is limited or restricted, the author's definition can embrace not only those privacy interests in personal information recognized by the prevailing approach to privacy but also the anomalous interests in privacy that have been legitimated by either judicial or legislative policies (for example, the privacy interests associated with intrusions by sound trucks and door-to-door salesmen, as well as the peripheral privacy claims to abortion and the use of contraceptives).

Viewing privacy as an existential condition of limited access presupposes a set of notions that oppose those relied on by the traditional approach to privacy. Specifically, the author's definition and analysis presuppose:

1. Privacy is both a necessary and a contingent condition of individuals' life experiences and engagements.
2. Privacy as a condition of limited access to one's experiences and engagements may be compromised by either causal or interpretive access.
3. Privacy as a condition is different from a right or claim.
4. Privacy is valuable for both its intrinsic worth and instrumental value.

The confusion of privacy and a right of privacy arose precisely because traditional analyses presumed that privacy entailed the notions of control, voluntariness, and individual freedom. On the contrary, privacy is an existential condition and hence not always chosen. Privacy may be both inevitable and contingent.

Inevitable and Contingent Privacy

In some respects individual experience and engagements are necessarily private. The nature of human experience is such that individuals must choose either to disclose or to refrain from disclosing to others. However, the very nature of thought, feeling, and communication renders impossible the communication of every trait or quality of the thought, feeling, or experience. Individual experiences can be comprehended by the individual in a way that they can never be understood by others. Since individuals cannot communicate all of their thoughts and feelings, the sharing of experiences is limited. Inevitable privacy results from a general limitation on individual communication. The necessary limitations on access to one's experiences and engagements thus derive from the nature of both human experience and communication.

By contrast, and of greater concern, is contingent privacy. Contingent privacy refers both to what individuals choose to disclose (or not to disclose) about themselves through communication and engagements with others and to the circumstances that impose limits on access to individuals. In daily life individuals enter into a large number of relationships; they range from solitude to intimacy with loved ones and friends, to social and business affairs, to passing acquaintances, to relatively impersonal social transactions. Through a variety of engagements, individuals voluntarily both limit and grant access to themselves. The privacy of individual relationships, however, does not always result from conscious choice and effort on the part of individuals to secure limited access. Often, individuals do not self-consciously choose to limit access to their affairs. At times they simply assume privacy because the very circumstances of their activities may dictate a modicum of privacy. Individuals' privacy is therefore contingent upon their conscious effort to limit access and upon the circumstances of their relationships, which may impose limitations on access by other parties.

Individuals have expectations about the privacy of their affairs, and their expectations are reinforced by social norms. When these expectations are compromised, individuals may seek vindication of their privacy interests through litigation or the political process. Judicial and political institutions therefore must determine (1) what constitutes an invasion of personal privacy, (2) whether a reasonable expectation of privacy exists, and (3) whether society through its institutions should afford protection and recompense for invasions of privacy. Such determinations require an understanding of the ways in which privacy may be compromised.

Causal and Interpretative Privacy

Privacy is compromised when unwanted access to an individual's experiences and engagements is gained. There are two ways in which privacy may be compromised: causal and interpretative access. This is because "it so happens that causation and interpretation are the two ways in which an entity [individual] can be conjoined with its [his] surroundings, or in which others can be introduced to it."[40]

Causal access refers to those intrusions upon individuals' engagements that influence those persons' enjoyment of their engagements and future relationships. Hence, causal privacy refers to the limitations on causal access to an individual. For example, trespass and nuisance laws restrict intrusions upon individual privacy, as do statutes regulating loudspeakers, music on public buses, and the like.

The privacy of individual engagements may also be compromised by interpretative access, which is gained by accumulating information about an individual's engagements and relationships. Interpretative privacy refers to the limitations on the accumulation and disclosure of information about an individual. Examples of interpretative privacy include unwanted publicity concerning an individual's engagements by the media and collection of personal information by government agencies or private organizations. Legitimate expectations of personal privacy may be compromised not only when personal information is collected unbeknown to an individual but also when that individual has voluntarily disclosed information that subsequently is made available to some third party, as when the Internal Revenue Service discloses personal financial information to the Justice Department or state and local welfare or Social Security offices. Notwithstanding the inability to control the access or disclosure of information, an individual may still have legitimate privacy expectations. Similarly, there are reasonable expectations of privacy with respect to personal records, because such disclosures to third parties compromise individuals' interpretative privacy and may also influence their futures, thereby restricting privacy, individual freedom, and personal autonomy. Causal access and interpretative access are thus two interdependent ways in which privacy may be compromised. Some forms of interpretative access presuppose causal access, such as eavesdropping or informers, and some forms of causal access presuppose interpretative access.

Normative Values of Privacy

Analyzing privacy invasions according to causal and interpretative access illuminates the normative values underlying privacy protection. Contrary to the prevailing assumption that privacy is valuable for either its intrinsic worth or its instrumental value, it is apparent that in most situations privacy is valuable for both. Consider the problems of safeguarding personal records held by governmental agencies. Individuals have interests both in the nature of the personal information contained in the records and in who will be permitted access to it, since the information is valuable intrinsically and instrumentally. The intrinsic value of personal information may well be intuitive, but the instrumental values of privacy can be demonstrated because disclosures may affect an individual's future activities. The instrumental values attached to privacy derive from its relation to individual freedom.

Since privacy is an existential condition, unwanted intrusions upon and disclosures of personal affairs contravene the value individuals place on privacy as well as their freedom and sense of personal autonomy in defining their engagements. Legislation safeguarding privacy therefore legitimates the value of privacy per se and those values that are associated with individual liberty and personal autonomy.

Contrary to the traditional approach to privacy, this analysis shows that there is not a single privacy interest underlying a right of privacy. Rather, privacy is an existential condition that gives rise to a broad range of privacy interests, and those privacy interests are meaningful in themselves as well as in relation to individual freedom and autonomy.

Yet, not every intrusion upon or disclosure of personal affairs gives rise to a privacy interest of sufficient weight to warrant legal safeguards. Privacy interests must be balanced with other interests, such as the public's right to know, administrative costs and needs, and broader societal objectives as, for example, crime control. Moreover, many privacy interests, such as those associated with personal autonomy or solitude, do not require explicit legislative recognition because of their association with more traditional legal categories, as in statutes relating to trespass, nuisance, peeping toms, and the like. In addition, nonlegal safeguards, such as physical seclusion, "natural" limits on dissemination of personal information, the relative indifference of most people in large urban areas, and the costs in time, money, and energy of acquiring information about individuals, ensure some individual privacy.

IMPLICATIONS OF THE PREVAILING PARADIGM OF PRIVACY

The critique of the prevailing approach to privacy uncovered problems with the analytical and normative presuppositions of defining privacy as control over personal information or knowledge. Such definitions do not provide adequately for the broad range of privacy interests, let alone the range of interests legitimated through litigation. Logical fallacies were found with the assumptions (1) that privacy denotes individual seclusion or withdrawal, (2) that privacy is chosen and voluntary, and (3) that acknowledgment of privacy interests entails legal recognition in the form of a right of privacy. The preoccupation with establishing a legal right of privacy prohibited adequate analysis of privacy, because it narrowed the focus of privacy definitions and neglected nonlegal safeguards of privacy as well as countervailing interests, which must be considered when affording legal protection to privacy interests.

Privacy and the Right of Privacy Differentiated

Shortcomings of the prevailing theoretical approach to privacy prompted an alternative analysis of privacy as an existential condition of limited access to an individual's experiences and engagements. That analysis established that privacy differs in significant ways from the right of privacy. Individuals may have a large degree of privacy without having chosen it, and, even when individuals voluntarily undertake to secure the privacy of their engagements, their expectations of privacy need not be legally enforceable. The right of privacy does not necessarily include the right to choose where, when, and how one will have privacy.

Since privacy is an existential condition of individuals' engagements, the right of privacy may encompass a broad range of privacy interests. The right of privacy is an abstract, not an absolute, right extending to a variety of privacy interests. Yet, not every assertion of a privacy interest need be legally recognized. Some privacy interests are adequately protected by nonlegal safeguards, while others are guaranteed through their association with more traditional legal categories. Some privacy claims are not of sufficient importance in particular contexts of litigation to justify legal recognition (as, analogously, not all exercises of free speech have been extended protection under the First Amendment's guarantee of free speech).

Critique of Privacy as a
Right to Control Information

Contrary to the prevailing view, there are many kinds of privacy interests that cannot be accommodated even with an expansive interpretation of the notion of control over personal information. Therefore, analyzing the concept of privacy in terms of control over personal information is like using a skeleton key that opens too many doors. The traditional approach to privacy, consequently, represents only a special kind of privacy interest, informational privacy, and cannot adequately account for the protection of other privacy interests. Even from within a framework of privacy as control over personnal information, analyses often fail to distinguish the ways in which informational privacy may be lost. Accordingly, they neglect both the different interests citizens may have in informational privacy and the sources of legal protection available. There are at least three different ways informational privacy may be lost. First, access to personal information can be gained directly from individuals, but against their wishes and expectations of privacy. Examples of such invasions of privacy include: ordinary searches and seizures of private papers and effects, electronic surveillance and eavesdropping, compelled self-disclosures, grand jury and legislative investigations, and mandatory personal disclosures as preconditions for enjoying some benefit, such as welfare benefits, charge accounts, obtaining credit, or government employment. Second, recipients of volunteered personal information may be compelled by a third party to disclose information that both the individual and the original recipient desire to keep private. Typically, these are instances where individuals have provided information to an attorney, bank, credit agency, or governmental agency, whereupon that party is required to produce the information for some third party. Third, recipients of personal information may disclose the information to some third party but against the wishes and privacy expectations of the individual, such as when an agency of the federal government provides individually identifiable information to another agency or a private organization. Distinguishing between the ways in which informational privacy may be lost manifests the variety of privacy interests in personal information as well as the complexity of protecting privacy interests. Individual interests in informational privacy defy generalization, as do the legal safeguards, remedies, and solutions to particular problems of information control.

Somewhat ironically, the prevailing approach to privacy, focusing as it does on informational privacy, does not provide an adequate framework for analyzing such controversies over personal informational privacy. Its focus not only fails to provide a systematic analysis of privacy but, more important, prejudges the problems of safeguarding informational privacy by equating privacy and the right of privacy and neglecting the interrelationships among privacy, individual freedom, and personal rights.

THE POLITICAL IDEAL OF PRIVACY

Examination of the concept of privacy led to the conclusion that privacy is an existential condition of limited access to an individual's experiences and engagements and, more specifically, to four propositions concerning privacy: (1) privacy is both a necessary and a contingent condition of individuals' life experiences and engagements, (2) privacy as a condition of limited access to individuals' experiences and engagements may be compromised by either causal or interpretative access, (3) privacy is valuable for both its intrinsic worth and instrumental value, and (4) privacy as a condition is different from a right or a claim.

Analysis of privacy in terms of an existential condition revealed difficulties with traditional analyses of privacy. Traditional analyses err not only by assuming that privacy is basically chosen but also by further assuming that acknowledgment of privacy entails the recognition of a right of privacy. Often such analyses idealize privacy politically, in the sense of a liberty or a right, and consequently obscure the relationships among privacy, freedom, and rights. Yet, in what sense may privacy be regarded as a political ideal? More exactly, how does privacy relate to individual freedom, civil liberties, and legal rights? A reexamination of the political ideal of privacy and the connections among privacy, freedom, liberty, and rights is necessary because in traditional analyses these interrelationships remain obscure, and because a more perspicuous view emerges on the basis of the preceding analysis of privacy as an existential condition.

Privacy and Freedom

Notwithstanding traditional analyses, privacy does not primarily denote the voluntary seclusion or withdrawal of an individual from public affairs, and, therefore, the association of privacy with freedom may well be misleading. Conceptually, privacy is broader than freedom because privacy does not always result from self-conscious (free) action on the part of individuals. In this regard, the distinction drawn earlier between inevitable and contingent privacy is instructive. All individual experiences necessarily limit access by others because of the very nature of human experience and communication; hence, individuals are not free to permit unlimited access or share quantitatively and qualitatively all their experiences. Of greater concern here, access may be limited contingently in two ways. Individuals may choose not to disclose their experiences in conversations, or they may choose to conduct their affairs away from public exposure. Alternatively, the circumstances of an individual's engagements may limit access. Only contingent privacy, in the first instance, relates directly to individual freedom, because the condition of limited access results from self-conscious action. In the second instance, privacy is the product of events and contexts surrounding individuals' activities. In other words, the privacy of personal engagements may be contingent upon, as in the first instance, individual actions designed to secure limited access by others, or, as in the second instance, externalities that accompany individual engagements. Contrary to the traditional analyses, then, privacy does not always result from the voluntary choice on the part of individuals. Privacy, therefore, may not be simply characterized as an aspect of individual freedom and control over personal engagements.

Some scholars may object that contingent privacy actually relates to two senses of freedom, freedom to do something (limit access by others) and freedom from something (unwanted disclosures or intrusions). When individuals consciously limit access by others to their engagements, privacy may be associated with freedom in the positive sense. For example, individuals are free to limit access to their engagements by purposefully conducting their affairs in secluded areas, such as the basement or bedroom of their houses, or by limiting their personal disclosures to confidential conversations with trusted friends. In such situations, invasions of privacy also diminish individuals' freedom. Contingent privacy, however, may also result simply from the externalities accompanying individual engagements. For example, the physical location of individuals' activities or the relative indifference of their fellow suburbanites may isolate them and thereby constitute limitations on access. In such situations, privacy is contingent upon externalities but also relates to individuals' freedom from access. Accordingly, contingent privacy relates to both senses of freedom.

Nevertheless, the parallel between the two senses of contingent privacy and positive and negative freedoms is dangerously misleading. Dichotomizing freedom is seductively simple. Yet, freedom always consists in both freedom to do or become something (positive) and freedom from something (negative). As Gerald C. MacCallum, Jr., lucidly explains:

> Whenever the freedom of some agent or agents is in question, it is always freedom from some constraint or restriction on, interference with, or barrier to doing, not doing, becoming, or not becoming something. Such freedom is thus always of something (an agent or agents), from something, to do, not do, become, or not become something; it is a triadic relation. Taking the format "x is (is not) free from y to do (not do, become, not become) z," x ranges over agents, y ranges over such "preventing conditions" as constraints, restrictions, interferences, and barriers, and z ranges over actions or conditions of character or circumstances. When reference to one of these three terms is missing in such a discussion of freedom, it should be only because the reference is thought to be understood from the context of the discussion. [41]

Positive and negative freedom are not referentially opaque. Rather, they are transparently obvious forms of an individual's basic freedom from some restraint or constraint to do something. Hence, contingent privacy in the first instance discussed only emphasizes that the individual self-consciously chooses privacy, whereas privacy in the second instance emphasizes those externalities that may condition and promote privacy and freedom from intrusions.

The important difference between the two senses of privacy, therefore, lies not with regard to individual freedom but with respect to the way in which privacy may be contingent upon individual activities. In some situations privacy results from self-conscious action on the part of individuals, and in other situations privacy may characterize individuals' engagements merely as an externality.

As events and circumstances change, reliance on externalities that provide for privacy may shift and, indeed, promote a privacy consciousness. For example, individuals may through no action of their own suddenly become objects of curiosity for their fellow suburbanites. In fact, since the late nineteenth century a variety of economic, geographic, and social changes took place in the United States that affected the ways in which individuals perceived and secured their privacy and thereby promoted a kind of privacy consciousness registered by increasing litigation in the twentieth century over a right of privacy.

Privacy as a Liberty and a Right

The political ideal of privacy as a liberty or a right may be interpreted as an individual's freedom to secure conditions free from unwanted access. Such a political ideal, however, is impermissibly broad, since privacy as an existential condition remains wider than both freedom and liberty. In other words, privacy per se remains primarily a nonpolitical and nonlegal concept.

The political ideal of privacy as a liberty or a right also may confuse liberty with freedom. Freedom depends on an individual's de facto abilities, whereas liberty is conferred by a system of rules and regulations established through social practices. Individuals may be free to do something if they are free from certain constraints or restrictions, while individuals have the liberty to do something if and only if they have no duty to refrain from doing so. In some circumstances, an individual might be free—have the ability—not to disclose personal information and yet not be at liberty to do so. Alternatively, as Joel Feinberg notes: "A person might be at liberty to do X, and yet not be free to do X because he is constrained by something other than a duty."[42] Thus, the political ideal of privacy as a liberty encompasses a narrower range of individual activities than those embraced by privacy construed as a freedom.

An acceptable political ideal of privacy moreover requires that the liberty of privacy be defined in terms of and on the basis of a theory of rights. A political ideal of privacy in the sense of an unqualified liberty of noninterference (that is, simply to be let alone, where "to be let alone" has no definition in terms of political or legal rights) appears less than exemplary. H. J. McCloskey points out:

> We are free, in this sense of liberty, if we are let alone.
> So we are free if we are let to starve, or to die for want
> of means of subsistence. We are free to read, to write,
> to acquire learning in a state in which the only education
> available is private education at a cost beyond our means,
> provided that no one interferes with us and prevents us
> seeking education when and if we can afford it. Thus we
> can enjoy the fullest liberty, yet be unable to do anything
> we wish to do, for we may lack the means to realize our
> wishes, but be free because we are let alone.[43]

Conceptually, liberties are circumscribed by rights. Individuals may have a liberty of privacy that is not also a right of privacy, but they may not have a right of privacy that is not also a liberty, since rights in a sense contain liberties as components. The relationship between liberties and rights may be explained in the following manner: "I have a right to X, then I cannot also have a duty to refrain from doing X. But to say that I lack a duty to refrain is to say that I have a liberty or privilege to do. Hence, if I have a right to do X, I must also be at liberty to do X. What the right adds to the liberty is the duty of others not to interfere."[44] Liberties are permissions without protections to act in certain ways, while rights are entitlements to exercise, have, and enjoy liberties. Hence, an ideal of privacy in the sense of an absolute liberty of noninterference is unacceptable because of its unconditional nature and its failure to provide a basis for entitlement to protected privacy. An acceptable political ideal of privacy requires a theory of rights, because rights contain and limit liberties and the liberty of noninterference requires qualification.

Rights in a strict and narrow sense are claim rights. "[L]egal claim rights are necessarily the grounds of other people's duties toward the right-holder. A legal right is a claim to performance, either action or forbearance as the case may be."[45] Rights have an affinity with claims. Claims are often assertions of rights, since in claiming individuals exercise their rights by showing that they are entitled legally or morally, despite the objections of others, to do or have something. Yet, rights are not the same as claims because rights may be possessed, exercised, or enjoyed, whereas individuals make claims but do not possess, exercise, or enjoy them. Similarly, Joel Feinberg explains that,

> [h]aving a claim to X is not (yet) the same as having a right to X, but is rather having a case, consisting of relevant reasons of at least minimal plausibility, that one has a right to X. The case establishes a right, not to X, but to a fair hearing and consideration. Claims, so conceived, differ in degree: some are stronger than others. Rights, on the other hand, do not differ in degree; no one right is more of a right than another.[46]

The activity of claiming consists in having a case for doing or having something; it involves the assertion of a right, or entitlement, to be at liberty to do or have something without interference. An individual who has a right, as Richard Flathman concisely states, may "decide whether, when, and how to exercise it, whether to alienate it, how vigorously to defend it, and so forth."[47]

Rights are entitlements signifying that no duty, obligation, or other moral or legal restriction may interfere with an individual's doing or having something. Legal rights as entitlements to act, therefore, are not powers conferred by or recognized by law. Rights are distinct from powers because an individual may have a right but not the power or capacity to exercise the right. For example, individuals may have a legal right to drive a car but remain powerless to do so because of temporary paralysis or because they cannot afford to buy or rent a car. The distance between rights and powers, therefore, resembles that betweeen liberty and freedom: just as an individual may be at liberty to do or have something and not be free to do so, an individual may also have a right to do or have something and yet remain powerless to do so.

A right of privacy, however, does not include the entitlement to legal protection of all privacy expectations because, like most rights, it is not absolute and unqualified in application; in addition, such a right would entail the protection of an unqualified liberty from noninterference. Instead, the right of privacy is a prima facie right. "[A] prima facie right is a right to do X except when there is 'some more urgent moral consideration,' its nature unspecified and open-ended, that stands in the way."[48] The right of privacy as a prima facie right entitles individuals to the protection of privacy when and where their privacy claims are reasonable and not overridden by other legal, moral, or political considerations. That the right of privacy is a prima facie right derives both from the nature of privacy and the practice of rights more generally.

The Political Ideal of Privacy
and the Practice of Rights

The legal scope of a right of privacy depends largely on the practice of rights in a society—that is, which claims to particular privacy expectations are legally recognized. The practice of rights is a social phenomenon; it involves a certain kind of interaction among people, namely, the activity of formally claiming and legitimating individual entitlements to do or have something. A legal right of privacy involves a rule-governed practice by which individuals formally claim entitlement to protection of their privacy. Viewing legal rights as constituting a practice enables examination of both the institutional processes and practices by which interests in privacy are raised to the status of legal rights and, simultaneously, the legal boundaries of the right of privacy (the occasions when and with regard to what other legal, moral, and political considerations an individual may legitimately assert the right of privacy).

Analyzing the legal protection of personal privacy in terms of the practice of rights, moreover, makes apparent the gap between the virtual and actual contours of the right of privacy. In historical perspective the practice of rights not only has an impact on but remains affected by the practices of other economic, political, and social institutions. Consequently, the contours of rights may shift with historic changes in other institutional practices. In this regard Ronald Dworkin observes: "Political rights are creatures of both history and morality: what an individual is entitled to have, in civil society, depends upon the practice and the justice of its political institutions."[49] As the activity of claiming entitlement to different kinds of privacy interests may change with new technological developments and theretofore unforeseen intrusions of personal privacy, so too the legal contours of a right to privacy may shift, as judicial policies legitimate new assertions of privacy interests over countervailing claims.

Within the practice of rights, the right of privacy is a prima facie right entitling individuals to the protection of their privacy only when and where their claims are reasonable and not overridden by some other legal or political consideration. As a prima facie right, the right of privacy is necessarily an abstract right that enables individuals to claim protection for a variety of particular privacy interests. In other words, an abstract right of privacy enables individuals in specific cases and controversies to assert concrete rights of privacy by claiming entitlement to particular privacy interests. The distinction between abstract and concrete rights may well be only one of degree and not of kind, but it remains crucial for understanding the practice of rights and constitutionally protected privacy. "Abstract rights, like the right to speak on political matters, take no account of competing rights; concrete rights, on the other hand, reflect the impact of such competition."[50] Dworkin explains the difference between abstract and concrete rights:

An abstract is a general political aim the statement of which does not indicate how that general aim is to be weighted or compromised in particular circumstances against other political aims. . . . Abstract rights in this way provide arguments for concrete rights, but the claim of a concrete right is more definite than any claim of abstract right that supports it. . . . Concrete rights . . . are political aims that are more precisely defined so as to express more definitely the weight they may have against other political aims on particular occasions.[51]

In litigation the right of privacy as an abstract prima facie right entitles individuals to claim that particular privacy interests should be protected. Yet, judicial construction of these claims, along with other legal and political considerations, determines whether individuals have legitimate claims or concrete rights of privacy. Hence, in the practice of rights an abstract right of privacy enables individuals to claim entitlement to protected privacy, whereas concrete rights, once legitimated, signify the scope of the broader abstract right of privacy.

Judicial decisions interpret the abstract right of privacy and, thereupon, enforce concrete rights of privacy. The decisions are permissible only if the abstract right of privacy is also a constitutional right rather than simply a moral or political right. Since the Constitution does not expressly guarantee a right of privacy, judicial construction of a right of privacy presupposes that the abstract right of privacy is also a background right of the Constitution. A constitutional background right is an abstract right based upon and justifiable in terms of both the general purposes and principles of constitutionally limited government and the specific guarantees of the Bill of Rights. The following chapters examine the political ideal of a constitutional background right of privacy in terms of the guarantees of the Constitution, the Bill of Rights, and the developing constitutional law of privacy in order to elucidate the scope of and principal justifications for constitutionally protected privacy.

NOTES

1. Poe v. Ullman, 367 U.S. 497, 521 (1960) (Douglas, J., dis. op.). A majority of the Court did not recognize a constitutional right of privacy until Griswold v. Connecticut, 381 U.S. 479 (1965).

2. Thomas Cooley, Torts (2d. ed., 1888) at 91.

3. Samuel D. Warren and Louis D. Brandeis, "The Right to Privacy," 4 Harvard Law Review 193 (1890).

4. Ibid., at 205.

5. Harry Kalven, Jr., "Privacy in Tort Law—Were Warren and Brandeis Wrong?" 31 Law and Contemporary Problems 326, at 328 (1966).

6. See, generally, Edward Shils, "Privacy: Its Constitutions and Vicissitudes," 31 Law and Contemporary Problems 281 (1966); and Arthur S. Miller, "Privacy in the Corporate State: A Constitutional Value of Dwindling Significance," 25 Administrative Law Review 231 (1973).

7. See Roscoe Pound, "Interests in Personality," 23 Harvard Law Review 343 (1915); Leon Green, "The Right of Privacy," 27 Illinois Law Review 237 (1932); Harold R. Gordon, "Right of Privacy in Name, Likeness, Personality, and History," 55 Northwestern University Law Review 553 (1960).

8. A. Bates, "Privacy—A Useful Concept?" 42 Social Forces 432 (1964).

9. F. S. Chapin, "Some Housing Factors Related to Mental Hygiene," 7 Journal of Social Issues 164 (1951).

10. Sidney M. Journard, "Some Psychological Aspects of Privacy," 31 Law and Contemporary Problems 307 (1966).

11. Frederick Davis, "What Do We Mean by 'Right to Privacy'?" 4 South Dakota Law Review 1, 4-5 (1959).

12. Ibid., at 20.

13. Louis Lusky, "Invasion of Privacy: A Clarification of Concepts," 72 Columbia Law Review 693, 703 (1972).

14. Ettore v. Philco Television Broadcasting Co., 229 F.2d. 481, 485 (3d cir. 1956) (Biggs., J.).

15. William Prosser, "Privacy," 48 California Law Review 383, 392 (1960).

16. Robert Dixon, "The Griswold Penumbra: Constitutional Charter for an Expanding Law of Privacy?" 64 Michigan Law Review 197, 197 (1965).

17. Edward Bloustein, "Privacy as an Aspect of Human Dignity: An Answer to Dean Prosser," 39 New York University Law Review 962, 1003 (1964). See also idem, "Privacy, Tort Law and the Constitution: Is Warren and Brandeis's Tort Petty and Unconstitutional as Well?" 46 Texas Law Review 611 (1978); and idem, "The First Amendment and Privacy: The Supreme Court and the Philosopher," 28 Rutgers Law Review 41 (1974).

18. Boyd v. United States, 116 U.S. 616, 630 (1886).

19. Gerald Dworkin, "The Common Law Protection of Privacy," 2 University of Tasmania Law Review 418, 433 (1967).

20. Hyman Gross, "The Concept of Privacy," 42 New York University Law Review 34, 53 (1967).

21. Ibid.

22. Ibid., at 35-36.

23. Ibid.

24. Hyman Gross, "Privacy and Autonomy," in Privacy, Nomos XIII, ed. Roland J. Pennock and John W. Chapman (New York: Atherton Press, 1971) 169, 170.

25. Charles Fried, An Anatomy of Values (Cambridge, Mass.: Harvard University Press, 1970) 138.

26. Ibid.

27. Charles Fried, "Privacy," 77 Yale Law Journal 475, 482-83 (1965).

28. Oscar M. Ruebhausen and Orville G. Brim, "Privacy and Behavioral Research," 65 Columbia Law Review 1184, 1189 (1965).

29. H. Proshansky, W. H. Ittelson, and L. G. Rivlin, eds., Environmental Psychology (New York: Holt, Rinehart and Winston, 1970).

30. Irwin Altman, "Privacy: A Conceptual Analysis," 8 Environment and Behavior 7, 8 (1976).

31. Ibid., at 8.

32. Arthur R. Miller, Assault on Privacy (Ann Arbor: University of Michigan Press, 1971) at 25.

33. Alan F. Westin, Privacy and Freedom (New York: Atheneum, 1970) at 7-8.

34. Richard B. Parker, "A Definition of Privacy," 27 Rutgers Law Review 275, 280-81 (1974).

35. Ibid., at 279.

36. Lusky, "Invasion of Privacy," at 695.

37. Fried, "Privacy," at 483.

38. H. J. McCloskey, "The Political Ideal of Privacy," 21 Philosophical Quarterly 303, 305-8 (1971).

39. Roland Garrett, "The Nature of Privacy," 18 Philosophy Today 263, 264 (1974).

40. Ibid., 275.

41. Gerald C. MacCallum, Jr., "Negative and Positive Freedom," in Contemporary Political Theory, ed. Anthony de Crespigny and Alan Wertheimer (New York: Atherton Press, 1970) 107, at 109.

42. Joel Feinberg, Social Philosophy (Englewood Cliffs, N.J.: Prentice-Hall, 1973) at 55.

43. H. J. McCloskey, "A Critique of the Ideal of Liberty," 74 Mind 483, 487 (1965).

44. Feinberg, Social Philosophy, at 66.

45. Ibid., at 58.

46. Ibid., at 66.

47. Richard Flathman, The Practice of Rights (Cambridge: At the University Press, 1976) at 1-2.

48. Feinberg, Social Philosophy, at 79.

49. Ronald Dworkin, "Hard Cases," 88 Harvard Law Review 1057, 1063 (1975).

50. Ibid., at 1075.

51. Ibid., at 1070.

PART II

PRIVACY AND THE CONSTITUTION

2

Constitutionally
Protected Privacy:
A Man's House is
His Castle

What infinite hearts' ease must
Kings neglect
That private men enjoy!
And what have kings, that privates
Have not too,
Save ceremony, save general
Ceremony?

William Shakespeare
Henry V, act 4, scene 1

The political ideal of privacy, in the sense of freedom from unwanted intrusions by the government, may have meaning in any polity
because all governments govern imperfectly; some individual conduct
inevitably escapes the exercise of political power and remains private. In this regard the system of free government in the United
States is perhaps both more imperfect in governance and affords
greater protection for individual privacy than do most governments.
By design the U.S. Constitution and Bill of Rights consecrated the
founding principle of limited government, which implies that both the
governors and the governed are subject to the rule of law and "that
governmental powers stop short of certain intrusions into the personal
life of the citizen."[1] Indeed, one purpose of the Bill of Rights "was
to withdraw certain subjects from the vicissitudes of political controversy, to place them beyond the reach of majorities and officials and
to establish them as legal principles to be applied by the courts."[2]
The Constitution and Bill of Rights established that individuals are
free to enjoy their basic liberties except for limitations imposed by
the exercise of valid governmental powers. The U.S. polity, then,
insofar as it embodies the principles and purposes of constitutionally

35

limited government, provides for a political ideal of privacy not
merely in the sense of freedom from governmental intrusions but in
the sense of a basic liberty and right of personal privacy.

Since only constitutionally permissible governmental activities
may constrain the exercise of citizens' liberties, from the standpoint
of the government, citizens have a right of privacy, or what Louis D.
Brandeis called a "right to be let alone." According to Brandeis:

> The makers of our Constitution undertook to secure condi-
> tions favorable to the pursuit of happiness. They recog-
> nized the significance of man's spiritual nature, of his
> feelings and of his intellect. They knew that only part of
> the pain, pleasure and satisfactions of life are to be found
> in material things. They sought to protect Americans in
> their beliefs, their thoughts, their emotions and their sen-
> sations. They conferred as against the Government, the
> right to be let alone—the most comprehensive of rights
> and the right most valued by civilized man.[3]

Brandeis's view and similar judicial characterizations of a constitutional right of privacy as "the beginning of all freedom" and "a fundamentally personal right emanating from the totality of the constitutional scheme under which we live"[4] are understandable, if not without qualification justifiable, in terms of the political ideals embodied
in the written Constitution.

The political ideal of a right of privacy nevertheless exists as a
kind of background right of the fundamental law of the Constitution.
That is, while not explicitly recognized in the Constitution, the right
of privacy as a political ideal remains a presumption of the basic purposes and principles of constitutionally limited government, as well
as the social and political practices that encouraged and maintain the
practice of rights in the United States.

The value of privacy and its connection with individuals' freedom and liberty to choose their relationships and places to enjoy private comforts have long been recognized in the social practices of
U.S. citizens. Although colonists, the revolutionists, and, later,
the framers of the Constitution often only tacitly acknowledged the
value of privacy, it connoted a strong moral sense of what was or
should be regarded as private rather than public. Privacy was never
held to be an absolute value, an unqualified freedom or liberty from
interference. Rather, privacy competed with other values, such as
civic order, sociability, and fraternity. Moreover, while early citizens respected privacy, when a controversy over personal privacy
occurred, apart from actual physical assault or destruction of private
property, the matter was treated as that of personal honor, which in

most instances resulted in a duel, a horsewhipping, or a shooting. An invasion of privacy was treated as a matter of personal honor, in part, because privacy had not risen to the status of a legal entity in seventeenth-century English common law or the biblical law of the Puritans, nor the mixture of both traditions that characterized the law of New England colonies.[5]

Colonists through their colonial charters, and later the drafters of the Constitution and Bill of Rights, enlarged upon traditional English liberties; in particular, freedom of religion, freedom of conscience, freedom of assembly, and the freedom from unreasonable searches and seizures. Still, the guarantees of religious freedom, due process, and protection from unreasonable searches and seizures appear at least one conceptual level removed from the explicit recognition of a right of personal privacy. That is, "freedom of religion, for example, guarantees a person the right to believe in the faith of his choice; while the right of privacy makes it possible for the individual to refuse to let anyone else know what his particular religious affiliation might happen to be."[6] From this standpoint, historian Thomas H. O'Connor correctly concludes: "Since American colonists were not yet secure in the fundamental rights themselves, it is obvious that they were not yet ready to concern themselves with a concept which presumes that those basic rights have already been achieved."[7] In other words, explicit recognition of a legal right of privacy depended upon first securing basic rights to personal liberty and property. Establishment of legal guarantees for interests in freedom of speech, press, religious exercise, and possession of private property was contingent on social practices that evidenced a modicum of respect for privacy. Yet, establishment of those guarantees remained a prerequisite for legal recognition of privacy itself. The incorporation of basic personal liberties and property rights into the Bill of Rights not only ensured those privacy interests associated with the effective exercise of explicit constitutional guarantees but made possible, through judicial construction, the legitimation of claims to a constitutional right of privacy.

Because the Bill of Rights was designed to secure basic civil liberties and, more broadly, it may be argued, individuals' "right to be let alone," the absence of explicit provision for a right of privacy necessitated that privacy interests lay dormant, until either constitutional interpretation acknowledged and legitimated their connection with express constitutional guarantees, or judicial creativity fashioned a right of privacy. The exercise of judicial power in legitimating claims to constitutionally protected privacy nevertheless has been controversial. Evaluation of the Supreme Court's fashioning a constitutional right of privacy and criticisms thereof, however, requires closer examination of the judicial construction of the Bill of Rights and constitutionally protected privacy. Fourth Amendment safeguards for individuals' privacy interests are examined in this chapter. Chapters 3 and 4 explore claims to constitutionally protected privacy under the Fifth and First Amendments. Chapter 5 concludes the examination of the developing constitutional law of privacy by considering privacy claims with regard to the Ninth and Fourteenth Amendments, along with the dynamics of judicial construction of a constitutional right of privacy.

HISTORICAL BASIS FOR FOURTH AMENDMENT-PROTECTED PRIVACY

From Paxton's Case to the Bill of Rights

Personal privacy attains perhaps its principal constitutional protection and the closest approximation of explicit recognition in the guarantees of the Fourth Amendment. The amendment, as similar provisions in state constitutions, was drafted in response to abuses connected with general warrants or writs of assistance employed by British officials in the colonies prior to the American Revolution. [8] The English Parliament had authorized searches and seizures as early as 1335 in granting innkeepers in port towns the right to search and seize illegally imported monies. However, during the reign of Charles I, with the cooperation of Parliament, the Privy Council, and the Star Chamber, general warrants resulted in "ransacking" and seizure of the personal papers of political dissidents, authors, and printers of seditious libel. Not until Entrick v. Carrington in 1765 were general warrants held illegal; Parliament in the next year declared them illegal. [9]

During this period colonists complained against the use of writs of assistance by royal officers. In Paxton's Case, James Otis declared in a historic indictment against the writs: "A man's house is his castle; and while is quiet, he is well guarded as a prince in his castle."[10] Otis registered a belief of both Englishmen and colonists. That belief was perhaps most eloquently articulated by William Pitt, the Elder:

> The Poorest man may in his cottage bid defiance to all the force of the Crown. It may be frail—its roof may shake——the wind may blow through it—the storm may enter—the rain may enter—but the King of England cannot enter—all his force dares not cross the threshold of the ruined tenement. [11]

The allusion of individuals' houses to castles is intelligible not merely because houses are fortresses and bastions of private property but also because they are the principal place in which individuals engage and conduct their affairs in private. Hence, the Virginia Declaration of Rights denounced general warrants as "grievous and oppressive," and later Patrick Henry urging the adoption of the Bill of Rights argued that:

> The officer of Congress may come upon you now, fortified with all the terrors of paramount federal authority. Excisemen may come in multitudes; for the limitations of their numbers no man knows. They may, unless the general government be restrained by a bill of rights, or some similar restrictions, go into your cellars and rooms, and search, ransack, and measure, everything you eat, drink, and wear. They ought to be restrained within proper bounds. [12]

James Madison drafted the initial proposal for limiting searches and seizures by the government:

> The right of the people to be secured in their persons, houses, papers, and effects, shall not be violated by warrants issuing without probable cause, supported by an oath or affirmation, and not particularly describing the place to be searched or the persons or things to be seized. [13]

Madison's proposal was altered when Elbridge Gerry changed "secured" to "secure" and inserted the clause "against unreasonable searches and seizures," and another delegate changed "by warrants issuing" to "and no warrant shall issue."[14] No further significant changes were made, and, thus, upon adoption of the Bill of Rights Madison's revised proposal became the Fourth Amendment to the Constitution.

The Language and Logic of the
Fourth Amendment

A literal reading of the amendment provides no basis for establishing a right of privacy per se. Yet, the historic Anglo-American concerns and social practices leading to the adoption of the Bill of Rights and, in particular, the Fourth Amendment support the conclusion that individuals have legitimate expectations of privacy when connected with the fundamental liberty against arbitrary governmental intrusions. The amendment guarantees individuals "the right to be secure in their persons, houses, papers, and effects . . . against unreasonable searches and seizures." The first clause affirmatively states a general right guaranteeing individuals' exercise of their protected liberty, whereas the second clause specifies procedural safeguards. Searches and seizures are reasonable when backed by a warrant issued upon "probable cause, supported by an Oath or affirmation, and particularly describing the place to be searched, and the persons or things to be seized." Fourth Amendment provisions therefore may be articulated either as ensuring individuals' substantive right to be secure in their persons and property or, alternatively, as procedural safeguards against unreasonable governmental intrusions into their private lives and affairs.

Because the Fourth Amendment guarantees individuals' right to be secure from unreasonable governmental intrusions, individuals have legitimate expectations of privacy with regard to the security of their "persons, houses, papers, and effects." The amendment's protections logically extend to those privacy interests associated with the fundamental liberty guaranteed therein. Hence, the Fourth Amendment's protection of certain privacy interests follows not only from the historical concerns reflected in the amendment but also from the logic of the language of the amendment.

Actually, the historic concerns and the logic of the amendment were interrelated in the social practices of early citizens of the United States. That interrelationship was most lucidly articulated in Judge Thomas Cooley's discussion of invasions of "one's privacy" within the context of that

> maxim of the common law which secures to the citizen immunity in his home against the prying eyes of the government, and protection in person, property, and papers even against the process of law, except in a few specified cases. The maxim that "every man's house is his castle" is made a part of our constitutional law in the clause prohibiting unreasonable searches and seizures.[15]

Judge Cooley's discussion of privacy within the context of citizens' houses, the affairs of the household, and the protection afforded by the Fourth Amendment not only reiterated the historic concerns with securing personal liberty and property rights but also anticipated judicial construction of the amendment's protection of "the sanctities of a man's home and the privacies of life."[16]

LIBERAL CONSTRUCTION AND
PROGENY—PRODIGAL SONS?

An Expansive Interpretation

While the Supreme Court noted the relationship between privacy and the Fourth Amendment in an 1877 case, which held that Congress could not authorize the postal service "to invade the secrecy of letters,"[17] the first discussion of the relationship did not occur until 1886 in Boyd v. United States.[18] In holding unconstitutional a statute that permitted the government to order the accused to produce shipping invoices of allegedly illegally imported goods, the Court set a liberal construction as its standard for interpreting the Fourth and Fifth Amendments. "[C]onstitutional provisions for the security of person and property should be liberally construed. A close and literal construction deprives them of half their efficacy, and leads to gradual deprecation of the right, as if it consisted more in sound than in substance."[19] With a liberal construction privacy interests may be protected when associated with the liberty safeguarded by the Fourth Amendment. Justice Bradley fervently argued:

> The principles laid down in Entrick v. Carrington, 19
> How. State Trials (K.B. 1765) affect the very essence
> of constitutional liberty and security. They reach far-
> ther than the concrete form of the case then before the
> court, with its adventitious circumstances; they apply to
> all invasions on the part of the government and its em-
> ployees of the sanctity of a man's home and the privacies
> of life. It is not the breaking of his doors, and rummaging
> of his drawers, that constitutes the essence of the offense;
> but it is the invasion of his indefeasible right of personal
> liberty and private property, where that right has never
> been forfeited by his conviction of some public offense—
> it is the invasion of this sacred right which underlies and
> constitutes the essence of Lord Camden's judgement.
> Breaking into a house and opening boxes and drawers are
> circumstances of aggrevation; but any forcible and com-
> pulsory extortion of a man's own testimony or of his pri-
> vate papers to be used as evidence to convict him of crime
> or to forfeit his goods, is within the condemnation of that
> judgement. In this regard the Fourth and Fifth Amend-
> ments run almost into each other.[20]

Justice Bradley's opinion emphasized an expansive role for the Fourth Amendment in securing personal privacy; indeed, in an appropriation of Justice Story's terminology, the Fourth Amendment guarantees an "indefeasible right of personal security, personal liberty and private property."[21]

While Justice Bradley noted the interrelationship between the Fourth and Fifth Amendments, his significant conclusion was that the purpose of the Fourth Amendment was to protect the security and privacy of "persons, houses, papers, and effects"; as a corollary, police could seize only instrumentalities of a crime but never an individual's papers as mere evidence of a crime. Justice Bradley's conclusion followed from his construction of the reasonableness clause of the amendment. He argued that individuals have an indefeasible property right at common law and under the Fourth Amendment, which renders unreasonable any governmental search and seizure of private papers or other property for mere evidence of a crime. Accordingly, no warrant or subpoena could reasonably issue for items not already owned by or forfeited to the state. In this connection Justice Bradley comments: "The unreasonable searches and seizures condemned in the Fourth Amendment are almost always made for the purpose of compelling a man to give evidence against himself, which in criminal cases is condemned in the Fifth Amendment."[22] Compelling an individual to produce private papers or other property is inherently unreasonable. Simply stated, it contravenes basic liberties and expectations of privacy associated with private property, as defined by common law property rights and as guaranteed by the procedural safeguards of the Fourth Amendment, as well as protected in criminal cases by the Fifth Amendment's right against self-accusation.

Constitutionally protected privacy, therefore, did not depend on the existence of an "intimate relationship" between the Fourth and Fifth Amendments. Rather, the amendments independently demarcate and provide alternative guarantees for particular liberties and interests in personal privacy. Justice Bradley's opinion emphasized that in some instances claims of personal privacy are especially well founded due to the intersecting and overlapping guarantees of both amendments. Thus, the intimate relationship between the amendments results from the kinds of privacy expectations individuals may assert under either amendment. In some situations privacy claims may derive constitutional justification from both the Fourth and Fifth Amendments. "That these two amendments should independently protect a person's books and papers was for Justice Bradley all the more reason to place the individual's private communications in a special position beyond the government's reach."[23]

Because courts have often relied upon a connection between the two amendments, it is critical to observe that privacy claims justifiably rely upon the independent guarantees of either amendment. A "convergence theory"[24] blurs the particular privacy interests associated with each amendment and neglects the significantly distinct functions served by both amendments. In some situations intrusions upon individuals' liberties and privacy expectations may suggest an intimate relation between the guarantees of the Fourth and Fifth Amendments, yet that relationship follows only because of the independent protections of each amendment. As Justice Clark reiterated in the majority opinion in Mapp v. Ohio:

> We find that, as to the Federal Government, the Fourth and Fifth Amendments and, as to the States, the freedom from unconscionable invasions of privacy and the freedom from convictions based upon coerced confessions do enjoy an "intimate relation. . . ." They express "supplementing phases of the same constitutional purpose—to maintain inviolate large areas of personal privacy." The philosophy of each amendment and of each freedom is complementary to, although not dependent upon, that of the other in its sphere of influence—the very least that together they assure in either sphere is that no man is to be convicted on unconstitutional evidence.[25]

Justice Bradley's construction of the Fourth Amendment and its underlying common law property principles ensured extensive protection for privacy. Privacy interests associated with common law proprietary interests received constitutional legitimacy under the amendment's guarantee against unreasonable governmental intrusions upon "persons, houses, papers, and effects." Indeed, although the amendment's applicability was limited to governmental intrusions, the Court never restricted constitutionally permissible claims of privacy against official intrusions to a literal reading of the Fourth Amendment.[26] While the Court in Hester v. United States held that the Fourth Amendment's protection of persons, houses, papers, and effects did not extend to "open fields,"[27] subsequent determinations established protection for individuals' houses, business offices, stores, hotel rooms, apartments, automobiles, and taxicabs.[28] Individuals could raise legitimate claims to privacy in such constitutionally protected areas.

Late nineteenth and early twentieth century courts thereby ensured personal privacy by focusing on the content and area of governmental searches and seizures. Furthermore, Justice Bradley's determination of an indefeasible right of privacy at common law and under the Fourth Amendment implied the constitutional protection of mere evidence and the exclusion of ill-gotten evidence, thereby establishing two further protections for individual privacy under the Fourth Amendment.

The Mere Evidence Rule

Judicial construction limits protected privacy under the Fourth Amendment to proscription of unreasonable governmental intrusions. The Court for almost a century endeavored on a case-by-case basis to determine what constitutes a reasonable search and seizure.[29] In 1920, for example, the Court reversed a contempt citation issued for refusal to produce certain books and papers because the subpoena was issued on information illegally obtained.[30] In the next year, in Gouled v. United States, the Court held that unlawfully seized papers could be suppressed at trial despite the acquiesced-in denial of the defendant's pretrial motion for their return.[31]

The Gouled decision reaffirmed Justice Bradley's construction of the reasonableness clause and his interpretation that the Fourth Amendment dovetailed with the Fifth Amendment's right against self-accusation in providing substantial protection for personal privacy. The Court held that the seizure of private papers violated the prohibition of the Fourth Amendment and that the introduction of the papers as evidence in the trial violated the Fifth Amendment. While the absence of a search warrant would have been sufficient grounds for excluding the papers seized as evidence, the Court, as in Boyd, argued that under the Fourth Amendment the government could permissible seize only that property that it could also assert a proprietary interest in at common law, as with warrants for stolen property. In reaffirming Boyd's underlying property principles, the Court fashioned a distinction between "mere evidence" and materials that served as "agency or instrumentality" of a crime. The Fourth Amendment protected evidentiary materials but not instrumentalities of crime, fruit of crime, and contraband that might be seized in order to prevent its use and possible injury to the public.

Construction of the mere evidence rule as a means of limiting governmental intrusions upon citizens "apparently constituted a crude attempt by the Supreme Court to strike a fourth amendment balance between the government's interest in gathering evidence of criminal activity and the individual's reasonable expectations of privacy."[32] Subsequent applications of the rule, however, led to inconsistent and illogical results.[33] Nevertheless, not until the 1960s did the Court indicate that it might depart from the interpretation of the Fourth Amendment received in Boyd and Gouled. In Jones v. United States, the Court suggested that the amendment's protections need not be confined to traditional property rights:

> We are persuaded, . . . that it is unnecessary and ill-advised to import into the law surrounding the constitutional right to be free from unreasonable searches and seizures

subtle distinctions, developed and refined by the common law in evolving the body of private property law which, more than almost any other branch of law, has been shaped by distinctions whose validity is largely historical.[34]

In 1967 the Court explicitly abandoned the justification for Fourth Amendment-protected privacy based upon property principles. In Warden v. Hayden the Court observed:

> The premise that property interests control the right of the Government to search and seize has been discredited. Searches and seizures may be "unreasonable" within the Fourth Amendment even though the Government asserts a superior property interest at common law. We have recognized that the principal object of the Fourth Amendment is the protection of privacy rather than property, and have increasingly discarded fictional and procedural barriers rested on property concepts.[35]

In the following year, in Mancusi v. DeForte, the Court reiterated that privacy claims under the amendment depend "not upon a proprietary right in the invaded place but upon whether the area was one in which there was a reasonable expectation of freedom from governmental intrusion."[36]

The confusion that arose in distinguishing between mere evidence and instrumentalities resulted in the abandonment of this distinction and contributed to the rejection of the underlying property principles of Boyd-Gouled. Yet, in the early twentieth century the Boyd-Gouled rationale provided a useful conceptual and constitutional approach to privacy protection. As Justice Marshall noted in his dissent in Couch v. United States: "These concepts attempted to define, however imprecisely, a sphere of personal privacy that the Government could not enter over objection."[37] Certainly, "the nature of what is seized is relevant to application of the Fourth Amendment in cases where the object's nature reveals, on its face, that special expectations of privacy are present."[38] The Boyd-Gouled rationale thus not only provided for a limitation on searches conducted under a valid warrant but also for a relatively objective standard for privacy protection. The shift in judicial protection of privacy away from the Boyd-Gouled rationale that conjoined privacy interests with proprietary interests, moreover, was concomitant with the Supreme Court's gradual repudiation of the basis for the exclusionary rule and its role in securing constitutionally protected privacy.

The Exclusionary Rule

In order to ensure the Fourth Amendment's historic purposes
of providing safeguards against general warrants and preventing arbitrary governmental intrusions into the privacy of a person's home,
as well as enforcing Boyd's liberal construction, the Supreme Court
in Weeks v. United States adopted the exclusionary rule prohibiting
admission in federal courts of illegally seized evidence.[39] Justice
Day, writing for the majority, refused to distinguish between the
seizure and the introduction of evidence at trial in holding that illegally obtained materials must be excluded as evidence. To allow the
introduction of illegally seized materials "would be to affirm by judicial decision a manifest neglect, if not an open defiance, of the Constitution."[40] Justice Day premised the exclusionary rule upon both
the disapproval of illegal governmental activity and the recognition of
the need to preserve the integrity of the judicial system.

Weeks clearly indicated that without an exclusionary rule claims
against unreasonable "invasions of the home and privacy of the citizens" would have little practical feasibility:

If letters and private documents can thus be seized and
held and used in evidence against a citizen accused of an
offense, the protection of the Fourth Amendment declaring
this right to be secure against such searches and seizures
is of no value, and, so far as those thus placed are concerned, might as well be stricken from the Constitution.[41]

Although the exclusionary rule functions only negatively on the suppression of evidence, its justification in Weeks rested with a constitutional right guaranteed by the Fourth Amendment rather than with a
judicial policy. The Fourth Amendment safeguards individuals from
unreasonable searches and seizures and therefore requires the exclusion at trial of any evidence unlawfully obtained.[42]

Because the Bill of Rights had been held not to apply directly to
the states, the Weeks-established exclusionary rule was likewise not
required in state courts.[43] After Weeks, in Wolf v. Colorado the
Court explicitly refused to apply the rule to the states.[44] Moreover,
despite the Court's recognition of legitimate privacy claims, the majority held that the rule was a nonconstitutional remedy. Justice
Frankfurter, however, observed that "[t]he security of one's privacy
against arbitrary intrusion by the police—which is at the core of the
Fourth Amendment—is basic to a free society. It is therefore implicit
in the concept of 'ordered liberty' and as such enforceable against the
states through the Due Process Clause."[45] Although acknowledging
that the core of the Fourth Amendment protects personal privacy, the

majority nevertheless declined to suggest a method for enforcing it
against the states. Justice Frankfurter termed the exclusionary rule
a mere "judicial implication" based neither on explicit constitutional
requirements nor congressional legislation enforcing the Constitution.

In contrast the dissenters argued that the right of privacy as
the core of the Fourth Amendment required that the states be prohibited from both unreasonable searches and seizures and the introduction of unconstitutionally obtained evidence. They observed that
the rule is the only means of giving content to the commands of the
Fourth Amendment. Justices Rutledge and Murphy further contended
that the Constitution itself requires an exclusionary privilege and expressed their belief that introduction of unconstitutionally obtained
evidence compromised judicial integrity. [46]

Eleven years later, in Elkins v. United States, the majority of
the Court accepted the Wolf dissenters' view of the exclusionary rule
but rejected their rationale. [47] The majority eliminated the distinction between Fourth Amendment requirements imposed on the federal
government and those requirements of the due process clause of the
Fourteenth Amendment imposed on the states. The Elkins majority
concluded that there is no logical distinction between evidence obtained in violation of the Fourth Amendment and that acquired in violation of the Fourteenth Amendment.

The majority thereby overruled Weeks, holding that evidence
unreasonably seized by state officials was inadmissible in federal
courts but accepted the reasoning in Wolf that the exclusionary rule
rested on the Court's supervisory power and not upon a constitutional
right. Because of "considerations of reason and experience," the
Court held that exclusion from federal courts of evidence illegally
seized by state officials was essential to protected privacy. "The
rule is calculated to prevent, not repair. Its purpose is to deter—to
compel respect for the constitutional guaranty in the only effectively
available way—by removing the incentive to disregard it." [48] Ironically, the Court extended the exclusionary rule, not by relying on the
constitutional principle of exclusion and protected privacy recognized
in Weeks, but by accepting Wolf's rationale of judicial policies aimed
at deterring official invasions of privacy and preserving judicial integrity.

Two years after Elkins the Supreme Court nevertheless concluded
that the exclusionary rule actually rests on constitutional principles.
In Mapp v. Ohio the Court found the rule to be an "essential ingredient"
of the Fourth Amendment and therefore to apply directly to state criminal proceedings. [49] Justice Clark, for the majority, stated:

> Since the Fourth Amendment's right of privacy has been de-
> clared enforceable against the States through the Due Pro-

cess clause of the Fourteenth, it is enforceable against
them by the same sanction of exclusion as is used against
the Federal Government. Were it otherwise, then just as
without the Weeks rule the assurance against unreasonable
federal searches and seizures would be "a form of words,"
valueless and undeserving of mention in a perpetual charter of inestimable human liberties so too, without that rule
the freedom from state invasions of privacy would be so
ephemeral and so neatly severed from its conceptual
nexus with the freedom from all brutish means of coercing
evidence as not to merit this Court's high regard as a freedom "implicit in the concept of ordered liberty."[50]

As in Boyd the Court recognized the "complementary" phases of the
Fourth and Fifth Amendments in constitutionally protecting privacy
but relied solely on the Fourth Amendment as the basis for excluding
evidence unlawfully seized.

Having once recognized that the right to privacy embodied
in the Fourth Amendment is enforceable against the States
. . . we can no longer permit that right to remain an empty
promise. . . . Our decision, founded on reason and truth,
gives to the individual no more than that which the Constitution guarantees him, to the police not more than that to
which honest law enforcement is entitled, and, to the courts,
that judicial integrity so necessary in the true administration of justice.[51]

Significantly, then, the Court justified the exclusionary rule upon constitutional principles extending to a right of personal privacy, noting
as supplementary justifications the Elkins rationale and the policy of
preserving judicial integrity.[52]

By contrast, in Linkletter v. Walker, decided the next year,
the Court retreated to its former position that claims to constitutionally protected privacy constitute only a privilege and not a right under
the Fourth Amendment.[53] In Linkletter the Court identified deterrence
as the principal rationale for the exclusionary rule and denied retroactivity to the Mapp holding:

We cannot say that this purpose [deterence] would be advanced by making the rule retroactive. . . . Nor would it
add harmony to the delicate state-federal relationship of
which we have spoken as part and parcel of the purpose
of Mapp. Finally, the ruptured privacy of the victims'
homes and effects cannot be restored. Reparation comes
too late.[54]

While Linkletter might have appeared sui generis, the decision actually indicated the Court's preference for a policy rationale over a constitutional principle as the basis for the exclusionary rule. Subsequent Burger Court decisions focused on deterrence as the rationale for the rule and, moreover, objected to both the rule and its rationale.[55] Indeed, in United States v. Calandra, where the exclusionary rule was held not to apply to questions asked of a grand jury witness, which were based on evidence obtained by an illegal search and seizure of his papers, the majority refused to recognize that a right of privacy shielded individuals from having to provide information to grand juries:

> The duty to testify may on occasion be burdensome and
> even embarrassing. It may cause injury to a witness's
> social and economic status. Yet the duty to testify has
> been regarded as "so necessary to the administration of
> justice" that the witness's personal interest in privacy
> must yield to the public's overriding interest in full dis-
> closure.[56]

In sum, as judicial interpretation divorced the exclusionary rule from its initial justification in terms of constitutional rights, the rule's role in safeguarding personal privacy diminished.

Although the rule operates only negatively on the suppression of evidence, the Weeks-Mapp rationale that the Fourth Amendment forbids use of unlawfully obtained evidence permitted extensive protection and legitimation of privacy claims. Admittedly, upon a "personal rights" rationale for the rule the Court might appear to be "making the tail of the exclusionary rule wag the dog of the Fourth Amendment."[57] As Robert McKay observes:

> The exclusionary rule of Mapp v. Ohio is a concededly blunt
> and somewhat imprecise instrument for the protection of
> individual privacy against official lawlessness. It is of
> course easier for law enforcement officers to proceed di-
> rectly against the homes, the business, the telephones and
> the persons of those suspected of wrong doing. But the
> United States Constitution forecloses that route in its em-
> phasis upon the higher call of privacy of person and effects.[58]

Still, in holding that a right of privacy is at the core of the Fourth Amendment, the Weeks-Mapp rationale for the exclusionary rule followed as a corollary of the liberal construction of the Fourth Amendment and the underlying principles of Boyd-Gouled.

By comparison, the Warren and Burger Courts increasingly fostered a policy orientation toward and a rationalization of the exclusionary rule as promoting judicial integrity and deterrence. The rule functions on a theory of judicial integrity to maintain the appearance and reality of judicial noncomplicity in illegal governmental activities.[59] Similarly, upon a deterrence theory the rule is not constitutionally required.[60] Instead, the rule serves an educative role in that it makes plain to law enforcement officers that unlawful seizures are futile. Consequently, the rule functions as only one possible means of implementing the values of the Fourth Amendment. With either rationale, since both depend on policy considerations rather than constitutional principles, the rule, and its safeguard for privacy, becomes contingent upon utilitarian calculations as to its effectiveness in achieving either police deterrence or judicial integrity. As Chief Justice Burger stated, in United States v. Checcolini, the Court must "balance the costs to society of losing perfectly competent evidence against the prospect of incrementally enhancing Fourth Amendment values."[61] Criticisms of the exclusionary rule's effectiveness from both within and without the Court have led to restrictive application of the rule.[62] Privacy claims under the rule are likely to be increasingly overridden by interests in the prosecution of criminals.[63]

Notwithstanding the Burger Court's policy orientation toward the exclusionary rule, the Weeks rationale rested upon constitutional principles, as had Gouled's mere evidence rule, logically deriving from the underlying jurisprudence of Boyd's liberal construction of the Fourth Amendment. Together, the Boyd–Gouled–Weeks extension of the amendment's guarantees to constitutionally protected areas, the prohibition of searches for and seizures of mere evidence, and the exclusion of illegally obtained evidence at trial promoted extensive safeguards for personal privacy. The Boyd–Gouled–Weeks rationale reflected what Alan Westin termed a "propertied privacy"[64] outlook, because the Court's construction of the amendment gave constitutional effect to the common law maxim "a man's house is his castle" by associating privacy interests with proprietary interests at common law.

Fourth Amendment-protected privacy as developed in Boyd–Gouled–Weeks presupposed a spatial conception of privacy. Legitimate claims to the privacy of individuals' engagements arose with regard to and were justifiable in terms of the locus of the individuals' engagements as defined by proprietary interests. Privacy claims were strongest in so-called "constitutionally protected areas,"[65] particularly in one's house, and were enforced by the express requirements of the Fourth Amendment as well as the judicially constructed mere evidence and exclusionary rules.

Technological changes in the early twentieth century posed anew the problem of determining what constitutes an unreasonable search and seizure under the Fourth Amendment.[66] The way in which the Court dealt with the potential and actual invasions of personal privacy

that resulted from law enforcement's adoption of new technology led
to demise of the doctrine of constitutionally protected areas, repudiation of the mere evidence rule, and subsequent, albeit gradual, modi-
fication of the rationale for the exclusionary rule. Within the practice
of rights and the patterns of judicially enforced privacy claims, the
repudiation of both the Gouled- and Weeks-established rules and rationales accompanied the rejection of the underlying jurisprudence of
Boyd. The next section examines the patterns of judicial construction
of the Fourth Amendment that led to the rejection of Boyd's jurisprudence of constitutionally protected privacy and encouraged a conceptual
and constitutional approach to protected privacy bearing only a family
resemblance to that fostered by Boyd.

FROM OLMSTEAD TO KATZ: REASONABLE
EXPECTATIONS OF PROTECTED PRIVACY

Olmstead's Strict Construction and Application

In the early twentieth century the development of new technological equipment such as the telephone and radio made it possible to conduct and eavesdrop on oral conversations at great distances. As a
result the question arose as to whether Fourth Amendment claims
could be legitimately asserted against nontrespassory government intrusions by means of wiretapping, eavesdropping, and other electronic
monitoring devices. In the 1928 landmark case Olmstead v. United
States, the Supreme Court's five-to-four decision implied that no legitimate privacy claims existed with regard to messages passing over
telephone lines outside a person's house or office. [67] The Court held
that since the interception of such messages is carried out without
entry into an individual's premises, there is no "search" of a constitutionally protected area and, further, telephone messages are not
things that can be "seized" under the Fourth Amendment. Ironically,
the Olmstead decision resulted from the Court's rigid adherence to
Boyd's jurisprudential basis and emphasis upon property principles
in interpreting the reasonableness clause of the Fourth Amendment.
That is, Olmstead's rigid application of Boyd's property principles
resulted in an illiberal construction of constitutionally protected privacy.

Olmstead denied recognition of privacy expectations against
nontrespassing intrusions because the Fourth Amendment literally prohibits "unreasonable searches and seizures," and the Court assumed
that prior to determining reasonableness there must be a "search"
involving physical trespass and a "seizure" of tangible material.
Chief Justice Taft's majority opinion found the property principles un-

derlying the amendment to imply, first, that listening by means of
electronic devices did not constitute a "search" since no physical
trespass occurred and, second, no unconstitutional "seizure" took
place as no tangible material was involved.

Chief Justice Taft's strict construction of the amendment and
its underlying property concepts and principles was a retrenchment
of Boyd inasmuch as the Court refused to recognize privacy claims
that were not identical with proprietary interests in tangible materials.
The petitioners admitted that "[i]t would indeed be difficult to attempt
to enumerate all those things coming within the phrase 'the privacies
of life,'" but also observed that "[i]f a private telephone line into a
man's home or office is not one of the 'privacies of life,' then it is
difficult for the human mind to conceive what would be included in that
phrase."[68] Nevertheless, Chief Justice Taft accepted a strict construction as had the majority in the court of appeals. "Whatever may
be said of the tapping of telephone wires as an unethical intrusion upon
the privacy of persons who are suspected of crime, it is not an act
which comes within the letter of the prohibition of constitutional provisions."[69] Noting that "the common law rule that evidence [is] not
rendered inadmissible in a criminal case by illegality of the means
by which it was obtained,"[70] Chief Justice Taft refused to find of constitutional significance any difference between evidence gathered by
wiretapping or obtained by looking through or listening at windows or
doors. Thus, accepting the traditional property principles underlying
previously liberal interpretations of the Fourth Amendment, Olmstead
adopted the strict construction of the amendment urged by the government:

> In every case in which a violation of the Fourth Amendment
> was found to have occurred the decision without exception
> dealt with a case in which the object of the search and
> seizure condemned was literally described in the language
> of the Amendment; that is, "persons, houses, papers, and
> effects," "effects" used in the sense of tangible personal
> property.[71]

Strict construction of both the amendment and the nexus between privacy and proprietary interests consequently narrowed constitutionally
recognizable claims to personal privacy. As William Beaney writes,
"In effect, the majority looked upon the Fourth Amendment as a guaranty against a particular method of invading privacy or personal security—as a ban on physical intrusion of the home and seizure of material objects—rather than a protection of the right of privacy itself
[that is, the recognition and protection of interests in the intrinsic
worth of privacy]."[72]

In his dissent Justice Butler endeavored to extend traditional property concepts and principles to the problem of wiretapping: "Wire tapping involves interference with the wire while being used. Tapping the wires and listening in by the officers literally constituted a search for evidence."[73] Justice Butler attempted to combine a strict construction of property principles with a liberal construction of protected privacy by finding proprietary interests in the wire violated by the tap. A broader range of claims to personal privacy could thereby be accommodated than under Chief Justice Taft's opinion. Yet Justice Butler, like Chief Justice Taft, assumed identification of privacy interests with traditional proprietary interests. Justice Butler permitted more extensive recognition of claims to privacy because of his liberal application of property principles. Still, Justice Butler's position, like Chief Justice Taft's, prohibited Fourth Amendment applicability to privacy invaded by the use of detectaphones and electronic surveillance equipment other than wiretaps. Justice Butler's strict construction yet liberal application of the underlying property principles of the amendment represented an untenable compromise between Chief Justice Taft's strict construction and application of the amendment and dissenting Justice Brandeis's liberal construction and application of the amendment.

Justice Brandeis emphasized a liberal construction and application of the Fourth Amendment. He argued that the amendment's guarantees impose general limitations on the government and those limitations should be interpreted so as to ensure the basic purposes of the amendment in theretofore unforeseen situations. Hence, constitutionally recognizable claims to personal privacy must not be confined to traditional categories of searches involving physical trespass and seizures of tangible materials. The amendment liberally construed, Justice Brandeis argued, was not limited to trespass on private property nor the seizure of tangible materials but extended "to protect . . . [against] every unjustifiable intrusion by the Government upon the privacy of the individual, whatever the means employed."[74] Judicial recognition of constitutionally protected privacy, therefore, did not depend on the government's violation of an individual's proprietary interests. Claims to protected privacy are not identical with proprietary claims, though privacy interests may be—and, indeed, historically were—associated with citizens' proprietary interests in their persons, houses, papers, and effects. According to Justice Brandeis's liberal construction and application of the amendment, governmental intrusions upon individuals' privacy in their homes, papers, effects, or personal engagements would be permissible if and only if the government could establish the reasonableness of the particular form of intrusion.

Historically, the Supreme Court accepted neither Chief Justice Taft's strict construction and application nor Justice Brandeis's liberal construction and application of the Fourth Amendment and its underlying property principles. The Court also rejected Justice Butler's version of a compromise, namely, a strict construction and liberal application of Fourth Amendment property principles. Instead, the Court gradually adopted a liberal construction of the underlying property principles of the Fourth Amendment but provided less than liberal application to privacy claims. Indeed, not until the mid-1960s did the Court denounce Olmstead's theory of physical trespass as a precondition for a "search" and reject its tangibles requirement for a "seizure" under the amendment.

Whittling Away at the Trespass Theory

Initially the Supreme Court circumvented Olmstead's trespass theory by construing the issue of unwanted access to personal communications by means of wiretaps as posing a problem of interpreting and applying Section 605 of the Federal Communications Act rather than the Fourth Amendment. The Court in Nardone v. United States used this act to evade the issue of electronic surveillance, that is, at least with regard to wiretaps. [75]

In 1942, however, the Court extended its trespass theory to the use of detectaphones, devices that when placed against a wall detect sounds on the other side of the wall. In Goldman v. United States federal agents without a warrant entered the defendant's office and planted a dictaphone with wires leading to an office next door, but the next day the dictaphone broke and the agents used a detectaphone instead. [76] The Court held that evidence obtained by the use of the detectaphone was admissible since no physical trespass had occurred; by contrast, evidence gathered from the dictaphone would have been inadmissible. Strict construction and application of the trespass distinction in this instance precluded recognition of constitutionally protected privacy.

Three years later in On Lee v. United States, the Court held that there was no trespass when a narcotics officer listened to conversations from a microphone hidden on the undercover agent. [77] The conversation was held admissible because On Lee had spoken voluntarily with the undercover agent. The majority accepted the court of appeals ruling that the presence of the microphone on the secret agent eliminated any constitutional difficulties. In an important dissent from the circuit court, however, Judge Frank reiterated Boyd's interpretation that the historic purposes and principles underlying the Fourth Amendment required protection of privacy rather than merely prohibition of intrusions by physical trespass. Judge Frank eloquently expressed the view that the amendment guarantees privacy in constitutionally protected areas:

> A man can still control a small part of his environment,
> his house; he can retreat thence from outsiders, secure
> in the knowledge that they cannot get at him without diso-
> beying the constitution. That is still a sizeable hunk of
> liberty—worth protecting from encroachment. A sane,
> decent, civilized society must provide some such oasis,
> some shutter from public scrutiny, some insulated enclo-
> sure, some enclave, some inviolate place which is a man's
> castle. [78]

The Supreme Court, by strict application of the trespass distinction,
rejected such liberal interpretations and confined its analysis to intrusions upon constitutionally protected areas.

Although still relying on Olmstead-Goldman's rigid trespass distinction, the Court in 1961 did allow the exclusion of a defendant's
conversation on Fourth Amendment grounds. In Silverman v. United
States, federal agents without a warrant drove a "spike-mike" into a
wall to overhear conversations. [79] They made contact with a heating
duct serving the defendant's house and, thus, were able to monitor
conversations throughout the house. The mike's connection with the
duct constituted an actual intrusion in a constitutionally protected area
and not merely a technical trespass. Justice Stewart, writing for the
majority, however, concluded: "We find no occasion to re-examine
Goldman [that is, consider the protection of personal conversations
absent intrusion into a constitutionally protected area], but we decline to go beyond it, by even a fraction of an inch."[80] Concurring in
Silverman, Justice Douglas urged that the Court renew a liberal construction of constitutionally protected privacy and abandon its trespass
distinctions and rigid adherence to property concepts and principles:

> The depth of the penetration of the electronic device—even
> the degree of its remoteness from the house—is not the
> measure of the injury. . . . Our concern should not be
> with the trivialities of the local law of trespass, as the
> opinion of the Court indicates. But neither should the com-
> mand of the Fourth Amendment be limited by nice distinc-
> tions turning on the kind of electronic equipment employed.
> Rather the sole concern should be with whether the privacy
> of the home was invaded. [81]

The Court nevertheless continued its property analysis in Lopez
v. United States. [82] Unlike On Lee, Lopez made incriminating statements to a known agent of the Internal Revenue Service. The deception
here was not the use of a secret agent but the use of a Minifon minia-
ture tape recorder that recorded Lopez's attempted bribe of the agent.

The Court found both that the agent's testimony was admissible because the agent was in Lopez's office with his consent and that the tape recording was admissible as independent evidence, because it was on the person of the agent who was lawfully present. Lopez had no constitutionally recognizable claims to privacy in his conversations. Rather, he simply "assumed the risk" that his words would be divulged to others; moreover, that "risk" included the possibility that his conversation "would be accurately reproduced in Court, whether by faultless memory or mechanical recording."[83]

In dissent, Justice Brennan rejected the majority's property analysis but apparently relied upon its implication in limiting the range of privacy claims under the amendment. Justice Brennan noted that the liberty of personal communications was particularly threatened by electronic devices that potentially could destroy all anonymity and all privacy by making the government privy to everything that goes on. Yet, Justice Brennan argued that the Fourth Amendment applied only to electronically secured evidence, not nonelectronically gathered evidence. Evidence obtained by eavesdropping or the testimony of secret agents would not unreasonably invade an individual's privacy, since each party takes the risk of divulgence of personal information by the other. Constitutionally recognizable claims to privacy therefore depended upon the manner of intrusion. The amendment would apply only to evidence gathered by electronic means but not that produced by eavesdropping or the testimony of secret agents.

Intangibles and Secret Agents

Contrasted with the Boyd-Gouled-Weeks rationale and its broad protection for privacy, until the mid-1960s the Supreme Court legitimated few claims to privacy because of its adherence to Olmstead's rigid property analysis. The Court refused to find Fourth Amendment protection for the privacy of personal communications, whether access was obtained by electronic means or eavesdropping and secret agents. In 1966, however, the Supreme Court in three secret agent cases rejected the tangibles requirement that previously had limited the scope of constitutionally recognizable privacy claims.[84] Still, the Court accepted an exceedingly narrow view of what constituted an invasion of privacy, rendering little more protection for privacy than Olmstead's rigid property analysis.

In Hoffa v. United States the Court stated that "the protections of the Fourth Amendment are surely not limited to tangibles, but can extend as well to oral statements."[85] The case arose out of the testimony of a Teamster Union official, who while secretly working for the Federal Bureau of Investigation had been a member of James

Hoffa's entourage in Nashville, Tennessee, during Hoffa's trial of alleged misappropriation of union funds. The official's testimony concerning statements he had heard in Hoffa's hotel suite was offered in support of the government's case against Hoffa for jury bribery. Justice Stewart, for the Court, acknowledged that a hotel room could be the object of Fourth Amendment protection but focused his discussion of the amendment's protections on the "security a man relies upon when he places himself . . . within a constitutionally protected area."[86] Since the teamster official was in the hotel room by invitation and had access to only what was "directed to him or knowingly carried on in his presence," Hoffa "was not relying on the security of his hotel room" and, consequently, had no constitutionally recognizable expectation of privacy.[87]

Similarly, in Lewis v. United States, the Court rejected the defendant's reliance on Gouled in support of his privacy claim to be free in his home from all governmental entries unless he properly consented.[88] Here, an undercover narcotics agent was admitted to Lewis's house on the pretext of buying marijuana. Chief Justice Warren, for the Court, distinguished Gouled as involving a general ransacking search and not merely the guileful entry of a secret agent. Lewis had no constitutionally recognizable claim to privacy, since his primary concern was whether the agent was a "willing purchaser who could pay the agreed price" and, further, since the agent during his visit did not "see, hear, or take anything that was not contemplated . . . as a necessary part" of the business transaction.[89] Again, in Osborn v. United States, the Court suggested, as it had in Hoffa, that the incriminating statements made in the presence of an undercover agent were simply instances of misplaced confidence and their use as evidence did not violate the Fourth Amendment.[90] Although in all three cases the Court held that the Fourth Amendment protects "intangibles," such as personal communications, it found no constitutionally significant difference in the privacy compromised by means of tape recordings and the testimony of secret agents; indeed, tape recorders simply aided undercover agents in testifying accurately.

Katz: "The Fourth Amendment
Protects People, Not Places"

After reaffirming in the secret agent cases Silverman's rejection of Olmstead's requirement that only seizures of tangible materials are constitutionally regulated by the Fourth Amendment, the Supreme Court in 1967 effectively overruled Olmstead's twin requirement of a physical trespass or penetration of a constitutionally protected area.

Katz v. United States, along with Warden v. Hayden's rejection of
the mere evidence rule in the same year, underscored the Court's
repudiation of the underlying property principles of the Fourth Amendment and their strict construction and application to claims of protected privacy.[91]

In Katz federal agents acting without a warrant attached an electronic listening device, similar to a detectaphone, to the outside of a
glass public telephone booth in which the defendant was making incriminating calls by relating gambling information. Counsel for both
sides argued the issues of whether the telephone booth was a constitutionally protected area in which Katz had a reasonable privacy claim.
Justice Stewart, for the majority, however, rejected the counsels'
formulation of the constitutional questions. In Justice Stewart's
opinion, analysis of protected privacy in terms of the Boyd-fostered
doctrine of constitutionally protected areas had been deceptive as
well as misguided in application. The doctrine was seductive in its
implication that the amendment primarily protects personal privacy.
Justice Stewart rejected that implication by noting that the amendment
should not be translated into a general constitutional right of privacy.
The doctrine was deceptive because recognizable claims to privacy
were contingent upon the locus of individuals' activities. He dispelled
that idea by saying that "the Fourth Amendment protects people, not
places. What a person knowingly exposes to the public, even in his
own home or office, is not a subject of Fourth Amendment protection.
. . . But what he seeks to preserve as private, even in an area accessible to the public, may be constitutionally protected."[92] Simply because Katz was in a public telephone booth did not imply that he had
forgone all privacy expectations and could not assert recognizable privacy claims.

The doctrine of "constitutionally protected areas" as strictly interpreted and applied by Olmstead-Goldman limited Fourth Amendment
guarantees and protected privacy to searches involving physical penetration of enclosed areas. Katz disposed of the physical trespass requirement as a prerequisite for privacy claims. Claims to Fourth
Amendment-protected privacy were constitutionally recognizable, independent of physical trespass or penetration into an enclosed area.
The constitutionally significant question in legitimating privacy claims
was not "whether there was physical trespass or whether the petitioner
was in a constitutionally protected area, but whether the petitioner intended to keep the seized evidence private or not."[93]

Instead of the traditional formulation based on constitutionally
protected areas, Justice Stewart emphasized that the Fourth Amendment protects people rather than places and then focused on whether
Katz justifiably relied on his privacy. The proposition that the Fourth
Amendment protects people and not places while accurate is neverthe-

less ambiguous. Moreover, <u>Boyd</u> never implied that the amendment protects places and not people. Rather, intrusions upon the security and privacy of people and their possessions were to be analyzed only with regard to common law proprietary interests.

The crucial question left open by <u>Katz</u> is: Under what circumstances does the Fourth Amendment protect people and their privacy? From <u>Boyd</u>'s rationale a relatively objective standard for appraising individuals' privacy expectations could be formulated: constitutionally protected claims of privacy were justifiable in terms of the locus of individuals' engagements as defined by proprietary interests. By comparison, Justice Stewart apparently provides only a subjective test with his notion of "justifiable reliance": "What a person seeks to preserve as private, even in an area accessible to the public, may be constitutionally protected."[94]

A completely subjective approach to privacy protection, however, leads—and, indeed, in lower courts led—to confusion as to the criteria for a "justifiable reliance" on privacy. The Court contributed to the confusion by stressing that analysis of Fourth Amendment–protected privacy turns on an evaluation of individuals' actual expectations of privacy and publicity. Further, the Court assumed that individuals have expectations of either total privacy or total publicity, and it consequently failed to consider the importance of the degree of individuals' expectations of privacy or publicity relative to the locus of their engagements.

Since the Court considered individuals' expectations of privacy and publicity only as contraries, reasonable expectations of privacy would, therefore, effectively block all searches. That is, "If a reasonable expectation of total privacy exists, the fourth amendment prescribes that the search becomes unlawful when the expectation arises; while if there is a reasonable expectation of total publicity, the fourth amendment imposes no restrictions on the search."[95] Equating searches and seizures that violate reasonable expectations of privacy with the Fourth Amendment's guarantee against unreasonable searches and seizures considerably narrows the coverage of the amendment. Moreover, a subjective conception of reasonable expectations of privacy is unacceptable because it "deprives people who clearly merit fourth amendment protection from the benefit of that protection. A person asleep or in a coma, for example, is incapable of entertaining any subjective expectations at all, and his unconscious state may last a lifetime. To deny him freedom from unreasonable governmental intrusion because of his unfortunate condition is absurd."[96]

A completely subjective analysis that equates the reasonableness of expectations of privacy with the Fourth Amendment's proscription against unreasonable searches and seizures, however, reads too much into <u>Katz</u>. Justice Stewart in rejecting the propertied conception of privacy pointed out that the amendment's protections often have nothing to do with privacy. Moreover, the Court found electronic eavesdropping unreasonable precisely because prior judicial approval had not been secured. Without prior judicial approval searches involving electronic eavesdropping are per se unreasonable under the amendment. The Court would have held lawful under the circumstances of Katz electronic eavesdropping backed by a valid search warrant. Judicial approval of a search warrant mitigates individuals' expectations of privacy; privacy claims perforce yield to valid warrants. Because individuals' privacy expectations do not change upon the issuance of a warrant, the reasonableness of the search and the applicability of the Fourth Amendment cannot depend on individuals' subjective reliance on privacy. In this regard Anthony Amsterdam suggests that:

> Mr. Katz's conversation in a pay telephone booth was protected because he "justifiably relied" upon its being protected—relied, not in the sense of an expectation [a psychological expectation], but in the sense of a claim of right. In the end, the basis of the Katz decision seems to be that the fourth amendment protects those interests that may justifiably claim fourth amendment protection. [97]

The Court's discussion of privacy expectations refers to individuals' rights under the Fourth Amendment to claim a right of privacy and not their actual subjective expectations of privacy.

What, then, is Katz's rationale for constitutionally protected privacy? It begs the question to say that the Fourth Amendment protects reasonable expectations of privacy, and reasonable expectations of privacy are those claims protected by the amendment. Such a conclusion provides little insight as to when and under what circumstances claims of privacy are recognizable under the Fourth Amendment.

Justice Harlan's concurring opinion in Katz clarifies and amplifies the majority's rationale for Fourth Amendment-protected privacy by discussing the notion of "reasonable expectation of privacy" in terms of two elements—individuals' actual expectations of privacy and societal recognition of those expectations as reasonable:

> My understanding of the rule ["the Fourth Amendment protects people, not places"] that has emerged from prior decisions is that there is a twofold requirement, first that a person have exhibited an actual (subjective) expectation of privacy and, second, that the expectation be one that society is prepared to recognize as "reasonable." Thus a man's home is, for most purposes, a place where he ex-

pects privacy, but objects, activities, or statements that
he exposes to the "plain view" of outsiders are not "protected" because no intention to keep them to himself has
been exhibited.[98]

Inasmuch as Justice Harlan obviously intends the first requirement
in a subjective sense, he remains vulnerable to the criticism that
Fourth Amendment guarantees are thereby greatly diluted. As Anthony Amsterdam observes:

> An actual, subjective expectation of privacy obviously has
> no place in a statement of what Katz held or in a theory of
> what the fourth amendment protects. It can neither add to,
> nor can its absence detract from, an individual's claim to
> fourth amendment protection. If it could, the government
> could diminish each person's subjective expectation of pri-
> vacy merely by announcing half hourly on television that
> 1984 was being advanced by a decade and that we were all
> forthwith being placed under comprehensive electronic sur-
> veillance.[99]

Yet, perhaps Justice Harland, unlike Amsterdam, discerns that the
practice of rights depends not only upon judicial legitimation of claims
of rights but also on the actual expectations and interests of individuals,
which led them to demand legal recognition and protection for their interests. Justice Harlan nevertheless qualifies his subjective conception with a second requirement and thereby improves upon the majority's opinion.
    Justice Harlan's second requirement that privacy expectations
are to be legitimated if and only if "society is prepared to recognize
[them] as 'reasonable'" provides the necessary criterion for protected privacy. Not without ambiguity, the second requirement may
either denote an empirical condition that society in fact evidences approval for certain expectations of privacy or a normative conception
that society ought to find some expectations of privacy reasonable.
Neither Justice Harlan nor his commentators provide conclusive support for either alternative; the requirement may lie somewhere between both conditions.[100] Determination of reasonable expectations
of privacy requires reference to "the structure of society, the patterns
of interaction, [and] the web of norms and values" yet the mere fact
of societal consensus alone may be normatively objectionable.[101] The
standard of "reasonableness" that "society is prepared to recognize"
therefore might be akin to that in criminal law: "An act is reasonable
in law when it is such as a man of ordinary care, skill, and prudence
would do under similar circumstances."[102] Indeed, Justice Harlan

stresses that it would be unreasonable for individuals to claim a right
to the privacy of their activities if those activities were in "plain view"
of the public and they made no attempt to foreclose access by others
to their engagements.

Justice Harlan's twin requirements suggest that the reasonableness of privacy claims must be logically related to the time and place
of the search relative to individuals' expectations and, ultimately,
societal judgments. His opinion, like the majority's, emphasizes
that privacy is not protected in the abstract (not every nor any expectation deserves recognition) but rather only those expectations of privacy that social practices and institutions generally acknowledge.
The problem remains as to which expectations are acknowledged as
reasonable. In this regard, Justice Harlan states:

> I join the opinion of the Court, which I read to hold only
> (a) that an enclosed telephone booth is an area where,
> like a home, Weeks v. United States . . . and unlike a
> field, Hester v. United States . . . a person has a consti-
> tutionally protected reasonable expectation of privacy; (b)
> that electronic as well as physical intrusion into a place
> that is in this sense private may constitute a violation of
> the Fourth Amendment; and (c) that the invasion of a con-
> stitutionally protected area by federal authorities is, as
> the Court has long held, presumptively unreasonable in
> the absence of a search warrant.
>
> As the Court's opinion states, "The Fourth Amendment
> protects people, not places." The question, however, is
> what protection it affords to those people. Generally, as
> here, the answer to that question requires reference to a
> "place."[103]

Justice Harlan implicitly acknowledges that most privacy is contingent upon the circumstances and contexts of individuals' engagements
and efforts to limit access by others. By returning to the Boyd-fostered doctrine of constitutionally protected areas, he correctly indicates that it would be impossible to determine the reasonableness of
privacy expectations without reference to the area and context of individuals' activities. Individuals' actual expectations of privacy and
societal judgments as to the reasonableness of those expectations presupposes consideration of the context and circumstances of individuals'
activities and the intrusions thereupon.

Katz's rationale as elaborated by Justice Harlan bears a family
resemblance to Boyd's liberal construction of protected privacy and
the doctrine of constitutionally protected areas. Katz's proclamation
that "the Fourth Amendment protects people, not places" emphasizes

that no area is inherently private. Rather, individuals' privacy claims are determined to be reasonable and protected only by reference to the place and circumstances of their activities. "It is not the nature of the area . . . but the relationship between the area and the person incriminated by the search that is critical."[104] In other words, "determination as to whether the area in question is or is not constitutionally protected is necessary. It is a mistake to view Katz as eliminating the latter possibility—all Katz dispensed with was slavish adherence to the technicalities of state trespass law."[105]

Katz's holding that "wherever a man may be, he is entitled to know that he will remain free from unreasonable searches and seizures" only abandoned Olmstead–Goldman's strict construction and application of the underlying property principles of the Boyd-fostered doctrine of constitutionally protected areas. Repudiating Olmstead's construction of protected privacy, Katz places a new focus on reasonable expectations of privacy yet continues to treat searches and seizures as violations of constitutionally protected places. "What [Katz] changed are the standards for determining private areas, as well as those for determining private affairs."[106]

Katz nevertheless departs from Boyd's reliance on common law property concepts and principles as determining Fourth Amendment-protected privacy. Whereas Boyd–Gouled–Weeks promoted extensive safeguards for personal privacy by focusing not only on the circumstances and area of the search and seizure but also on the content of the governmental intrusion, Katz signifies that the Court approaches privacy claims by focusing on individuals' expectations within constitutionally protected areas and "the act compelled by a government warrant or subpoena rather than by considering the content of the evidence sought."[107] Katz's rejection of strict construction and application of property principles to privacy claims permits protection of intangibles, such as conversations, and at the same time allows for seizures of evidence that may fall outside societal judgments as to the "privacies of life."

Katz stands as a landmark of constitutional analysis of protected privacy, midway between Boyd's liberal construction and application of Fourth Amendment principles and Olmstead's strict construction and application of property concepts and principles. Thus, Katz provides the jurisprudential basis for the contemporary Court's liberal construction of an abstract right of privacy but strict application of the Fourth Amendment to privacy claims.

LIBERAL CONSTRUCTION AND ILLIBERAL PROTECTION

Notwithstanding the Supreme Court's shifting rationales for Fourth Amendment-protected privacy, the fundamental principle emerges that constitutionally recognizable claims to privacy are limited to unreasonable governmental intrusions. The reasonableness of those intrusions is determined by the area and circumstances of the search and by the nexus between individual privacy interests and the governmental interest in searching and seizing. The principal privacy safeguard, therefore, lies with the requirement that prior to government searches a warrant be obtained enabling a "disinterested determination" of probable cause by a "neutral and detached magistrate."[108] The requirement that a warrant be issued only upon cause itself limits intrusive searches and seizures only to those people who there is reason to believe are criminally culpable. Justice Douglas's discussion in <u>McDonald</u> v. <u>United States</u> exemplifies the Court's view of the relationship between privacy and the warrant requirement:

> We are not dealing with formalities. The presence of a
> search warrant serves a high function. Absent some
> grave emergency, the Fourth Amendment has interposed
> a magistrate between the citizen and the police. This was
> done not to shield criminals nor to make the home a safe
> place for illegal activities. It was done so that an objec-
> tive mind might weigh the need to invade that privacy in
> order to enforce the law. The right of privacy was deemed
> too precious to entrust to the discretion of those whose job
> is the detection of crime and the arrest of criminals.
> Power is a deadly thing; and history shows that the police
> acting on their own cannot be trusted. And so the Constitu-
> tion requires a magistrate to pass on the desires of the
> police before they violate the privacy of the home.[109]

The issuance of a search warrant upon determination of probable cause crucially defines the point at which individuals' privacy claims are overridden by a governmental interest. In the early twentieth century the Court recognized only two exceptions to the requirement that a search be conducted in compliance with the warrant requirement.[110] Subsequent judicial policies allowed exceptions to the requirement not only where a search was made incident to arrest but also in so-called "hot-pursuit" and "stop-and-frisk" situations."[111] The increasing number of permissible exceptions reflects in part the Court's adoption of <u>Katz</u>'s analytical framework for personal privacy. In 1968 the Court elaborated <u>Katz</u>'s holding that "wherever an individual may harbor a reasonable 'expectation of privacy,' . . . he is entitled to be free from unreasonable governmental intrusion" by noting that "the specific content and incidents of this right [of privacy] must be shaped by <u>the context in which it is asserted</u>."[112] Contrary to <u>Katz</u>'s dichotomy of individuals' expectations of either total privacy or total publicity, Terry v. Ohio found individuals' expectations of privacy dependent on the context and circumstances of their activity. [113] Reasonable expectations of privacy, like the reasonableness of a search, are context-dependent. [114] Determination of reasonableness requires juxtaposition of the government's interest in searching and individuals' interests in privacy within the context and circumstances of the intrusion. [115] Courts, for example, found justifiable expectations of privacy against warrantless intrusions into citizens' homes, apartments, dormitory rooms, business offices, and with regard to materials sent through the mail, stored in rented lockers, and in garbage; but rejected privacy claims in jails, open fields, yards, abandoned property, goods under bailment, financial records of bankrupt companies, records of long distance calls, vehicle identification numbers, and Social Security numbers. [116]

The Supreme Court, while maintaining Katz's liberal construction of a Fourth Amendment-protected privacy, nevertheless promotes less than liberal protection for personal privacy. Indeed, although "it is settled for the purposes of the amendment that 'except in certain carefully defined classes of cases, a search of private property without proper cause is "unreasonable" unless it has been authorized by a valid search warrant, '"[117] the Burger Court has weakened this principal safeguard for Fourth Amendment-protected privacy by extending the number of exceptions to the warrant requirement and considerably relaxing the standard for probable cause. [118]

United States v. Santana illustrates the Burger Court's strict application of the amendment to claims of protected privacy. [119] Santana, standing in the doorway of her house holding a paper bag containing envelopes of heroin, retreated upon the approach of police officers into the vestibule where she was subsequently apprehended. Justice Rehnquist, for the Court, observed that while "under the common law of property the threshold of one's dwelling is 'private,' as is the yard surrounding the house, it is nevertheless clear that under the cases interpreting the Fourth Amendment Santana was in a 'public' place. Santana was not in an area where she had any expectation [that is, claim] of privacy."[120] Because the doorway of her house was not in an area in which the Court recognized any expectation of privacy, the police, who had probable cause, lawfully made a warrantless arrest. Santana's retreat into the vestibule of her house provided grounds for "hot pursuit" by the police in order to prevent the destruction of evidence and, thus, justified the warrantless entry of her home. [121] Justices Marshall and Brennan dissented on the ground that the majority's decision did not rest upon whether the exigency of the situation required the arrest on private property but on the fact that notwithstanding Santana's presence in the doorway of her house she was "so exposed to public view, speech, hearing and touch" as to be "in the unprotected outdoors,"[122] a constitutionally unprotected area in which individuals have no reasonable expectation of privacy.

Santana illustrates the Burger Court's strict application of the amendment to privacy claims. Although Katz had reasonable expectations of privacy in a public telephone booth, Santana did not in the doorway and vestibule of her house. Nor do citizens have reasonable expectations of privacy, though they have assertable proprietary interests, in their family automobiles.[123] The Court has contrasted individuals' expectations of privacy in their houses and automobiles in several cases. Although "[a] search even of an automobile is a substantial invasion of privacy,"[124] individuals have "a lesser expectation of privacy in a motor vehicle because its function is transportation and it seldom serves as one's residence or as the repository of personal effects."[125] The Court upholds warrantless searches of automobiles because of their mobility and "because the expectation of privacy with respect to one's automobile is significantly less than [that] relating to one's home or office."[126]

The Warren and Burger Courts' liberal construction of the Fourth Amendment but strict application to the areas and circumstances in which citizens may assert valid privacy claims limits the contours of Fourth Amendment-protected privacy. Ironically, whereas Boyd promoted extensive protection for personal privacy in constitutionally protected areas upon proprietary concepts and principles, contemporary courts relying on Katz's liberal construction of individuals' expectations of privacy have limited protection of privacy, even where individuals may have common law proprietary interests. Strict application of the Fourth Amendment has characterized the judicial policies of both the Warren and Burger Courts with respect to the areas of eavesdropping and informers, administrative searches, and issues of so-called informational privacy.

Eavesdropping and Informers

In 1967, along with Katz, the Supreme Court in Berger v. State of New York addressed the issue of what constitutes a reasonable search and seizure by electronic eavesdropping.[127] Because "eavesdropping involves an intrusion on privacy that is broad in scope," the Court established specific constitutional requirements: (1) authorization to eavesdrop only on a showing of probable cause, (2) description with specificity of the object to be seized, (3) notice to the subject of the search, (4) a determined limitation on the time of the search, and (5) a mandatory return to the magistrate specifying the items to be seized.

Still, the Burger Court's approach to the problem of personal privacy posed by governmental informers and secret agents under-

scores its predominantly strict application of the Fourth Amendment
to claims of constitutionally protected privacy. The Court's decision
in United States v. White illustrates its strict application of the amendment's guarantees, reminiscent of the cases fostered by Olmstead's
strict application of property principles.[128] The Court upheld the
conviction of White based on evidence gathered by an electronic trans-
mitter concealed on an informer. Justice White, for the majority,
specifically dealt with Katz's holding that what a person reasonably
seeks to preserve as private is constitutionally protected but found
no constitutionally significant difference between electronically
equipped and nonequipped informers:

> Our problem is not what the privacy expectations of particu-
> lar defendants in particular situations may be or the extent
> to which they may in fact have relied on the discretion of
> their companions. Very probably, individual defendants
> neither know nor suspect that their colleagues have gone
> or will go to the police or are carrying recorders or trans-
> mitters. Otherwise, conversation would cease and our
> problem with these encounters would be nonexistent or far
> different from those now before us. Our problem in terms
> of the principles announced in Katz, is what expectations of
> privacy are constitutionally "justifiable"—what expectations
> the fourth amendment will protect in the absence of a war-
> rant. So far, the law permits the frustration of actual ex-
> pectations of privacy by permitting authorities to use the
> testimony of those associates who for one reason or another
> have determined to turn to the police, as in the manner ex-
> emplified by Hoffa and Lewis.[129]

Justice White implicitly acknowledges that privacy claims against informers involve the assertion of entitlement to control personal information but finds of no constitutional significance the qualitative difference in effectiveness and exactitude between disclosures by the old-
fashioned Hoffa type of informer and an electronically equipped informer.

Ostensibly accepting Katz's liberal construction of Fourth Amendment-protected privacy, the Court limits the amendment's application
by following the On-Lee-Lopez-Hoffa-Lewis-Osborn assumption of
risk rule. Actually, the Court's reliance on the assumption of risk
rule and restrictive application of the Fourth Amendment to claims of
privacy against bugged informers and the admissibility of evidence
gathered by tape recordings permit it to circumvent Katz's analysis
of reasonable expectations of privacy.

In terms of the scope of constitutionally protected privacy, the
Fourth Amendment does not protect voluntarily relinquished personal

information. Citizens have neither reasonable expectations nor valid claims of privacy against loss of personal information by means of a bugged informer or an old trustworthy friend-turned-informer.

Administrative Searches and
a Man's House Is His Ruined Tenement

The Supreme Court permits a lower standard of probable cause for issuance of warrants in the area of administrative searches, though such searches arguably affect a greater number of individuals and present more serious invasions of privacy than those searches pursuant to criminal prosecution. In fact, not until the 1960s did the Court entertain privacy claims with regard to administrative searches.

The Court's initial inquiry dealt with whether the Fourth Amendment had any application to administrative searches. In Frank v. Maryland the Court held that the Fourth Amendment confers no right to forbid warrantless administrative searches conducted at reasonable times and places, which are designed to facilitate enforcement of health regulations.[130] Ostensibly the Fourth Amendment applied only to criminal searches, not civil searches. Only searches designed to obtain incriminating evidence impinge on the right of self-protection and require prior judicial approval. Administrative searches are permissible without judicial safeguards so long as the potential loss of privacy is counterbalanced by gains in social welfare. Justice Frankfurter declared for the majority that even "giving the fullest scope to this constitutional right of privacy," administrative searches lie outside the purview of the Fourth Amendment.

Contrariwise, Justices Warren, Black, Douglas, and Brennan complained that the majority's decision greatly diluted the right of privacy. The dissenters argued that the basic fallacy in the majority's opinion was the insistence that the amendment applies principally to criminal searches, thereby providing no safeguards for invasions of personal privacy by other governmental officials. In particular, Justice Douglas urged a liberal application of the amendment to privacy claims.

> [The fourth amendment] was designed to protect the citizen against uncontrolled invasion of his privacy. It does not make the home a place of refuge from the law. It only requires the sanction of the judiciary rather than the executive before that privacy may be invaded. History shows that all officers tend to be officious; and health inspectors, making out a case for criminal prosecution of the citizen are no exception. . . . One invasion of privacy by an offi-

cial of government can be as oppressive as another. . . .
It would seem that the public interest in protecting privacy
is equally as great in one case as another.[131]

In 1960 the dissenters again rejected the formalistic dichotomy
between criminal and civil searches in Abel v. United States and Ohio
ex rel. Eaton v. Price, pointing out that "[i]t is the individual's interest in privacy which the Amendment protects, and that would not appear to fluctuate with the 'intent' of the invading officers."[132] In an
important dissent, however, Justice Brennan argued that the proper
course would be to require inspectors to obtain a warrant whenever a
householder objected to the entry.

Seven years later Justice Brennan's suggestion was adopted by
a Supreme Court with two new members joining the Frank dissenters
in the majority opinion (Justices White and Fortas took the seats of
two members of the Frank majority). In Camara v. Municipal Court
and its companion case, See v. City of Seattle, the Court acknowledged
the implications of a liberal construction and application of the Fourth
Amendment:

> The basic purpose of this Amendment, as recognized in
> countless decisions of this Court, is to safeguard the pri-
> vacy and security of individuals against arbitrary invasions
> by government officials. The Fourth Amendment thus gives
> concrete expression to a right of the people which is "basic
> to a free society."[133]

The majority ruled, on the one hand, that the Fourth Amendment bars
prosecution of a person for refusing to permit administrative officials
to conduct warrantless inspections and, on the other hand, that an administrative warrant nevertheless might be issued on a showing of
less than the probable cause required in criminal cases. Justice
White outlined the necessary requirements:

> Such standards, which will vary with the municipal program
> being enforced, may be based upon the passage of time, the
> nature of the building (e.g., a multifamily apartment house),
> or the condition of the entire area, but they will not neces-
> sarily depend upon specific knowledge of the conditions of
> the particular dwelling. It has been suggested that so to
> vary the probable cause test from the standard applied in
> criminal cases would be to authorize a "synthetic search
> warrant" and thereby to lessen the overall protections of
> the Fourth Amendment. . . . But we do not agree. The
> warrant procedure is designed to guarantee that a decision

> to search private property is justified by a reasonable gov-
> ernmental interest. But reasonableness is still the ulti-
> mate standard. If a valid public interest justifies the in-
> trusion contemplated, there is probable cause to issue a
> suitably restricted search warrant.[134]

The Court thus affirmed the safeguard against official intrusions in
the requirement that a warrant be issued upon a showing of probable
cause but permitted the standard of probable cause to vary with the
type and manner of the search.

Camara and See indicate a hierarchy in the standard of probable
cause and concomitantly the relative merits of privacy claims. The
traditional standard of probable cause remains required of criminal
searches. Privacy attains a high degree of protection because of its
association with the fundamental liberty to be secure from arbitrary
governmental intrusions. Administrative searches, however, require a lower standard of probable cause upon "balancing the need to
search against the invasions which the search entails."[135] Administrative searches of commercial property, for example, require a
prior determination of probable cause upon a balancing of privacy and
societal interests, but claims of privacy have less weight. In Marshall v. Barlow's Inc., the Court did assert that in heavily regulated
industries the businessman's right of privacy included the right to
have a magistrate determine the reasonableness of the search according to an "administrative plan containing specific neutral criteria."[136]
Writing for the majority, Justice White stated: "If the government intrudes on a person's property, the privacy interest suffers whether
the government's motivation is to investigate violations of criminal
laws or breaches of other statutory or regulatory standards."[137]
Nevertheless, legal recognition of privacy claims varies with the type
of administrative program (health inspections, welfare visits, parole
and probation searches, airport and border searches) and the manner
in which officials conduct the search.[138]

The Court's treatment of administrative searches underscores
its continuing reliance on the doctrine of constitutionally protected
areas in determining the reasonableness of privacy claims. The
Court's decision in G. M. Leasing Corporation v. United States illustrates its strict application of the Fourth Amendment to privacy
claims. In G. M. Leasing Corporation, the Court declined to interpret the Internal Revenue Code "as giving carte blanche for warrantless invasions of privacy."[139] The Internal Revenue Service for the
purpose of jeopardy assessments may make warrantless automobile
seizures occurring in public streets or other open areas, since they
involve no unconstitutional invasion of privacy. But a warrantless entry into the privacy of a business office may not be justified on the

grounds that assets are "seizable" to satisfy tax assessments. Justice Blackmun, for the Court, observed: "It is one thing to seize without a warrant property resting in an open area or seizable by levy without an intrusion into privacy, and it is quite another thing to effect a warrantless seizure of property, even that owned by a corporation, situated on private premises to which access is not otherwise available for the seizing officer."[140] Not surprisingly, the Burger Court upholds privacy claims against the warrantless seizure of private property in constitutionally protected areas. The Court unanimously held unlawful the warrantless entry and seizure of assets in a business office by agents of the Internal Revenue Service because the circumstances of the case established a nexus between privacy and proprietary interests in a constitutionally protected area.

Papers, Property, and Informational Privacy

The so-called property bias of the Supreme Court in the nineteenth and early twentieth century continues, but, with the opposite effect of promoting strict application of the Fourth Amendment and illiberal protection for privacy. Although following Katz's liberal construction of reasonable expectations of privacy, the Burger Court continues to strictly apply Fourth Amendment guarantees in validating claims to informational privacy only when privacy and proprietary interests are conjoined. "Katz has not eliminated property considerations—ownership, possession, occupancy—but has changed their role from legal touchstones for the Fourth Amendment to standards by which expectations of privacy are evaluated."[141]

Actually, the Supreme Court's strict application of Fourth Amendment guarantees and illiberal protection for privacy expectations in personal information derives from the interplay of three judicial policies: legitimating administrative searches on a lower standard of probable cause than required of criminal investigations; circumventing a privacy analysis by an assumption of risk rule, applicable when individuals disclose personal information to bugged informers or trusted friends-turned-informers; and reembracing Fourth Amendment property concepts, thereby converting analysis of "expectations of privacy into expectations of ownership, possession, or occupancy."[142]

Individuals' expectations of informational privacy may be compromised in three ways. Access to personal information may be obtained directly from individuals by means of electronic eavesdropping or by compelling their disclosure on threat of criminal sanction. Recipients of volunteered information may be required by some third party, such as the government, to disclose personal information against their wishes and those of the individuals concerned. Alternatively recipients of personal information may voluntarily disclose information to the government against the wishes and privacy expectations of the individual concerned. In the first situation, when personal information is gathered surreptitiously, Fourth Amendment guarantees provide some protection, but, generally, the principal privacy protection in such situations derives from the Fifth Amendment. The second situation characterizes that presented in the cases of California Bankers Association v. Shultz and United States v. Miller. Whereas the third situation involves those cases in which a bugged informer or Hoffa-type informer discloses personal information. In the latter two situations the Fourth Amendment ostensibly provides the principal guarantee for privacy interests.

While analytically distinguishable, privacy interests in all three situations have received illiberal protection. In the first, the Court has fashioned Fourth Amendment requirements for wiretapping and other forms of electronic surveillance by which access to personal information is gathered directly from but unbeknown to an individual. Yet, it narrowed the breadth of Fifth Amendment guarantees protecting against compelled personal disclosures. In the second situation, privacy claims have been denied since the Court found no legitimate expectations of privacy. Rather, the Court circumvented an analysis of individuals' privacy expectations by its assumption of risk rule. Similarly, in the third situation, the Court has failed to find any "societal judgment" as to the reasonableness of individuals' privacy expectations and, furthermore, reemphasized proprietary concepts in application of the Fourth Amendment.

Notwithstanding the broad range of privacy interests that receive Fourth Amendment protection under its requirement that "no warrant [for search and seizure] shall issue, but upon probable cause," judicial enforcement leaves open the possibility of serious invasions of privacy by administrative summonses and subpoena duces tecum of papers in the possession of third parties, but in which individuals retain expectations of privacy.[143] The Court construes the Fourth Amendment to only prohibit overly broad and sweeping summonses. The nature of the papers sought by a subpoena duces tecum usually is not considered in applying the guarantees of the amendment. Instead, subpoenas must only satisfy the requirement that "the inquiry is within the authority of the agency, the demand is not too indefinite and the information sought is reasonably relevant."[144] Hence, administrative subpoenas and summonses need only satisfy the amendment's requirement that warrants not be overly broad so as to constitute a general search. An Internal Revenue Service summons, for example, need only describe documents and papers sought with "reasonable particularity" so that respondents may produce such records for inspection.[145]

Since the Court has held that administrative investigations are analogous to grand jury proceedings, in that both are basically inquisitional, administrative summonses require no showing of probable cause. In <u>United States</u> v. <u>Powell</u>, the Supreme Court held that the Internal Revenue Service "need not meet any standard of probable cause to obtain enforcement of [its] summons."[146] Administrative subpoenas are lawful if: (1) the underlying investigation has a legitimate civil purpose authorized by Congress, (2) the documents sought are relevant and material to the investigation, (3) the subpoena is sufficiently specific so that compliance will not be unreasonable burdensome, and (4) other procedural requirements are met.[147]

Both litigation and statutory scheme provide broad powers for the Internal Revenue Service to examine papers, books, and records with respect to tax liability or for the purpose of ascertaining the correctness of tax returns. Internal Revenue Service summonses, while administratively issued, however, are enforceable only by a federal district court in an "adversary proceeding" affording the opportunity for challenge by and protection of the witness.[148] Still, only when the government attempts to obtain papers or documents by judicial enforcement of an administrative summons may an individual intervene and contest the wrongfulness of the summons. <u>Donaldson</u> v. <u>United States</u> indicates the problems of individuals' intervention with administrative summonses as well as the Court's tendency to focus on proprietary interests in determining the applicability of Fourth Amendment guarantees.[149] While <u>Donaldson</u> was primarily concerned with intervention under the Federal Rules of Civil Procedure and not the Fourth Amendment, the Court implied that without a proprietary interest no Fourth Amendment claim was permissible against a summons or subpoena of records. The Court denied Donaldson's attempt to intervene with an Internal Revenue Service summons directed at his former employer and ordering production of salary payments and other transactions relating to him, because he could not demonstrate a "significantly protectable interest."[150] Donaldson had no significantly protectable interest inasmuch as he did not own or possess the records.

Individuals ostensibly have no reasonable expectations of privacy under the Fourth Amendment in documents that they do not own or possess. Still, corporate or bank record keeping of individuals' transactions may reveal a substantial amount of information about individuals' activities and associations. The Court nevertheless has long held that Congress may require record keeping as part of the requirements of law enforcement, and those records are subject to government inspection under the conditions established by the enacting legislation.[151] Audits by bank examiners, for example, are permissible, even if deemed searches by depositors. In general, warrantless searches and record-keeping requirements are reasonable where necessary for governmental supervision of a regulated business.

Accordingly, the Supreme Court in California Bankers Association upheld the reporting requirements of the Bank Secrecy Act as "controlled by existing legal process."[152] The Court refused to acknowledge any legitimate privacy expectations on the part of banks or their depositors. Indeed, although the district court dealt squarely with the issue of what "expectations of privacy" are protected by the Fourth Amendment, Justice Rehnquist, for the Court, held that the Fourth Amendment claims by the California Bankers Association were asserted vicariously. He evaded the privacy claims of the depositor-plaintiffs by denying standing on the grounds that the plaintiffs had not alleged that they had or would engage in transactions involving more than $10,000, which at least at that time was the only type of domestic transaction the regulations required banks to report.

Justices Douglas, Brennan, and Marshall dissented. Both Justices Douglas and Marshall focused upon the consequences of the act's record-keeping and reporting requirements. Justice Douglas pointed out that previously compulsory record keeping was confined to monitoring record keepers or their businesses, but this act required the bank in keeping records to act as the government's agent in monitoring its customers and clients. Thereupon, Justice Douglas contended: "One's bank accounts are within the 'expectations of privacy' category. For they mirror not only one's finances but his interests, his debts, his way of life, his family and his civic commitments. . . . A checking account, as I have said, may well record a citizen's activities, opinion, and beliefs as fully as transcripts of his telephone conversations."[153]

Although the majority opinion in California Bankers Association evaded the claims to protected privacy, in 1976 the Court dealt with the issue of privacy and the Bank Secrecy Act. In United States v. Miller, the government appealed a court of appeals ruling that documents subpoenaed duces tecum under the Bank Secrecy Act fell within a constitutionally protected area of privacy.[154] The Supreme Court reversed, relying on Hoffa for the proposition: "No interest legitimately protected by the Fourth Amendment is implicated by government investigative activities unless there is an intrusion into a zone of privacy, into 'the security a man relies upon when he places himself or his property within a constitutionally protected area.'"[155] Miller argued that the combination of the Bank Secrecy Act's record-keeping requirements and the issuance of a subpoena duces tecum to obtain those records permitted the government to circumvent Fourth Amendment guarantees that would have been applicable if the government had proceeded directly against him.

The Court rejected Miller's argument, first, by distinguishing Boyd as well as signifying the importance of ownership and possession of documents and, second, by examining whether depositors have any legitimate expectations of privacy in their banking transactions. While acknowledging Katz's rejection of "the narrow view that 'property interests control the right of the Government to search and seize,'" the Court placed greater emphasis on another proposition in Katz, namely, "[w]hat a person knowingly exposes to the public . . . is not a subject of Fourth Amendment protection."[156] Thereupon, the Court determined that it "must examine the nature of the particular documents sought to be protected in order to determine whether there is a legitimate 'expectation of privacy' concerning their contents."[157] Because the checks were found not to be confidential communications but negotiable instruments for commercial transactions, depositors had no Fourth Amendment privacy claims. The Court also implied that in dealing with personal information contained in or that may be inferred from required records, it might employ the rationale of those cases dealing with informers, in which individuals simply were held to assume a risk of disclosure and of access to their personal communications. "The depositor takes the risk, in revealing his affairs to another, that the information will be conveyed by that person to the Government."[158] Thus, the majority in United States v. Miller, relying on Katz's liberal construction of Fourth Amendment guarantees for privacy nevertheless strictly applied the amendment's protections because of the nature of the documents sought and the presumption that individuals have reasonable expectations of privacy only in papers that they own or possess. The Court also suggested that its strict application of the amendment could be buttressed by circumventing a privacy analysis with the assumption of risk rule.

California Bankers Association v. Shultz and United States v. Miller illustrate the Burger Court's refusal to "conceptualize the intangible nature of the injury, the chilling effect upon privacy, when information systems [are] set up to record"[159] private transactions and the activities of depositors. "Taking a practical look at the [Bank Secrecy] Act, it is apparent the Government is not interested in the transaction itself, but its real inquiry is into the background of the financial transactions—a background which the individual may seek to keep private."[160] The Court nevertheless evaded its own privacy analysis by reemphasizing proprietary concepts and by failing to consider not only the value of informational privacy but also how access to that information may influence individuals' future activities. Notwithstanding the Court's observation in United States v. United States District Court that "[t]hough physical entry of the home is the chief evil against which the wording of the Fourth Amendment is directed, its broader spirit now shields private speech from unreasonable surveillance," claims to informational privacy that have no clearly established contextual nexus with proprietary interests fail.[161]

Individuals' expectations of privacy with regard to their banking transactions arguably are not as great as their expectations of privacy

with respect to papers located within the fortress they call home.
Still, the Supreme Court has not addressed the policy issues of record
keeping and reporting, the potential for discretionary injustice, and
the consequences for personal privacy. There are at least two separate issues in governmental requirements for record keeping and
reporting. First, what kind of files and information may reasonably
be collected and maintained. Second, what kinds of procedural safeguards should be established for the collection, maintenance, and access to information gathered. In neither California Bankers Association nor United States v. Miller did the Court entertain an analysis of
the reasonableness of bank record keeping and reporting or of the potential effect on personal privacy. As one commentator observed of
the Court's strict application of the Fourth Amendment, "Not only does
it provide limited protection against the overly broad collection of
personal information, but it provides practically no limitation on what
officials may do with information they gather by lawful means."[162]

PRIVACY, PROPERTY,
AND THE FOURTH AMENDMENT

Contemporary privacy litigation poses constitutional and public
policy issues not unlike those of the early twentieth century. While
privacy issues in the 1920s and 1930s arose with the government's
use of technology permitting electronic surveillance, in the 1960s and
1970s privacy issues revolve around the government's use of third-
generation computers allowing extensive information collection, maintenance, and exchange. The present Court, like the Taft Court, however, fails to "conceptualize Fourth Amendment interests in terms
more appropriate to a [increasingly] technological society in which
property and privacy are no longer unified."[163] The Warren Court,
in Katz, reembraced the Boyd-fostered liberal construction of Fourth
Amendment-protected privacy by repudiating Olmstead's strict construction and application of the amendment and its underlying property
concepts and principles. Katz nevertheless failed to promote an adequate conceptual framework for constitutional recognition of individuals' claims to Fourth Amendment-protected privacy and, in particular, informational privacy. The Burger Court further circumscribed
the amendment's guarantees and retreated from Katz's analysis of
reasonable expectations of privacy by reemphasizing proprietary concepts in determining legitimate privacy interests and areas of Fourth
Amendment protection.

Historically, both in common law and constitutional law, privacy
interests were intimately linked with proprietary interests because
"property rights reflect society's explicit recognition of a person's

authority to act as he wishes in certain areas, and therefore should be considered in determining whether an individual's expectations of privacy are reasonable."[164] Although "Katz held that capacity to claim the protection of the Fourth Amendment depends not upon a property right in the invaded place but upon whether the person who claims the protection of the Amendment has a legitimate expectation of privacy in the invaded place," the Supreme Court never "altogether abandoned use of property concepts in determining the presence or absence of privacy interests protected by [the Fourth] Amendment."[165] The Burger Court's reliance on proprietary concepts in determining the legitimacy of individuals' privacy claims, however, permitted it to retreat from Katz and thereby contract the contours of Fourth Amendment-protected privacy, as well as avoid extension of the amendment's protection to claims of informational privacy.

The Burger Court's 1978 decision in Rakas v. Illinois reaffirmed its reliance on proprietary concepts and strict application of the Fourth Amendment to privacy claims. In Rakas, Justice Rehnquist, for a five-member majority, emphatically rejected as too broad a measure for construction of protected privacy and application of Fourth Amendment guarantees, including the exclusionary rule, the doctrine that "anyone legitimately on premises where a search occurs may challenge its legality."[166] Justice Rehnquist held that passengers in an automobile have no valid Fourth Amendment claims or legitimate expectations of privacy against searches of automobiles or seizure of evidence therein. Here, the passengers asserted neither property nor possessory interest in the automobile, or seized property, and the fact that they were "legitimately on the premises," in the sense that they were in the automobile with the owner's permission, provided no basis for legitimate expectations of privacy. While Justice Rehnquist expressly denied the four dissenters' view that Rakas "holds that the Fourth Amendment protects property, not people," he did suggest that passengers in automobiles or visitors in apartments or homes might "contest the lawfulness of the seizure of evidence or the search if their own property were seized during the search."[167] Thus, Justice White, for the dissenters, concluded: "Though professing to acknowledge that the primary purpose of the Fourth Amendment's prohibition of unreasonable searches is the protection of privacy—not property—the Court nonetheless effectively ties the application of the Fourth Amendment and the exclusionary rule in this situation to property law concepts."[168]

Although Rakas, along with Santana, California Bankers Association, and Miller, underscored the Burger Court's reliance on property concepts in determining the reasonableness of individuals' privacy claims, the exact relationship between individuals' privacy and proprietary claims remains ambiguous. In Rakas, Justice Rehnquist argued that property concepts are not irrelevant to the Court's determination of legitimate privacy claims, yet noted, on the one hand, that privacy claims "need not be based on a common-law interest in real or personal property" (as in Katz) and, on the other hand, that "even a property interest in premises may not be sufficient to establish a legitimate expectation of privacy" (as in Santana). Justice Powell, concurring, attempted to clarify the Court's analysis by urging that "whether one's claim to privacy from governmental intrusion is reasonable [emerges only] in light of all the surrounding circumstances . . . no single factor invariably will be determinative."[169]

While in historical perspective the Supreme Court demonstrates a property bias in fashioning the contours of the Fourth Amendment and protected privacy, the Court has established considerable protection for personal privacy consistent with the Fourth Amendment's underlying principles. In terms of the developing constitutional law of Fourth Amendment-protected privacy, however, the Burger Court's renewed emphasis upon proprietary concepts not only precludes protection for individuals' interests in informational privacy, as in California Bankers Association and Miller, but also, as with Santana and Rakas, circumscribes the contours of Fourth Amendment-protected privacy.

NOTES

1. Thomas Emerson, "Nine Justices in Search of a Doctrine," 64 Michigan Law Review 219, 229 (1965).

2. West Virginia Board of Education v. Barnette, 319 U.S. 624, 638 (1943).

3. Olmstead v. United States, 277 U.S. 438, 478 (1928) (Brandeis, J., dis. op.).

4. Public Utilities Commission v. Pollak, 343 U.S. 451, 467 (1952) (Douglas, J., dis. op.); Poe v. Ullman, 367 U.S. 497, 521 (1961) (Douglas, J., dis. op.).

5. See David H. Flaherty, Privacy in Colonial New England (Charlottesville: University Press of Virginia, 1972).

6. Thomas H. O'Connor, "The Right to Privacy in Historical Perspective," 53 Massachusetts Law Quarterly 101, 102 (1968).

7. Ibid.

8. See United States v. Chadwick, 433 U.S. 1, 7-8 (1977); Marcus v. Search Warrant, 367 U.S. 717, 724 (1961); Frank v. Maryland, 359 U.S. 360, 363 (1959); Olmstead v. United States, 277 U.S. 438, 463 (1928); Boyd v. United States, 116 U.S. 616, 624-30 (1886); Jacob W. Landynski, Search and Seizure and the Supreme Court (Baltimore: Johns Hopkins Press, 1966); Nelson B. Lasson, The History

and Development of the Fourth Amendment to the United States Constitution (Baltimore: Johns Hopkins Press, 1937).

9. Entrick v. Carrington, 19 Howard State Records 1029, 95 Eng. Rep. 807 (K.B. 1765).

10. Paxton's Case, Quincy's Reports 51 (Mass. 1761). See T.T.F. Rudox, Life of James Otis 66 (1823). On the maxim, see J. Clarke, Parcemiologia Anglo-Lantina . . . Or Proverbs English and Latin 101 (1639).

11. Frank v. Maryland, 359 U.S. 360, 378-79 (1959) (quoting Pitt, Speech on the Excise Bill).

12. Quoted in III The Debates in the Several Conventions on the Adoption of the Federal Constitution, Jonathan Elliot, ed., 1836 (New York: Burt Franklin Reprints, 1974) 448-49.

13. Ibid., at 448-49.

14. Landynski, Search and Seizure, at 41.

15. Thomas Cooley, A Treatise on the Constitutional Limitations Which Rest upon the Legislative Power of the States of the American Union, 1st ed. (Boston: Little, Brown, 1868) 305.

16. Boyd v. United States, 116 U.S. 616, 630 (1886).

17. Ex Parte Jackson, 96 U.S. 727, 733 (1878). See also United States v. Chadwick, 433 U.S. 1, 9-10 (1977); United States v. Van Leewven, 397 U.S. 249 (1970).

18. Boyd v. United States, 116 U.S. 616 (1886).

19. Idem, at 635.

20. Idem, at 630.

21. Joseph Story, Commentaries on the Constitution of the United States, 1st ed. (Boston: Hilliard, Gray, 1833) 1895.

22. Boyd v. United States, 116 U.S. 616, 633 (1886).

23. Note, "Formalism, Legal Realism, and Constitutionally Protected Privacy under the Fourth and Fifth Amendments," 90 Harvard Law Review 945, 956 (1977).

24. Andresen v. Maryland, 427 U.S. 463, 472 n.6 (1976).

25. Mapp v. Ohio, 367 U.S. 643, 656-57 (1961).

26. The Court has held that the amendment only guarantees against unreasonable governmental searches and seizures; it provides no protection against private searches and seizures. See Burdeau v. McDowell, 256 U.S. 465, 475 (1921).

27. Hester v. United States, 265 U.S. 57 (1924).

28. See Weeks v. United States, 232 U.S. 383 (1914) (houses); Silverthorne Lumber Company v. United States, 251 U.S. 385 (1920) (business offices); Almos v. United States, 255 U.S. 313 (1921) (stores); Lustig v. United States, 338 U.S. 74 (1949), United States v. Jeffers, 342 U.S. 48 (1951), Stoner v. California, U.S. 483 (1964) (hotel rooms); Jones v. United States, 362 U.S. 257 (1960) (apartments); Henry v. United States, 361 U.S. 98 (1959) (automobiles); and Rios v. United States, 364 U.S. 253 (1960) (taxicabs).

29. See United States v. Robinson, 414 U.S. 218, 235 (1973), wherein the Court held that as a matter of judicial policy it would no longer promote a case-by-case approach in determining reasonableness.

30. Silverthorne Lumber Company v. United States, 251 U.S. 385 (1920).

31. Gouled v. United States, 255 U.S. 298 (1921).

32. Comment, "Papers, Privacy and the Fourth and Fifth Amendments: A Constitutional Analysis," 69 Northwestern University Law Review 626, 633 (1974).

33. Compare Marron v. United States, 275 U.S. 192 (1927) with United States v. Lefkowitz, 285 U.S. 452 (1932). Courts often had to strain to make evidence admissible. See Note, "Evidentiary Searches: The Ruler and the Reasons," 54 Georgetown Law Journal 593, 607-21 (1966).

34. Jones v. United States, 362 U.S. 257, 266 (1960); and Stanford v. Texas, 379 U.S. 476 (1965); but see Rakas v. Illinois, 99 S. Ct. 421 (1978).

35. Warden v. Hayden, 387 U.S. 294, 304 (1967).

36. Mancusi v. DeForte, 392 U.S. 364, 368 (1968).

37. Couch v. United States, 409 U.S. 322, 344 (1973) (Marshall, J., dis. op.).

38. Note, "Papers, Privacy and the Fourth and Fifth Amendments," at 635.

39. Weeks v. United States 232 U.S. 383 (1914).

40. Idem, at 394; but see Adams v. New York, 192 U.S. 245 (1904).

41. Weeks v. United States, 232 U.S. 383, at 390, 393 (1914).

42. See, for example, Agnello v. United States, 269 U.S. 20 (1925) (excluding contraband cocaine seized without a warrant); Almos v. United States, 255 U.S. 313 (1921) (excluding contraband whiskey seized without a warrant).

43. Barron v. Baltimore, 7 Pet. 243, 32 U.S. 243 (1833).

44. Wolf v. Colorado, 338 U.S. 25 (1949).

45. Idem, at 27.

46. Idem, at 41 (Murphy, J., dis. op., accorded with Douglas, J., dis. op.), and at 46 (Murphy, J., dis. op., joined by Rutledge, J.).

47. Elkins v. United States, 364 U.S. 206, 238 (1960).

48. Idem, at 217.

49. Mapp v. Ohio, 367 U.S. 643, 651 (1961).

50. Idem, at 655.

51. Idem, at 660.

52. Idem, at 656 and 659.

53. Linkletter v. Walker, 381 U.S. 618, 635 (1965).

54. Idem, at 636-37.

55. See Bivens v. Six Unknown Named Agents of the Federal Bureau of Narcotics, 403 U.S. 388, 414-17 (1971), wherein Chief Justice Burger outlines his objections to the rule. See also United States v. Calandra, 414 U.S. 338 (1974).

56. United States v. Calandra, 414 U.S. 338, 345 (1974), quoting Blair v. United States, 250 U.S. 273, 281 (1919).

57. Anthony Amsterdam, "Perspectives on the Fourth Amendment," 58 Minnesota Law Review 349, 369 (1974). See also Brown v. United States, 411 U.S. 223, 230 (1973); and Adderman v. United States, 394 U.S. 165, 174 (1969).

58. Robert B. McKay, "Mapp v. Ohio, the Exclusionary Rule and the Right of Privacy," 15 Arizona Law Review 327, 340-41 (1973). See also Thomas Shrock and Bob Welsh, "Up from Calandra: The Exclusionary Rule as a Constitutional Requirement," 59 Minnesota Law Review 251 (1974).

59. See Terry v. Ohio, 392 U.S. 1, 12-13 (1968); Harrison v. United States, 392 U.S. 219, 224 n.10 (1968); Mapp v. Ohio, 367 U.S. 643, 659 (1961); Olmstead v. United States, 277 U.S. 438 (1928) (Brandeis, J., dis. op.).

60. In United States v. Calandra, 414 U.S. 338, at 348 (1974), the Court stated: "In sum, the rule is a judicially created remedy designed to safeguard Fourth Amendment rights generally through its deterrent effect, rather than a personal constitutional right of the party aggrieved." See also Bivens v. Six Unknown Named Agents of the Federal Bureau of Narcotics, 403 U.S. 388, 416 (1971) (Burger, C.J., dis. op.); and Terry v. Ohio, 392 U.S. 1, 12-13 (1968).

61. United States v. Checcolini, 98 S. Ct. 1054, 1064 (1978).

62. Perhaps the most severe criticism has come from Chief Justice Burger's dissenting opinion in Bivens v. Six Unknown Named Agents of the Federal Bureau of Narcotics, 403 U.S. 388, 414-17 (1971). See also Dallin Oaks, "Studying the Exclusionary Rule in Search and Seizure," 37 University of Chicago Law Review 665, 755 (1970).

63. See Rakas v. Illinois, 99 S. Ct. 421 (1978); Stone v. Powell, 428 U.S. 465 (1976); United States v. Janis, 428 U.S. 433 (1976); United States v. Peltier, 442 U.S. 531, 536-39 (1975); and United States v. Calandra, 414 U.S. 338 (1974).

64. Alan F. Westin, Privacy and Freedom (New York: Atheneum, 1970) 339-41.

65. While the phrase describes the Court's approach to Fourth Amendment protections and protected privacy, in particular, it was formulated by Judge Frank dissenting in United States v. On Lee, 193 F.2d 306, 314 (2d Cir. 1951), aff'd 343 U.S. 747 (1952), and summarized the view that, "A sane, decent, civilized society must provide

some such oasis, some shelter from public scrutiny, some insulated enclosure, some enclave, some inviolate place which is a man's castle." Idem, at 315-16 (footnote omitted).

66. See, generally, Westin, Privacy and Freedom; and Arthur R. Miller, Assault on Privacy (Ann Arbor: University of Michigan. Press, 1971).

67. Olmstead v. United States, 277 U.S. 438 (1928).

68. Brief for Petitioner McInnis et al., at 9, and Brief for Petitioner Green et al., at 10, quoted by William Beaney, "The Constitutional Right of Privacy," in Supreme Court Review, ed. Philip Kurland (Chicago: University of Chicago Press, 1962) at 221.

69. Olmstead v. United States, 19 F.2d 842, 847 (9th Cir. 1927).

70. Olmstead v. United States, 277 U.S. 438, 448 (1928).

71. Brief for the United States, at 38-39, quoted by Beany, "Constitutional Right of Privacy," at 221.

72. Ibid., at 219.

73. Olmstead v. United States, 277 U.S. 438, 487 (1928).

74. Idem, at 478.

75. Nardone v. United States, 302 U.S. 379 (1937). In Nardone, the Court interpreted the act to prohibit the interception of telephone and telegraph communications. Fifteen years later, however, in Schwartz v. Texas, 344 U.S. 199 (1952), the Court held that wiretapped evidence could be divulged in state courts if obtained by state agents. In 1957 the Court nevertheless extended the act to exclude illegally state-gathered wiretap evidence in federal courts in Benanti v. United States, 355 U.S. 96 (1957). Finally, in Lee v. Florida, 392 U.S. 378 (1968), the Court overruled Schwartz, holding that the act prohibited the admission of state-gathered evidence even in state courts.

76. Goldman v. United States, 316 U.S. 129 (1942).

77. On Lee v. United States, 343 U.S. 747 (1952).

78. United States v. On Lee, 193 F.2d 306, 315-16 (2d Cir. 1951) (Frank, J., dis. op.).

79. Silverman v. United States, 365 U.S. 505 (1961).

80. Idem, at 512.

81. Idem, at 513.

82. Lopez v. United States, 373 U.S. 427 (1963).

83. Idem, at 439.

84. Lewis v. United States, 385 U.S. 206 (1966); Hoffa v. United States, 385 U.S. 293 (1966); Osborn v. United States, 385 U.S. 323 (1966).

85. Hoffa v. United States, 385 U.S. 293, 301 (1966).

86. Idem.

87. Idem, at 302.

88. Lewis v. United States, 385 U.S. 206 (1966).

89. Idem, at 210.

90. Osborn v. United States, 385 U.S. 323, 327 (1966).

91. Katz v. United States, 389 U.S. 347 (1967).

92. Idem, at 351.

93. See Note, "From Private Places to Personal Privacy: A Post-Katz Study of Fourth Amendment Protection," 43 New York University Law Review 968, 976-77 (1968).

94. Katz v. United States, 389 U.S. 347, 351-52 (1967).

95. Note, "Types of Property Seizable under the Fourth Amendment," 23 U.C.L.A. Law Review 963, 972 (1976).

96. Ibid., at 972 n.41.

97. Amsterdam, "Perspectives on the Fourth Amendment," at 385 (footnote omitted).

98. Katz v. United States, 389 U.S. 347, 360-61 (1967).

99. Amsterdam, "Perspectives on the Fourth Amendment," at 384.

100. Justice Harlan apparently altered his subjective conception in United States v. White, 401 U.S. 745, 786 (1972) (Harlan, J., dis. op.).

101. Arnold Simmel, "Privacy Is Not an Isolated Freedom," in Privacy, ed. J. R. Pennock and J. W. Chapman (New York: Atherton Press, 1971) 71-88, 84.

102. Howard, "The Reasonableness of Mistake in the Criminal Law," 4 University of Queensland Law Journal 45 (1961).

103. Katz v. United States, 389 U.S. 347, 361 (1967).

104. Kitch, "Katz v. United States: The Limits of the Fourth Amendment," Supreme Court Review, ed. Philip Kurland (Chicago: University of Chicago Press, 1968) 133, 136.

105. Comment, "Criminal Law—Unreasonable Visual Observation Held to Violate Fourth Amendment," 55 Minnesota Law Review 1255, 1263 (1971).

106. Comment, "The Concept of Privacy and the Fourth Amendment," 6 University of Michigan Law Review 154, 176 (1972).

107. Note, "Formalism, Legal Realism," at 946.

108. See Johnson v. United States, 333 U.S. 10, 13-14 (1948); and Aguilar v. Texas, 378 U.S. 108, 110-11 (1964); but see United States v. Santana, 427 U.S. 38, 43 (1976).

109. McDonald v. United States, 335 U.S. 451, 455-56 (1948).

110. In Carroll v. United States, 267 U.S. 132, 162 (1925), the Court stated that a search is justified when "the facts and circumstances within [the officers'] knowledge and of which they had reasonably trustworthy information were sufficient in themselves to warrant a man of reasonable caution in the belief that intoxicating liquor was being transported in the automobile which they stopped and searched."

111. See Terry v. Ohio, 392 U.S. 1 (1968); Warden v. Hayden, 387 U.S. 294 (1967); Harris v. United States, 331 U.S. 145, 150-51 n.11, 152 nn. 12 and 13 (1947).

112. Terry v. Ohio, 392 U.S. 1, 9 (1968).

113. See United States v. Dionisio, 410 U.S. 1, 8 (1973); Terry v. Ohio, 392 U.S. 1 (1968).

114. See Cady v. Dombrowski, 413 U.S. 433, 447-48 (1973); Chimel v. California, 395 U.S. 752, 765 (1968); Go-Bart Importing Co. v. United States, 282 U.S. 344, 357 (1931). But see United States v. Robinson, 414 U.S. 218 (1973) (once a suspect is under custodial arrest, he may be searched incident to that arrest without inquiry into the circumstances of that search).

115. See United States v. Brignoni-Ponce, 422 U.S. 873, 879-80 (1975); United States v. United States District Court, 407 U.S. 297, 322-23 (1972); Terry v. Ohio, 392 U.S. 1, 20-21 (1968); Camara v. Municipal Court, 387 U.S. 523, 535-37 (1967).

116. For a discussion of lower court reliance on Katz, see Richard Aynes, "Katz and the Fourth Amendment," 23 Cleveland State Law Review 63 (1974).

117. Mancusi v. DeForte, 392 U.S. 364, at 370 (1968), quoting Camara v. Municipal Court, 387 U.S. 523, at 528-39 (1967).

118. The Supreme Court permitted exceptions to the warrant requirement in Schneckloth v. Bustamonte, 412 U.S. 218 (1973) (permitted search upon third-party consent); Almeida-Sanchez v. United States, 413 U.S. 266 (1973) (allowed car search by roving border patrol); Cardwell v. Lewis, 417 U.S. 583 (1974) (allowed nonexigent seizure of paint sample from car); United States v. Watson, 423 U.S. 411 (1976) (finding of voluntary consent despite no proof defendant could withhold same). The Court relaxed the standard for probable cause in United States v. Harris, 403 U.S. 573, 580-81 (1971) ("substantial basis" for search); Texas v. White, 423 U.S. 67 (1975) (warrantless search of car in police custody though procurement of warrant was possible); South Dakota v. Opperman, 428 U.S. 364 (1976) (approved routine warrantless inventory searches of impounded automobiles); United States v. Martinez-Fuerte, 428 U.S. 543 (1976) (no violation of Fourth Amendment to stop and question occupants of automobile with no reason to believe they were illegal aliens).

119. United States v. Santana, 427 U.S. 38 (1976).

120. Idem, at 42. See also United States v. Watson, 423 U.S. 411 (1976), wherein the Court held permissible the warrantless arrest, without probable cause, of an individual in a public place.

121. United States v. Santana, 427 U.S. 38 (1976). The Court distinguished Warden v. Hayden, 387 U.S. 294 (1967), based on the "exigencies of the situations" for warrantless arrests, and Johnson v. United States, 333 U.S. 10 (1948), which first recognized the element of "hot pursuit" in a chase and relied only on the latter.

122. United States v. Santana, 427 U.S. 38, at 47 (1976) (Marshall, J., dis. op.).

123. See United States v. Martinez-Fuerte, 428 U.S. 543 (1976); United States v. Brignoni-Ponce, 422 U.S. 873 (1975); and Almeida-Sanchez v. United States, 413 U.S. 266 (1973).

124. United States v. Ortiz, 422 U.S. 891, 896 (1975).

125. Cardwell v. Lewis, 417 U.S. 583 (1974).

126. South Dakota v. Opperman, 428 U.S. 364, 367 (1976).

127. Berger v. State of New York, 388 U.S. 41 (1967).

128. United States v. White, 401 U.S. 745 (1972).

129. Idem, at 751-52.

130. Frank v. Maryland, 359 U.S. 360, 367 (1959).

131. Idem, at 376-81.

132. Abel v. United States, 362 U.S. 217, 255 (1960); and Ohio ex rel. Eaton v. Price, 364 U.S. 246 (1959).

133. Camara v. Municipal Court, 387 U.S. 523 (1967), at 528 quoting Wolf v. Colorado, 338 U.S. 25, at 27 (1949). See also See v. City of Seattle, 387 U.S. 541 (1967).

134. Idem, at 538-39.

135. Idem, at 537.

136. Marshall v. Barlow's Inc., 98 S. Ct. 1816, 1826 (1978).

137. Idem, at 1820.

138. See Colonade Catering Corp. v. United States, 397 U.S. 72 (1970), and Camara v. Municipal Court, 387 U.S. 523 (1967) (health inspections); Wyman v. James, 400 U.S. 309 (1971) (welfare inspections); United States v. Martinez-Fuerte, 428 U.S. 543 (1976), United States v. Brignoni-Ponce, 422 U.S. 873 (1975), Almeida-Sanchez v. United States, 413 U.S. 266 (1973) (border searches); Zurcher v. Stanford Daily, 98 S. Ct. 1970 (1978) (upholding of search of third party's premises). The Court has evaluated privacy claims in terms of both the nature and manner of governmental intrusion; see Camara v. Municipal Court, 387 U.S. 523, at 539 (1967) (dictum) (warrantless area inspections in certain health emergencies); Wyman v. James, 400 U.S. 309 (1971) (warrantless welfare inspections conducted at reasonable times); Colonade Catering Corp. v. United States, 397 U.S. 72 (1970) (warrantless inspection of federally licensed liquor dealer under 25 U.S.C. § 5146[b] [1970]); United States v. Biswell, 406 U.S. 311, 316 (1972) (warrantless nonforcible searches conducted in random fashion as long as they occur during business hours are permissible under the Gun Control Act of 1968, 18 U.S.C. § 921 [1970]). But see Marshall v. Barlow's Inc., 98 S. Ct. 1816 (1978) (struck down Section 8[a] of the Occupational Safety and Health Act of 1970, 29 U.S.C. § 657[a] [1970], which permitted warrantless searches of businesses in interstate commerce for purposes of insuring safety of workers); and Michigan v. Tyler, 98 S. Ct. 1942 (1978)

(held that unless the exigencies of proper fire prevention require the presence of fire fighters, a warrant is required when fire department personnel conduct a search to determine the cause of a fire).

139. G.M. Leasing Corp. v. United States, 429 U.S. 338, 358 (1977).

140. Idem, at 359-60.

141. Comment, "Government Access to Bank Records," 83 Yale Law Journal 1439, 1461 (1974).

142. Idem.

143. Subpoena duces tecum is a traditional common law writ for compelling production of documents. Fed. R. Crim. P. 17(c). Administrative agencies may also issue summonses requiring similar production of documents. See 26 U.S.C. § 7602(2) Tax Reform Act of 1976, P.L. 94-455, Sec. 1205; see, generally, John Wigmore, Evidence, ed. John McNaughton, vol. 8, § 2200 (Boston: Little, Brown, 1961).

144. United States v. Morton Salt Co., 338 U.S. 632, 652 (1950); see also Stanford v. Texas, 379 U.S. 476 (1965); United States v. Powell, 379 U.S. 48 (1964); and Hale v. Henkel, 201 U.S. 43 (1906) (holding a subpoena duces tecum that requires so many documents from a corporation that it would stop the business represented an overly burdensome request); Federal Trade Commission v. American Tobacco Co., 264 U.S. 298, 305-6 (1924) (dictum) (Fourth Amendment prohibits searches that constitute "fishing expeditions"). But see United States v. Lefkowitz, 285 U.S. 452, 464-65 (1932) (documents of evidentiary value only ruled to be improperly seized); United States v. Miller, 425 U.S. 435, 442 (1976).

145. See Oklahoma Press Publishing Co. v. Walling, 327 U.S. 186 (1846) ("specifies a reasonable period of time, and with reasonable particularity the subjects to which the documents called for relate"); Wheeler v. United States, 226 U.S. 478 (1912) ("[not] too broad as to be objectionable"); and Wilson v. United States, 221 U.S. 361 (1911) ("suitably specific and properly limited in scope").

146. United States v. Powell, 379 U.S. 48, 57 (1964); Ryan v. United States, 379 U.S. 61 (1964); United States v. Morton Salt Co., 338 U.S. 632, 642 (1950); and Blair v. United States, 250 U.S. 273, 281 (1919).

147. United States v. Powell, 379 U.S. 48, at 57-58. See also United States v. Morton Salt Co., 338 U.S. 632, 652-53 (1950); Oklahoma Press Publishing Co. v. Walling, 327 U.S. 186, 208-11 (1946); Federal Trade Commission v. American Tobacco Co., 264 U.S. 298, 305-7 (1924); and Donaldson v. United States, 400 U.S. 517, 530-36 (1971) (subpoena may not be used in support of ongoing criminal prosecution); United States v. Bisceglia, 420 U.S. 141 (1975).

148. Reisman v. Caplin, 375 U.S. 440 (1964).

149. <u>Donaldson</u> v. <u>United States</u>, 400 U.S. 517 (1971). See also <u>United States</u> v. <u>United States District Court</u>, 407 U.S. 297, 313-18 (1972).

150. Idem, at 531.

151. See <u>Almeida-Sanchez</u> v. <u>United States</u>, 413 U.S. 266, 271 (1973); <u>Colonade Catering Corp.</u> v. <u>United States</u>, 397 U.S. 72 (1970); and <u>United States</u> v. <u>Biswell</u>, 406 U.S. 311, 316 (1972).

152. <u>California Bankers Association</u> v. <u>Shultz</u>, 416 U.S. 21, 35-38, 59-61, 63-75 (1974).

153. Idem, at 89-90.

154. <u>United States</u> v. <u>Miller</u>, 425 U.S. 435 (1976).

155. Idem, at 440, quoting <u>Hoffa</u> v. <u>United States</u>, 385 U.S. 293, at 301-2 (1966).

156. Idem, at 442, quoting <u>Katz</u> v. <u>United States</u>, 389 U.S. 347, at 353 (1967), quoting <u>Warden</u> v. <u>Hayden</u>, 387 U.S. 294, at 304 (1967).

157. Idem. See also <u>Couch</u> v. <u>United States</u>, 409 U.S. 322, 335 (1973) (<u>Couch</u> is principally a Fifth Amendment case, although Couch raised a Fourth Amendment privacy claim in intervening with a subpoena duces tecum of her records held by her accountant).

158. <u>United States</u> v. <u>Miller</u>, 425 U.S. 435, at 443 (1976).

159. Comment, "The Constitutional Right of Privacy: An Examination," 69 <u>Northwestern University Law Review</u> 263, 291 (1974). See also <u>Laird</u> v. <u>Tatum</u>, 408 U.S. 1 (1972); <u>United States</u> v. <u>United States District Court</u>, 407 U.S. 297 (1972); <u>California Bankers Association</u> v. <u>Shultz</u>, 416 U.S. 21 (1974); <u>United States</u> v. <u>Miller</u>, 425 U.S. 435 (1976).

160. Note, "Constitutional Law—Searches and Seizures—Banks and Banking—Witnesses—Rights of Privacy," 8 <u>Akron Law Review</u> 181, 189 (1974).

161. <u>United States</u> v. <u>United States District Court</u>, 407 U.S. 297 (1972) (emphasis added). See also <u>Katz</u> v. <u>United States</u>, 389 U.S. 347 (1967); <u>Warden</u> v. <u>Hayden</u>, 387 U.S. 294 (1967); and <u>Mancusi</u> v. <u>DeForte</u>, 392 U.S. 364 (1968).

162. Robert Bogomolny, "The Right to Nondisclosure," 5 <u>Human Rights</u> 153, 233 (1976). Also, compare <u>G.M. Leasing Corp.</u> v. <u>United States</u>, 429 U.S. 338 (1977) with <u>Brown</u> v. <u>United States</u>, 411 U.S. 223, 229 (1973) (defendants not on premises at the time of a police search, nor having any proprietary interest in the premises, have no standing to challenge the propriety of the search).

163. Comment, "Government Access to Bank Records," at 1474.

164. <u>Rakas</u> v. <u>Illinois</u>, 99 S. Ct. 421, 435 (1978) (Powell, J., con. op.).

165. Idem, at 430 and 431 n.12.

166. Idem, at 429. The Court, thereby, limited <u>Jones</u> v. <u>United States</u>, 362 U.S. 257 (1960).

167. Idem, at 430 n.11.
168. Idem, at 437 (White, J., dis. op.).
169. Idem, at 435 (Powell, J., con. op.).

3

Personal Disclosures: No Man is Bound to Accuse Himself

There is no witness so dreadful, no accuser so terrible as
the conscience that dwells in the heart of every man.
                    Polybius
                    History, Book 18, Section 43

By comparison with the broad range of privacy interests that
may receive protection under the Fourth Amendment's guarantee
against unreasonable searches and seizures, a considerably narrower
range of privacy interests is embraced by the Fifth Amendment's
guarantee that no person "shall be compelled in any criminal case to
be a witness against himself." Whereas the Fourth Amendment's
proscription against unreasonable searches and seizures safeguards
privacy with regard to the permissible ways in which the government
may intrude upon individuals and their houses, papers, and effects,
the Fifth Amendment limits only governmental procedures by which
personal information may be gathered. Since the Fifth Amendment
proscribes the government from coercing and compelling individuals
to divulge personal information about their thoughts and activities,
the amendment ostensibly provides the principal guarantee for claims
to informational privacy.

HISTORY AND CONTOURS OF THE FIFTH AMENDMENT

Historical Background

The Fifth Amendment's provision that "No person . . . shall be
compelled in any criminal case to be a witness against himself" gave
constitutional effect to the maxim, "Nemo tenetur prodere scripsum"

—"No man is bound to betray [accuse] himself."[1] The maxim can be traced to John Lambert, an obdurate heretic, who in 1537 while chained to a stake protested the inquisitorial practices of ecclesiastical judges. Not until the middle of the seventeenth century, however, was the principle that no individual is bound to self-accusation established as a rule of evidence in English common law. Yet, by the close of the century the principle as part of the common law tradition was incorporated into colonial legal systems. As Leonard Levy's careful study of the history of the Fifth Amendment concludes, "By 1776 . . . the principle [that a man is not bound to accuse himself] . . . was simply taken for granted and so deeply accepted that its constitutional expression had a mechanical quality of a self-evident truth needing no explanation."[2] The Fifth Amendment, like the Fourth Amendment, evolved in the United States out of the reception of the English common law and, in particular, its accusatorial system of criminal procedure.[3]

The common law principle that "no man is bound to accuse himself" underlies the constitutional right guaranteed by the Fifth Amendment. Still, the drafters of the Bill of Rights were apparently unsure of the precise scope of the common law maxim. Initially, George Mason, as author of the Virginia Declaration of Rights, urged the constitutionality of the common law rule of evidence:

> That in all capital or criminal prosecutions a man hath a
> right to demand the cause and nature of his accusation,
> to be confronted with the accusers and witnesses, to call
> for evidence in his favor, and to a speedy trial by an im-
> partial jury of twelve men of his vicinage, without whose
> unanimous consent he cannot be found guilty; nor can he
> be compelled to give evidence against himself; that no
> man be deprived of his liberty, except by the law of the
> land or the judgment of his peers.[4]

Mason's formulation was not without ambiguity because the guarantee appeared within a list of enumerated rights of the accused and, consequently, failed to extend protection to anyone but the accused, nor to apply in any proceeding other than a criminal prosecution. Moreover, since in the seventeenth and eighteenth centuries the common law right extended to all stages of all equity and common law proceedings and to all witnesses, Mason's formulation provided only a "stunted version" of the common law maxim.

By comparison, James Madison's draft of the proposed amendment provided a guarantee that embraced the broad scope of the traditional common law maxim:

> No person shall be subject, except in cases of impeach-
> ment, to more than one punishment or trial for the same
> offense; nor shall be compelled to be a witness against
> himself; nor be deprived of life, liberty, or property,
> without due process of law, nor be obliged to relinquish
> his property, where it may be necessary for public use,
> without a just compensation.[5]

Madison's proposal broadly applied to civil and criminal proceedings,
as well as to any stage or forum of the legal process. Indeed, because Madison's proposal apparently collapsed the maxim "no man
is bound to accuse himself" with the maxim "no man should be a witness in his own case"—"Nemo debet esse testis in propria causa"—
his formulation would apply to not only self-incriminating but also
self-accusatory testimony, and, moreover, would extend protection
to third-party witnesses in civil, criminal, or equity proceedings. In
this regard Madison's proposal transcended the guarantees of most
state constitutions in order to embrace the broadest practices at common law.[6]

In committee John Lawrence suggested that the clause constituted
"a general declaration in some degree contrary to laws passed" and,
consequently, should be "confined to criminal cases"; thereupon, the
clause was amended without discussion and adopted unanimously.[7]
Thus, the present formulation "No person shall . . . be compelled
in any Criminal Case, to be a witness against himself. "

The Text and Strict Construction

The text of the Fifth Amendment indicates that the guarantee
applies only "when the accused is himself compelled to act, either by
testifying in court or producing documents."[8] Inclusion of the phrase
"in any criminal case" literally limits the scope of the guarantee,
precluding invocation of the right during police interrogations and by
parties and witnesses in civil and equity suits, as well as witnesses
before nonjudicial proceedings, such as grand jury investigations.
While a strict construction definitively, albeit narrowly, defines the
scope of the amendment's protection, it provides no clear guidance
for determining what constitutes compulsion of an individual's self-
accusation. Nevertheless, commentators have inferred that the
amendment, literally applied, protects against compelled self-incrimination alone, and not self-accusation that leads to infamy or
public disgrace.

Although historically the Supreme Court rejected such a strict
construction of the amendment's scope, the proclivity of modern jurists

to refer to the amendment as conferring a privilege against self-incrimination imposes two restrictions that do not necessarily follow from a strict construction of the amendment.

First, the inference that the amendment grants only a privilege rather than a right has great jurisprudential significance. Privileges differ from rights: whereas privileges are granted and, hence, revocable by the government, rights are not granted nor do they derive from the government. Rather, rights impose limitations on the exercise of governmental power, thereby defining the relationship between citizens and the government. To be sure, the practice of rights in the United States depends on judicial and legislative legitimation of claims to exercise rights, but the government does not create those rights—it merely validates claims of rights in litigated or contested circumstances. Therefore, "to speak of the 'privilege' against self-incrimination, degrades it, inadvertently, in comparison to other constitutional rights."[9] Provisions of the amendment confer the same constitutional status of protection against the exercise of governmental power as do other guarantees of the Bill of Rights.

Second, a literal reading and strict construction of the amendment does not perforce confine its protection only to self-incrimination. Since in criminal cases individuals' personal disclosures may expose them to civil liabilities or infamy, individuals may be forced into self-accusation, but that which falls short of self-incrimination. As Leonard Levy observes:

> To speak of a right against self-incrimination stunts the wider right not to give evidence against oneself. . . . The previous history of the right, both in England and America, proves that it was not bound by rigid definition. . . . The "right against self-incrimination" is a short-hand gloss of modern origin that implies a restriction not in the constitutional clause. The right not to be a witness against oneself imports a principle of wider reach, applicable at least in criminal cases, to the self-production of any adverse evidence, including evidence that made one the herald of his own infamy, thereby publicly disgracing him. The clause extended, in other words, to all the injurious as well as incriminating consequences of disclosures by witness or party.[10]

With a literal reading of the clause, then, the shorthand version of a privilege against self-incrimination appears to limit unnecessarily the scope of the Fifth Amendment.

A strict construction severely limits the contexts in which individuals may invoke the amendment and, in particular, the occasions on which individuals may legitimately claim Fifth Amendment-protected privacy. A strict construction promotes legitimation of privacy interests only when an individual is "compelled in any criminal case to be a witness against himself." The contours of Fifth Amendment-protected privacy, therefore, would be limited to the circumstances of individuals divulging personal information—not necessarily incriminating information—about their thoughts or engagements, under duress and compulsion of the government and only in criminal cases.

The judicially fashioned contours of the Fifth Amendment and protected privacy, however, are broader than entailed by the logic of a literal reading of the amendment. As Justice Frankfurter once observed, "the privilege against self-incrimination is a specific provision [sic] of which it is peculiarly true that 'a page of history is worth a volume of logic.'"[11] Both the history of the amendment and judicial interpretation have ensured broader protection than suggested by a literal reading of the Fifth Amendment.

The Supreme Court and the
Scope of the Fifth Amendment

The primary effect of the Fifth Amendment is that in criminal trials the accused cannot be required to take the witness stand, and, moreover, it is improper for judges to comment on the failure to testify.[12] Witnesses must explicitly claim the right, or otherwise they are considered tacitly to waive it; yet they do not possess final determination of the validity of their claims to exercise Fifth Amendment guarantees.[13] The Supreme Court never accepted the principle that witnesses in civil suits may refuse to testify because of possible adverse effects on civil or proprietary interests or because the result may be self-disgrace.[14] Even in criminal cases, the accused may refuse to answer only questions tantamount to admissions of guilt or inexorably leading to such evidence, but not where self-incrimination is "of an imaginary and unsubstantial character, having reference to some extraordinary and barely possible contingency, so improbable that no reasonable man would suffer it to influence his conduct."[15]

Although inclusion of the phrase "in any criminal case" literally limits the amendment's applicability to criminal trials, there exists compelling historical support that the framers bequeathed "a large and still growing principle."[16] As a matter of constitutional history, judicial policies tend to support the view that the Fifth Amendment's clause "is as broad as the mischief against which it seeks to guard."[17] The Supreme Court extended the contours of the amendment beyond criminal trials to grand jury proceedings as well as legislative investigations, and, in some circumstances, to witnesses or parties in civil

and criminal cases, where truthful assertions might result in forfeiture, penalty, or criminal prosecution. The Warren Court's landmark
decision in Miranda v. Arizona "expanded the right beyond all precedent, yet not beyond its historical spirit and purpose"[18] in extending
the right to police interrogations at the time of arrest or in the station
house. Thus, as a product of judicial policies, the Fifth Amendment's
protection extends from the time the inquiry "has begun to focus on a
particular suspect," through "custodial interrogation," to the trial itself as well as other quasi-judicial and nonjudicial proceedings.[19]

Judicial infidelity to the text of the Constitution, however, is
Janus-faced. Whereas constitutional interpretation broadened the
scope of the amendment in terms of the contexts in which individuals
may invoke their right to remain silent, loose construction of the
amendment also fostered policies that compromise Fifth Amendment
protection.

Since 1896 the Supreme Court has upheld grants of immunity on
the assumption that although the amendment permits a witness "to refuse to disclose or expose him to unfavorable comments," its primary
function is only "to secure the witness against prosecution which might
be aided directly or indirectly by his disclosure."[20] An individual
may be forced to forgo the Fifth Amendment right to remain silent
when offered immunity. The practical value of the amendment was
further restricted by the Burger Court's legitimation of limiting immunity grants—so-called transactional immunity—to "use" or "testimonial" immunity barring only use of disclosed information in criminal trials.[21] In addition to the policy of permitting grants of immunity to circumvent Fifth Amendment guarantees, the Burger Court
continues to uphold so-called "implied consent" and "required record"
statutes that impose upon privacy interests and may lead to self-incrimination.[22] Moreover, the Burger Court endorses the policy distinction by which the amendment protects individuals' evidence only
of a "testimonial" or "communicative" nature but not "real" or "physical" evidence, such as blood tests or handwriting samples.[23]

The contours of the Fifth Amendment and protected privacy,
thus, have been circumscribed by judicial policies permitting grants
of immunity, required records, and the distinction between real and
testimonial evidence. The Burger Court promotes, but did not origi-
nate, these policies. Instead, the Burger Court's extension of these
policies is based upon a reconsideration and reevaluation of the jurisprudential basis of the privilege against self-incrimination.

The contraction or extension of the scope of the Fifth Amendment and protected privacy depends upon judicial construction of the
purposes and policies behind the amendment. In Murphy v. Waterfront Commission of New York Harbor the Court perhaps most concisely elucidated the "complex of values" underlying the amendment:

It reflects many of our fundamental values and most noble
aspirations: our unwillingness to subject those suspected
of crime to the cruel trilemma of self-accusation, perjury,
or contempt; our preference for an accusatorial rather than
an inquisitorial system of criminal justice; our fear that
self-incrimination will be elicited by inhumane treatment
and abuses; our sense of fair play which dictates a "fair
state-individual balance by requiring the government . . .
in its contest with the individual to shoulder the entire
load"; . . . our respect for the inviolability of the human
personality and of the right of each individual "to a private enclave where he may lead a private life" . . .; our
distrust of self-deprecatory statements; and our realiza-
tion that the privilege while "a shelter to the guilty," has
often "a protection to the innocent."[24]

From this complex of values, three basic rationales for the amendment may be discerned: (1) the necessity to maintain a responsible
accusatorial system; (2) the desire to prevent cruel and inhumane
treatment of individuals by forcing them into a "trilemma of self-accusation, perjury, or contempt"; and (3) the belief that compelled
confessions are serious invasions of personal privacy. Significantly,
each of these justifications for the Fifth Amendment implies different
normative orientations toward the amendment and protection for personal privacy. The following section examines each of these rationales
and their implications for judicial policies and construction of the Fifth
Amendment and protected privacy.

RATIONALES OF A FOX HUNTER, AN OLD WOMAN, AND A HERMIT

The Fox Hunter's Reason

The "fox hunter's reason" was Jeremy Bentham's phrase for
the "preference for an accusatorial system rather than an inquisitorial
system of criminal justice." As Bentham characterizes the fox hunter's reason:

[It] consists in introducing upon the carpet of legal procedure the ideal of fairness, in the sense in which the
word is used by sportsmen. The fox is to have a fair
chance for his life: he must have (so close is the analogy) what is called law: leave to run a certain length of
way, for the express purpose of giving him a chance for
escape.[25]

The fox hunter's rationale justifies the Fifth Amendment by drawing an analogy between a fox hunt and an accusatorial system of criminal justice. Just as in a fox hunt certain rules define permissible and impermissible ways by which fox hunters may capture the fox, so too rules of criminal procedure define an acceptable process for prosecuting suspects of criminal activity in an accusatorial system. Moreover, both the rules of the sport of fox hunting and of the adversary system of criminal prosecution are predicated upon the notion of fairness—fair treatment of the fox and the criminal suspect. The Fifth Amendment is justified as an "essential mainstay of our adversary system"[26] precisely because an accusatorial system requires fair treatment of suspects of criminal activity. The analogy between fox hunts and accusatorial systems, thus, illuminates the basis for and function of the Fifth Amendment. Significantly, the fox hunter's rationale implies that the amendment cannot be justified on its own merits. Instead the amendment is only a rule and a policy objective of accusatorial systems.

In what sense is the Fifth Amendment a policy objective? How does the privilege serve the ideal of justice as fair treatment in accusatorial systems? According to the fox hunter's rationale, "the essence [of accusatorial systems and, hence, the amendment] is the requirement that the state which proposes to convict and punish an individual produce the evidence against him by the independent labors of its officers, not by the single, cruel expedient of forcing it from his own lips."[27] As the Warren Court reiterated in Miranda v. Arizona:

> The constitutional foundations underlying the privilege is
> the respect a government—state or federal—must accord
> to the dignity and integrity of its citizens. To maintain a
> "fair state-individual balance," to require the government
> "to shoulder the entire load, . . . to respect the inviola-
> bility of the human personality, our accusatorial system
> of criminal justice demands that the government seeking
> to punish an individual produce the evidence against him
> by its own independent labours, rather than by cruel,
> simple expedient of compelling it from his own mouth.[28]

The Fifth Amendment's guarantee against self-accusation is a policy objective of accusatorial systems, because it functions as an instrument for securing and maintaining a "fair state-individual balance."

The normative import of the amendment therefore relates to its role in maintaining a relationship between the individual and the state, aptly characterized as "equals meeting in battle." As Abe Fortas observed:

The principle that a man is not obliged to furnish the
state with ammunition to use against him is basic to this
conception. Equals, meeting in battle, owe no such duty
to one another, regardless of the obligations that they may
be under prior to battle. A sovereign state has the right
to defend itself, and within the limits of accepted procedure, to punish infractions of the rules that govern its
relationships with its sovereign individual to surrender
or impair his right of self-defense. [29]

The fox hunter's rationale for the amendment, as Fortas explained,
"reflects the individual's attornment to the state and in a philosophical
sense insists upon the equality of the individual and the state."[30]
Since the primary value is a relationship of equality between the individual and the state, "the privilege against self-incrimination represents a basic adjustment of the power and rights of the individual
and the state."[31] The amendment serves merely as a policy objective
of accusatorial systems in which the government must provide compelling proof of an individual's culpability without compelling the individual into self-incrimination.

The normative significance of the Fifth Amendment, therefore,
centers on its instrumental value for other ends—securing conditions
for a "fair fight" and maintaining a "fair state-individual balance"—
and not as an end in itself. Before discussing the implications for
judicial policy making, a brief examination of arguments, which presuppose that the amendment has only instrumental value, further clarifies the fox hunter's rationale and illustrates its importance in contemporary discussions of the Fifth Amendment and protected privacy.

The fox hunter's rationale underlines several main arguments.[32]
Foremost among the arguments is that historical abuses, exemplified
by the Star Chamber, High Commission, and Inquisition, justify the
adoption of the principle that "no man is bound to accuse himself" in
securing a "fair fight" between the individual and the state in criminal
prosecutions.[33] A corollary argument urges the usefulness of the
Fifth Amendment in frustrating "bad laws" and "bad procedures" relating to government inquiries into citizen's political and religious
beliefs.[34] Whether or not convincing, such arguments from history
are designed to be persuasive of the fact that unless individuals themselves are permitted to limit governmental inquiries, potentially serious abuses of power may result. Notwithstanding a history of prosecutory abuses, it would be imprudent and inefficient to allow in all
instances witnesses themselves to frustrate governmental inquiries.
Historical practices, moreover, do not settle the question of when
and to what extent witnesses should be allowed to decide whether they
should exercise their right to remain silent. Yet, absent an effective

First Amendment privilege, the Fifth Amendment does provide a con-
cededly blunt but "particularly effective [device for] frustrating belief
probes. "[35]

Additionally, some commentators argue that the Fifth Amendment actually defines the practical limits of governmental power.
That is, a kind of "futility argument" urges that "truthful self-incriminating answers cannot be compelled, so why try?"[36] The merit of
the futility argument, however, remains dubious as controversy rages
over whether witnesses will resort to brinkmanship when testifying
(thereby giving advantage to the fox rather than the fox hunter) and,
hence, whether other uses of the amendment can justify its promi-
nence in accusatorial systems.

Other arguments for the amendment's utility indeed may be
found. Supplementary arguments urge that the amendment protects
innocent defendants from convicting themselves by bad performance
on the witness stand; third-party witnesses are encouraged to appear
and testify since they need not fear self-incrimination; and, finally,
as a consequence of the amendment courts will not be burdened by
false testimony.[37] These arguments corroborate a further argument
that the Fifth Amendment contributes to "respect for the legal process."[38] Respect for the legal process, however, may be only derivative inasmuch as the amendment necessitates that the government
conduct competent and independent investigations. Still, regardless
of whether the Fifth Amendment directly or indirectly contributes to
respect for the legal process, the import of the argument emphasizes
again the interplay between the amendment and the values of the accusatorial system.

In identifying symbolic and practical uses of the Fifth Amendment, the preceding arguments presuppose that the amendment has
only instrumental value and no intrinsic worth. Quite apart from the
relative merits of each argument, together the arguments underscore
the significance of the fox hunter's rationale for and evaluation of the
amendment. What, then, are the implications of the fox hunter's rationale and the preceding arguments for judicial policies toward the
Fifth Amendment?

If the amendment is understood to have only instrumental value,
then its scope and applicability may be narrowly drawn, because "the
argument from the need to maintain an accusatorial system would only
apply where there was some danger of prosecution."[39] Where personal disclosures are not incriminating or where an individual receives immunity, claims under the amendment have no legitimacy.
Grants of immunity are permissible and justifiable in accusatorial
systems because immunity removes culpability for self-accusatory
statements and, thus, leaves undisturbed the state-individual balance.
The fair state-individual balance remains undisturbed, however, only

in the sense that an individual is not culpable for accusatory self-disclosures. An individual's privacy interests are necessarily forfeited by grants of immunity. Furthermore, if individuals refuse to testify after being granted immunity from prosecution, they may be jailed for contempt.[40] As Robert McKay observes:

> Even though protection against certain harmful consequence is assured through a sufficient grant of immunity, the privacy interest is relinquished upon disclosure compelled in return for a grant of immunity. Moreover, there is no way to protect against the related hazard of damage to reputation. It is not easy to square the privacy interest (which arguably is) a prime purpose of the privilege with immunity statutes that require surrender of privacy.[41]

In other words, while under the fox hunter's rationale the individual and the state ostensibly remain on equal footing, the individual faces the prospect of protecting personal privacy only when self-disclosures are incriminating. The individual must forgo privacy interests when personal disclosures are self-accusatory but not self-incriminating and is required to testify upon a grant of immunity, regardless of privacy interests, at the risk of being jailed for contempt for refusal to do so. In sum, given the fox hunter's jurisprudential basis for the Fifth Amendment, personal privacy receives little or no consideration and protection. Privacy interests are tangential, to say the least, and receive limited recognition, at best, if the amendment merely embodies a policy objective of accusatorial systems.

Still, more fundamentally, given the fox hunter's rationale, the Fifth Amendment confers only a privilege and not a right against self-accusation. That is, the amendment may be extended or contracted, depending upon judicial evaluations of its utility in different circumstances for maintaining an accusatorial system. This crucial implication of the fox hunter's rationale is well illustrated by Henry J. Friendly's argument:

> What is important is that on any view the Fifth Amendment does not forbid the taking of statements from a suspect; it forbids compelling them. That is what the words say, and history and policy unite to show that is what they meant. Rather than being a "right of silence," the right, or better the privilege [sic], is against being compelled to speak. This distinction is not mere semantics; it goes to the very core of the problem.[42]

As Friendly argues, the amendment's justification rests with its utility for prohibiting the government from compelling persons to be witnesses against themselves, because only in compelling an individual does the government rupture the fair state-individual balance. The "very core of the problem" for judicial construction, therefore, becomes one of determining what constitutes personal compulsion. Yet, governmental compulsion may be a matter of degree, dependent upon the circumstances of governmental inquiries. Consequently, if the Fifth Amendment is justified only in terms of its utility, and "compulsion is not a yes-or-no matter rather a continuum," then the privilege need not have the same contours in the police station as in the courtroom. [43] Instead, the scope of the Fifth Amendment will vary with judicial evaluation of the degree of personal compulsion and the utility of the privilege relative to the maintenance of a fair state-individual balance.

The Burger Court's efforts at line drawing in evaluating the degree of governmental compulsion, moreover, indicate that the threshold requirement for effective exercises of the privilege is a demonstration of "genuine compulsion of testimony." [44] As the Court in United States v. Washington reiterated:

> Absent some officially coerced self-accusation the Fifth
> Amendment privilege is not violated by even the most
> damning admissions. . . . The constitutional guarantee
> is only that the witness be not compelled to give self-in-
> criminating testimony. The test is whether, considering
> the totality of the circumstances, the free will of the wit-
> ness was overborne. [45]

Hence, not only are the legitimate occasions for invoking the privilege limited to where an individual makes self-incriminating disclosures, but, moreover, effective exercise of the amendment remains conditional upon showing that the government exerted "genuine compulsion" in securing an individual's statements of self-culpability.

The fox hunter's rationale, when endorsed in judicial construction of the amendment, therefore, severely limits the scope of the Fifth Amendment and its protection for personal privacy. Indeed, given an instrumental basis, the amendment provides only a relative constitutional guarantee. As a relative constitutional guarantee, the Fifth Amendment confers only a privilege against self-incrimination and not a right against self-accusation. As such the privilege against self-incrimination is context-dependent, and its effective exercise turns upon judicial evaluation of the degree of compulsion rather than self-accusation per se.

An Old Woman's Reason

Justice Douglas, dissenting in <u>Ullmann</u> v. <u>United States</u>, urged the unconstitutionality of immunity grants on the grounds that the Fifth Amendment embodies more than an instrumental value and policy objective of the accusatorial system:

> The guarantee against self-incrimination contained in the Fifth Amendment is not only a protection against conviction and prosecution but a safeguard of conscience and human dignity and freedom of expression as well. . . . [T]he Framers put it well beyond the power of Congress to <u>compel</u> anyone to confess his crimes. <u>The evil to be guarded against was partly self-accusation under legal compulsion. But that was only a part of the evil.</u> The conscience and dignity of man were also involved. [46]

Justice Douglas's rejection of the fox hunter's rationale embraced what Bentham termed "an old woman's reason"—namely, that the Fifth Amendment reflects the belief that it is cruel and inhumane to force a person to partake in his own undoing.

In Bentham's view, "The essence of [the old woman's] reason is contained in the word <u>hard</u>: 'tis hard upon a man to be obliged to criminate himself":

> Hard it is upon a man, it must be confessed, to be obliged to do anything that he does not like. That he should not much like to do what is meant by his criminating himself, is natural enough; for what it leads to, is, his being punished. What is no less hard upon him, is, that he should be punished. . . . Whatever hardship there is in a man's being punished, that, and no more, is there in his thus being made to criminate himself. [47]

According to Bentham, the old woman's rationale is a bit of "nonsense on stilts," which if legally accepted would only serve the guilty and foster bad evidence.

Notwithstanding Bentham's curt dismissal of the old woman's rationale, there exists considerable historical evidence that the rationale served as an important jurisprudential basis for the development and establishment of a right against self-accusation. In the late sixteenth century, for example, Thomas Cartwright and other Puritan leaders attacked the ex officio oath on the grounds that:

> Much more is it equall that a mans owne private faults should remayne private to God and him selfe till the Lord

> discover them. And in regard of this righte consider howe
> the Lord ordained wittnesses where by the magistrate should
> seeke into the offenses of his subjects and not by oathe rifle
> the secrets of theare hearts.[48]

Colonial common law practices and constitutional history demonstrate
that a crucial basis for the Fifth Amendment was the belief that individuals should be protected "against physical compulsion and against
the moral compulsion that an oath to a revengeful God commands of a
pious soul."[49] As Zechariah Chafee observed, "Nothing else in the
Constitution prevents government officials and policemen from exort-
ing confessions from American citizens by torture and other kinds of
physical brutality."[50]

While history supports both the fox hunter's and the old woman's
rationale for the Fifth Amendment, the old woman's rationale finds
the Fifth Amendment's primary purpose in preventing the torture and
inhumane treatment of individuals; a right against self-accusation respects the dignity of human beings. As David Louisell argues:

> [T]he best justification [for the Fifth Amendment] is simply
> this: It is essentially and inherently cruel to make a man
> an instrument of his own condemnation. The human tragedy
> having evinced as much cruelty as it has, any nurtured sen-
> timent against sadism is indeed a welcome brake on human
> passion, a valued friend, not likely to be discarded for
> newer ones.[51]

In other words, the old woman's rationale, contrary to that of the fox
hunter, recognizes that the Fifth Amendment embodies an end in itself, namely, respect for the moral dignity of the individual. Hence,
the amendment does not confer merely a privilege, as does the fox
hunter's rationale, but rather constitutionally denominates a right to
remain silent.

According to the old woman's rationale, the significance of the
Fifth Amendment does not depend on its instrumental role as a policy
preference of accusatory systems, rather it lies simply in the constitutional recognition that human beings should be respected. The
old woman's rationale requires that one takes rights seriously and not
dilute a constitutional guarantee by transposing a privilege against
self-incrimination for a right against self-accusation. If the practice
of rights and, in particular, the Fifth Amendment's guarantee are
taken seriously, then "third degree" methods of interrogation are necessarily proscribed. So it is that the Supreme Court and its commentators often justify the Fifth Amendment in terms of respect for the
dignity and inviolability of the individual, not only to foreclose brow-

beating and bullying but also to preclude the trilemma of reluctant witnesses. Reluctant witnesses must choose among the alternatives of disclosure, a "stultifying thing"; bringing contempt upon themselves by not testifying, an "unnatural act" of inflicting injury on oneself; or committing perjury.[52] By illuminating the perilous moral consequences of confronting and compelling individuals to testify against themselves, such arguments support the right against self-accusation and underscore the significance of the old woman's rationale for the Fifth Amendment.

The old woman's rationale, however, not only cautions judicial construction of the Fifth Amendment to foreclose the possibility of third-degree interrogations and confronting witnesses with a cruel trilemma of testifying, bringing themselves into contempt, or committing perjury. Also, upon the old woman's rationale, the Fifth Amendment extends protection to any claim against compulsory self-disclosure. Hence, the Court need not engage in line drawing with regard to the degree of governmental compulsion or attempt to define "genuine compulsion of testimony." Indeed, compelled disclosures, even on grants of immunity, constitute inhumane treatment because individuals are forced into self-condemnation by publicly testifying as well as by forgoing their privacy interests.

The old woman's rationale, thus, provides an alternative to the fox hunter's jurisprudential basis for the Fifth Amendment. The old woman's justification of the amendment in terms of respect for the dignity and inviolability of the individual contrasts sharply with the fox hunter's instrumental evaluation. Concomitantly, the implications of the old woman's rationale for judicial construction of the scope of the Fifth Amendment differ radically from those fostered by the fox hunter's rationale. Since the Fifth Amendment is interpreted to embody an end in itself, not merely an instrumental value, judicial interpretation must take seriously the notion of rights, and, in particular, a right against self-accusation. It is, therefore, extraconstitutional to diminish the practical value of the amendment by construing it to confer a privilege against self-incrimination and not a right against self-accusation. If the Fifth Amendment does not confer a privilege but a right, then it is also wrong for the Supreme Court to fashion the contours of the amendment to different circumstances upon their construction of what constitutes "genuine compulsion of testimony" or, in other instances, to allow the constitutional guarantee to be superseded by immunity grants. Furthermore, the old woman's rationale points to the ultimate dilemma that the fox hunter's rationale poses for constitutional interpretation: the Fifth Amendment is justified in terms of its instrumental value for securing and maintaining a fair state-individual balance; yet, judicial construction of the amendment's relative utility may lead to a narrow context-dependent privilege

against self-incrimination, with its effective exercise turning on judicial evaluation of the degree of governmental compulsion on an individual. Consequently, individuals, while not criminally culpable,
may still face public disgrace, infamy, self-condemnation and, thus,
dubiously remain on an equal footing with the state.

   Notwithstanding these arguments for and the moral appeal of the
old woman's rationale, it too poses a paradox for constitutional interpretation. The old woman's rationale arguably "confronts the clear
fact that the rule against self-incrimination is psychologically and
morally unacceptable as a general governing principle in human relations."[53] Defenders of the fox hunter's rationale, such as Sidney
Hook, appeal to common sense in countering the old woman's moral-
ism: "Let any sensible person ask himself whether he would hire a
secretary, nurse, or even a sitter for his children, if she refused to
reply to a question bearing upon the proper execution of her duties
with a response equivalent to the privilege against self-incrimination."[54] Friendly reiterates the argument:

> No parent would teach such a doctrine to his children; the
> lesson parents preach is that a misdeed, even a serious
> one, will generally be forgiven; a failure to make a clean
> breast of it will not be. Every day people are being asked
> to explain their conduct to parents, employers, and
> teachers.[55]

The old woman's rationale indeed leads to paradox. On the one hand,
the right against self-accusation is justified by its acknowledgment of
the moral dignity and inviolability of the individual. On the other
hand, the justification runs contrary to moral and social practices.
In other words, an individual's nondisclosure might be acceptable and
justifiable in legal proceedings but not in family affairs or social relationships.

   The paradox of the old woman's rationale appears more pressing
with regard to claims of Fifth Amendment-protected privacy. The old
woman's rationale, unlike the fox hunter's, assures extensive Fifth
Amendment protection for privacy interests as derivative of the intrinsic worth of individuals. Claims to informational privacy or nondisclosure of personal thoughts or engagements have merit because
of their association with respect for the dignity of individuals, which
itself requires that individuals not be forced to suffer the pain of self-
accusation. Like the fox hunter's rationale, the old woman's rationale
recognizes only the instrumental value of personal privacy, albeit for
a different end: whereas the former rationale acknowledges privacy
interests when associated with an equilibrium between the individual
and the state, the latter rationale recognizes personal privacy as an

essential aspect of the dignity and conscience of individuals. Moreover, unlike the fox hunter's rationale, the old woman's rationale legitimates privacy claims whenever and wherever individuals are compelled inhumanely and regardless of immunity from legal culpability
to disclose personal information. Although Fifth Amendment-protected
privacy under the old woman's rationale rests on moral principle and,
hence, may not justifiably be forfeited by grants of immunity, privacy
claims suffer the paradox of the old woman's rationale: disclosure of
personal information that is self-accusatory or self-incriminating may
not be legally compelled, but it may be compelled, on ethical grounds,
by an individual's lover, parents, friend, or employer.

A Hermit's Reason

As an alternative to the rationales of the fox hunter and the old
woman, contemporary commentators have proposed that a privacy rationale, or what might be termed the "hermit's rationale," justifies
the Fifth Amendment. The hermit's rationale holds that compelled
confessions are serious invasions of privacy and, furthermore, that
invasions of privacy are to be taken seriously. To compel disclosure
of personal information not only disturbs the fair state-individual balance and denies the dignity of individuals but also diminishes the intrinsic worth of personal privacy.

For the hermit the normative significance of individual privacy
is an end in itself, which attains constitutional expression and protection in the Fifth Amendment. As Leonard Ratner urged:

> The privilege against self-incrimination is a constitutional
> facet of the right of privacy. The right of each individual
> to remain unmolested in the absence of independent evi-
> dence connecting him with the commission of a crime is
> but an aspect of the limitation which the privilege places
> upon the powers of the police. The privilege reflects the
> further principle, however, that a person's own knowledge
> of whether or not he has any connection with a criminal
> act is private to him and should not be subjected to com-
> pulsory disclosure.[56]

That a privacy rationale underlies the amendment was increasingly acknowledged during the years of the Warren Court.[57] In particular, Justice Douglas urged the import of the value of privacy and
its relation to the Fifth Amendment.

> Privacy involves the choice of the individual to disclose or
> to reveal what he believes, what he thinks, what he pos-

sesses. . . . That dual aspect of privacy means that the
individual should have the freedom to select for himself
the time and circumstances when he will share his secrets
with others and decide the extent of that sharing. This is
his prerogative, not the State's.[58]

Yet, if as Justice Douglas suggests, the Fifth Amendment constitutionally embodies a privacy principle, how is it that this rationale
has gained currency in only the last 20 years? Indeed, critics of the
Supreme Court's recognition of Fifth Amendment-protected privacy
point out that the fox hunter's and the old woman's rationales have
historical support in the development of common and constitutional
law, whereas privacy was neither recognized in seventeenth and
eighteenth century common law nor given express recognition in the
Bill of Rights. Although not entirely persuasive, Judge Frank correctly countered such criticisms when he observed: "The critics of
the Supreme Court, however, in their over-emphasis on the history
of the Fifth Amendment, overlook the fact that a noble principle often
transcends its origins, that creative misunderstandings account for
some of our most cherished values and institutions."[59] Fortunately,
Judge Frank, unlike Justice Douglas, further explicated the relationship between the Fifth Amendment and personal privacy in countering
critics of the hermit's justification.

They ignore the fact that the privilege—like the constitutional barrier to unreasonable searches, or the client's
privilege against disclosure of his confidential disclosures
to his lawyer—has, inter alia, an important "substantive"
value, as a safeguard of the individual's "substantive"
right of privacy, a right to a private enclave where he may
lead a private life.[60]

Judge Frank thus makes explicit the import of and crucial difference
between the rationales of the fox hunter and the hermit. Whereas the
fox hunter views the Fifth Amendment as merely a procedural rule
deriving its justification from its utility within an accusatorial system,
the hermit's rationale justifies the amendment in terms of a constitutional principle or right, which fidelity to the Constitution requires
that one takes seriously.

In contrasting the fox hunter's and hermit's rationales, Judge
Frank, like Ratner and Justice Douglas, unfortunately does not indicate the significance of the hermit's rationale for judicial construction
of the contours of the Fifth Amendment and protected privacy. Indeed,
too often proponents of the hermit's rationale simply assert the normative import of Fifth Amendment-protected privacy but fail to artic-

ulate definite consequences for constitutional interpretation. The Warren Court's endorsement of a privacy rationale for the amendment, for example, ironically led to the denial of claims to Fifth Amendment-protected privacy. The Warren Court acknowledged that "the federal privilege against self-incrimination reflects the Constitution's concern for the essential values represented by 'our respect for the inviolability of human personality and of the right of each individual' to a private enclave where he may lead a private life," only to deny the retroactivity of Griffin v. California's no-comment rule.[61] Previously, the Court had employed a privacy rationale to deny the retroactivity of the exclusionary rule under the Fourth Amendment.[62] Acknowledgment of the import of a privacy rationale for the Fifth Amendment is not sufficient; instead a perspicuous view of the implications of the rationale for judicial construction is required.

Robert McKay, drawing from the Supreme Court's dicta on the interrelationship between the Fourth and Fifth Amendments, argues that a privacy principle underlies the Fifth Amendment:

> The limitation on searches and seizures prohibits only that which is "unreasonable," thus leaving the privacy of the home home imperfectly secured in order to accomodate genuine necessities of the state. But the privacy of the mind, at least against the compulsion of self-accusation, is absolute. Is it not sound as a modern expression of the original urge to protect freedom of conscience, that mind-freedom should be complete? Moreover, this respect of the fifth amendment appears as a logical corollary to the protections accorded to speech, press, and conscience in the first amendment.[63]

McKay's statement that "the privacy of the mind, at least against compulsion of self-accusation, is absolute" interpreted normatively is little more than bare assertion. It points, however, to a crucial implication of the hermit's rationale, namely, that grants of immunity should not be permitted to supersede the strictures of the Fifth Amendment. McKay admits, it is "not easy"—impossible is a more accurate adjective—"to square the privacy interest as a prime purpose of the privilege with immunity statutes that require surrender of privacy."[64] Nevertheless, the critical questions remain: what is the distinctive relationship between the Fifth Amendment, as opposed to the First and Fourth Amendments, and privacy interests; and what are the criteria for and consequences of judicial construction of the amendment?

McKay elaborated by discussing the connection between the guarantees of the First and Fifth Amendments: "The First Amendment

notion that no man may be compelled to worship or to speak in any
particular way—or at all—may be regarded as an enlarged version of
the more specific Fifth Amendment notion that no man shall be required to convict himself out of his own mouth."[65] First Amendment-
protected privacy indeed may be broader (that is, the range of privacy
interests that may be asserted under the amendment) than that guaranteed by the Fifth Amendment (the Court's construction of First
Amendment-protected privacy is examined in Chapter 4.) Yet the
First Amendment, literally, only prohibits Congress from legislating
on the establishment of or free exercise of religion or otherwise
abridging the freedom of speech or of the press, or the right of the
people to assemble peaceably. Strictly construed, the First Amendment does not guarantee the privacy of what people profess or do;
citizens may be required to make some disclosures. The Fifth Amendment does not simply guarantee a smaller version of the First Amendment; rather, it serves a significantly distinct function, namely, guaranteeing individuals that they will not be compelled by the state to bear
witness against themselves. McKay's argument for personal privacy
also appears circular: a privacy rationale is asserted as justifying
the Fifth Amendment, yet McKay argues from the amendment (or
amendments) for the constitutional protection of personal privacy.
Actually, McKay hedges his argument by concluding: "In sum, from
all the welter of reasons given in justification of the privilege against
self-incrimination, it seems to me that only two have any probative
force, and they are perhaps opposite sides of the same coin: (1) preservation of official morality, and (2) preservation of individual privacy."[66] Thus, McKay appears to collapse the rationales of the fox
hunter and hermit. In so doing, McKay emphasizes that the Fifth
Amendment protects privacy interests associated with "the privacy
of the mind" but fails to specify when and by what criteria individuals
should be allowed to exercise the amendment in order to protect their
privacy interests.

Individuals may have a wide range of privacy interests in limiting access by others, including the government, to their thoughts
and engagements. Consistent with this perspective that the Fifth
Amendment safeguards "one's mental and emotional state including:
personal thoughts, beliefs, ideas and information," Michael Dann endeavors to clarify the functions of the Fourth and Fifth Amendments
and their respective guarantees for personal privacy:

> [T]here are significant differences between the fourth and
> fifth amendment safeguards. The amendments differ in
> the general nature of the evidence prohibited. Unlike the
> fifth, the fourth amendment emphasizes protection against
> official intrusion into one's <u>physical</u>, as opposed to mental

psychological, privacy. This is indicated by the fourth amendment's comparatively explicit enumeration of "persons, houses, papers, and effects." Also, while the fourth amendment only prohibits, as a means by which the state can obtain evidence, "unreasonable" searches and seizures, the fifth absolutely prohibits the state from obtaining certain types of evidence against a person's will. Thus, our accusatorial system contemplates at least some degree of compulsion in the prosecution of what may be incriminating evidence by requiring submission to reasonable searches and seizures involving one's physical privacy. [67]

Dann correctly stresses that the Fourth Amendment only limits governmental access to "reasonable" searches and seizures and that the Fifth Amendment provides an absolute bar to compelled, incriminating personal disclosures. Dann, however, mistakenly finds that the amendments differ "in the general nature of the evidence prohibited." Dann's identification of privacy interests in "physical" seclusion with the Fourth Amendment's safeguards and "mental" privacy with the Fifth Amendment's guarantee bespeaks a false dichotomy between privacy interests associated with the respective amendments. Privacy is an existential condition of life that may be compromised by either causal access (intrusions that influence or causally affect individuals' engagements or future relationships) or interpretative access (intrusions that obtain information about individuals' thoughts and engagements). The Fourth Amendment's regulation of governmental searches and seizures ostensibly provides a broad protection for individuals' interests in causal privacy—governmental intrusion upon and interference with individuals' "persons, houses, papers, and effects"—and interpretative privacy—governmental intrusions designed to gather information about individuals' engagements. The Fifth Amendment prohibits the government from compelling individuals to be witnesses against themselves by disclosing personal information, thereby, protecting interpretative or informational privacy associated with self-accusatorial disclosures. In addition, causal privacy is protected insofar as governmental demands for personal disclosures, no less than governmental intrusions into a person's "constitutionally protected area" under the Fourth Amendment, causally affect individuals' activities and future relationships.

The constitutionally significant difference between the Fourth and Fifth Amendments, therefore, lies in their respective restrictions upon and regulation of the ways by which the government may obtain incriminating evidence and coterminously invade individuals' privacy. Dann's dichotomy between physical and mental privacy and two kinds of evidence protected under the amendments is too simple and, therefore, misleading. Differences between privacy interests protected under either amendment derive not from the kinds of evidence safeguarded but rather from the distinctive ways in which the amendments define the manner by which the government may legitimately obtain access to individuals' lives in order to secure evidence of culpability. Since the crucial difference between the Fourth and Fifth Amendments relates not to the nature of the evidence sought but to the manner by which the government may obtain evidence, judicial interpretation of both amendments' restrictions on the exercise of governmental power becomes crucial for each amendment's safeguards for personal privacy.

Still, the hermit's rationale, and McKay's and Dann's arguments in particular, are subject to the criticism that "while the impact of claiming the privilege can result in the protection of certain aspects of one's privacy, privacy will not explain the Fifth Amendment privilege."[68] Similarly, Bernard Meltzer argues: "There is no coherent notion of privacy that explains the privilege; rather it is the privilege that produces a degree of privacy by insulating the suspect or defendant to produce oral or documentary evidence."[69] To be sure, personal privacy receives protection whenever claims asserted under the amendment are found legitimate; privacy and rights of privacy are not synonymous. The Fifth Amendment, even when justified solely on the fox hunter's rationale, provides in some instances derivative protection for privacy interests. What nevertheless remains obscure in such criticisms is the demand for an "explanation" of the amendment in terms of privacy. Justifications differ from explanations: the privacy rationale may provide compelling reasons for validating claims under the amendment, yet, not explain the patterns of judicial construction and application of the amendment. Indeed, neither the fox hunter's nor the old woman's rationale provides explanations as such for the Fifth Amendment.

Perhaps what most perturbs critics of the privacy rationale is that every day individuals are compelled to disclose personal information about their thoughts and engagements—so why talk about privacy as a basis for the Fifth Amendment? In short, the hermit's rationale can be useful and comforting only for hermits. Judge Friendly's criticisms of the privacy rationale exemplify this view. Friendly finds that "to such extent as the privacy proponents offer any explanations of their thesis, they are disturbing in the last degree" and assumes quick defeat of the rationale merely because testimonial compulsion and grants of immunity are part and parcel of our accusatorial system.[70] Friendly cites the Supreme Court's approval of John Wigmore's observation: "For more than three centuries it has been recognized as a fundamental maxim that the public . . . has a right to everyman's evidence."[71] Fundamentally, Friendly revels in assuming that privacy must be absolute and therefore "the privacy theory . . . [must] lead to the absurd conclusion that the state cannot compel evidence from anybody."[72] Friendly nevertheless rejoices in the defeat of a strawman.

The hermit's rationale need not entail protection of every privacy claim under the Fifth Amendment. As Robert Gerstein argues: "The right of privacy cannot be understood as embodying the rule that 'privacy may be never violated.' The alternative is to look at the right of privacy not as an absolute rule but as a principle which would establish privacy as a value of great significance, not to be interfered with lightly by governmental authority."[73] Gerstein accepts Charles Fried's analysis of privacy "as the control we have over information about ourselves," but departs from his view "that a man cannot [should not] be forced to make public information about himself."[74] Gerstein suggests: "If the argument for privacy is made so broad as to sweep away tax returns, accident reports, and the capacity to compel testimony on personal matters in civil cases, for example, it must surely be rejected."[75] The privacy of individuals' thoughts and engagements has intrinsic worth, yet not every claim of privacy must be protected.

Gerstein, unlike McKay, Dann, and Fried, furthermore endeavors to define the kinds of disclosures of personal information that should receive Fifth Amendment protection. Gerstein argues:

> I think we are dealing here with a special sort of information, a sort of information which it is particularly important for an individual to be able to control. . . . It is not the disclosure of the facts of the crime, but the mea culpa, the public admission of private judgement of self-condemnation, that seems to be of real concern.[76]

Gerstein's argument that the amendment protects only against compelled disclosures of personal information that force individuals to make judgments as to their own culpability, however, leads back to the paradox of the old woman's rationale. Characteristically, Friendly overstates his counterargument:

> Far from being a moral doctrine, the privacy justification is about as immoral as one could imagine. To be sure, there may be offenses, for example, fornication and adultery, where the individual's right to be left alone may transcend the state's interest in solving them. . . . [Yet] can it be seriously argued that when a murder or rape or kidnapping has been committed, a citizen is morally justified

in withholding his aid simply because he does not want to
be bothered and prefers to remain in a "private enclave"
from which the state has cause to believe he departed in
order to do violence to another?[77]

Friendly concludes that the privacy argument is immoral only because
he interprets the argument in an extreme form, namely, that privacy
entails an unqualified mutual noninterference by individuals.

Contrary to Friendly, the hermit's rationale does not necessarily
entail an ideal of unconditional noninterference by individuals. Instead, the privacy argument simply holds that the government should
respect the moral autonomy of individuals. Governmental intrusions
—intrusions whether in the form of searches and seizures, regulated
by the Fourth Amendment, or demands for self-disclosure, which the
Fifth Amendment limits by its proscription of compelled self-accusa-
tions—should be circumspect and limited. The hermit's rationale,
like that of the old woman, is based on moral principle and not, as
the fox hunter's rationale, policy considerations.

Notwithstanding the moral appeal of the hermit's rationale, privacy arguments are ambiguous and incomplete with regard to guidance
for the Court's determination of the contours of the Fifth Amendment.
Failure to articulate independent standards for exercising the privilege suggests that the hermit's rationale may not usefully serve as
the primary basis for the amendment. Rather the hermit's rationale
may serve as an ancillary justification. It is not surprising that proponents of the hermit's rationale often rely on other justifications for
the privilege when fashioning their privacy arguments. McKay's
argument, for example, combined the rationales of the fox hunter and
the hermit so that the Fifth Amendment extends protection to claims
of privacy while according consideration to the needs of law enforcement. In other words, the hermit's rationale serves to limit the extent to which policy considerations should control the application of
the amendment. That is, there are good reasons, given the fox hunter's instrumental evaluation, for not limiting the Fifth Amendment's
protection only to those contexts of third-degree interrogations that
manifest genuine compulsion of testimony. Still, good reasons for
extending the contours of the Fifth Amendment to one context (for example, custodial interrogations) may not hold for another context (for
example, tax returns or accident reports). Gerstein's argument com-
bining the hermit's and old woman's rationales also illustrates how the
privacy argument may serve as an ancillary basis yet not entail absolute Fifth Amendment protection for personal privacy. The hermit's
rationale, thus, as an independent, unconditional basis for the amendment, proves unacceptable, but as an ancillary justification it may
serve as a crucial consideration in judicial construction of the contours of the Fifth Amendment.

The preceding discussion suggests that the fox hunter's, old woman's, and hermit's rationales by themselves are each insufficient in justifying the Fifth Amendment. Each rationale provides a significant analysis and justification for the Fifth Amendment, yet each neglects too much. Certainly, as Gerstein argues, "[t]he case for allowing the privilege would be strongest when all of these purposes would be served by its application."78 The import of the rationales for constitutional interpretation is nevertheless demonstrated by the fact that, as Justice Harlan candidly and accurately observed, "The Constitution contains no formulae within which we can calculate the areas . . . to which the privilege should extend, and the Court has therefore been obliged to fashion for itself standards for the application of the privilege."79

The following section examines judicial construction of Fifth Amendment-protected privacy. While the privacy rationale has become increasingly popular in the last 20 years, Fifth Amendment privacy claims have long received judicial recognition. Yet, as a matter of constitutional history, the Supreme Court has moved from a broad to a narrow construction of Fifth Amendment-protected privacy. In particular, the Burger Court's treatment of privacy claims (with regard to private papers and documents, required records, and the contexts and circumstances in which individuals may enjoy the benefits of the amendment) promotes a narrow construction of the amendment and diminishes protection for interests in personal privacy.

JUDICIAL CONSTRUCTION OF
FIFTH AMENDMENT-PROTECTED PRIVACY

Judicial construction of Fifth Amendment-protected privacy prohibits the government from compelling an individual to disclose incriminating personal information except on grants of immunity. Still, the contours of Fifth Amendment-protected privacy may be broadly or narrowly drawn, depending upon the Court's interpretation of the amendment's underlying principles and policies.

As with Fourth Amendment-protected privacy, Boyd v. United States provides the watershed for a broad construction of personal privacy under the Fifth Amendment. 80 Boyd's construction of the Fourth and Fifth Amendments foreclosed the possibility of overbearing governmental intrusions upon individuals' activities not only where the government searched and seized without a warrant or elicited compelled disclosures of personal information, but also where the government through the use of administrative summonses intruded upon individuals' privacy. The Boyd-fostered broad construction acknowledged the validity of the rationales of the old woman and hermit in holding that the amendment guarantees a constitutional right, not simply a procedural rule, which extends to interests in personal privacy. As the Court reiterated in Counselman v. Hitchcock: "This provision must have a broad construction in favor of the right which it was intended to secure. . . . The privilege is not limited to criminal matters, but it is as broad as the mischief against which it seeks to guard."[81] The Boyd-fostered broad construction acknowledges that the amendment may serve functions not suggested by a literal reading yet logically related to the amendment's proscription of compelled personal disclosures. Accordingly, late nineteenth and early twentieth century courts extended the Fifth Amendment not only to defendants in criminal proceedings but also to witnesses in criminal, civil, grand jury, legislative, and administrative proceedings, as well as to privacy claims regarding materials possessed by third parties, such as an individual's accountant or attorney.[82]

Boyd's broad construction of Fifth Amendment-protected privacy, however, never gained wide acceptance. Rather, a broad construction of the amendment was often confined to dicta and dissent. Historically, the Supreme Court limited the contours of Fifth Amendment-protected privacy by a narrow construction of the amendment based on the fox hunter's rationale. The fox hunter's rationale, as earlier explored, fosters an analysis of the amendment in terms of policy considerations of an accusatorial system. In contrast to the broad construction promoted by the old woman's and the hermit's rationales, which view the amendment as denominating a constitutional principle or right, an instrumental evaluation fosters a narrow construction of both the amendment and protected privacy. Whereas a broad construction acknowledges the intrinsic worth of individuals' privacy, a narrow construction minimizes even the instrumental values of privacy, because it holds that the Fifth Amendment "does not in any way protect expectations of privacy, but rather serves exclusively to prevent the state from compelling an individual to personally produce self-incriminating evidence."[83] More specifically, a narrow construction limits the criteria for determining "personal compulsion" in terms of the degree of governmental pressure exerted on an individual to disclose personal information and the kinds of evidence protected by the amendment, as well as the circumstances or contexts for raising Fifth Amendment claims.

The remainder of this chapter examines the basic tenets of the Supreme Court's narrow construction of the Fifth Amendment and protected privacy. Particular attention is given to the Burger Court's treatment of claims to constitutionally protected privacy with regard to private papers, required records, and the circumstances and contexts in which individuals may claim the benefits of the amendment.

Personal Compulsion and Private Papers

The Supreme Court's narrow construction of "the fundamental purpose of the fifth amendment [as] the preservation of an adversary system"[84] permits an individual to evoke the Fifth Amendment only when "genuine compulsion of testimony" has been demonstrated, or when, considering the totality of the circumstances, the free will of the witness was overborne."[85] The implications and significance for the contours of the Fifth Amendment are well illustrated by the Burger Court's treatment of privacy claims with regard to private papers, documents, and business records.

The Court has long adhered to a distinction between individuals and corporations in applying the Fifth Amendment, so that only "natural" persons and not corporations may claim protection.[86] Since the amendment was viewed as establishing a personal right, it was often maintained that individuals must own or possess any private papers in which they had an assertible Fifth Amendment claim. The Burger Court has firmly established, upon policy considerations, that, "A party is privileged from producing . . . evidence, but not from its production."[87] Individuals may claim Fifth Amendment-protected privacy and, for example, quash an administrative subpoena duces tecum requiring them to produce papers or documents in which they have privacy interests. However, they have no legitimate expectations of informational privacy or Fifth Amendment claims against compulsion of papers held by a banking institution, their accountants, or their attorneys.[88]

In Couch v. United States the petitioner was denied any reasonable expectation of privacy and claim under the Fifth Amendment to intervene with an Internal Revenue Service summons to her accountant for her business records. The Court held that, "[N]o Fourth or Fifth Amendment claim can prevail where, as in this case, there exists no legitimate expectation of privacy and no semblance of governmental compulsion against the person of the accused."[89] While the Court discussed concurrently, rather than independently, Fourth and Fifth Amendment protections for privacy and, thereby, collapsed the issues of reasonableness of individuals' expectations of privacy and governmental compulsion of personal disclosures, the Court noted, as an exception, that Fifth Amendment claims might be legitimate where individuals retained "constructive possession" of the materials held by a third party. Although refusing to establish a per se rule to that effect, as well as declining to specify the types of recognizable forms of constructive possession, the Court emphasized: "Possession bears the closest relationship to the personal compulsion forbidden by the fifth amendment. To tie the privilege against self-incrimination to a concept of ownership would be to draw a meaningless line."[90]

The Burger Court, thus, appeared sub silentio to overrule earlier decisions regarding ownership as a prerequisite for Fifth Amendment claims in limiting the amendment's protection to where an individual retains possession of the papers or documents.[91] Indeed, the Court concluded that "The criterion for Fifth Amendment immunity remains not the ownership of property, but the 'physical or moral compulsion exerted.'"[92]

In 1976 the Court indicated that it would strictly construe the nature of both compulsion of testimony and "constructive possession" of private papers. In Fisher v. United States, taxpayers, under investigation for possible civil or criminal liability under federal income tax laws, obtained from their accountants documents related to their accountants' preparation of their tax returns, and they transferred the documents to their attorneys.[93] Subsequently, the Internal Revenue Service served summonses on their attorneys, but they refused to comply. The Court, relying on Couch, held that individuals have no valid Fifth Amendment claims against their attorneys' production of such documents because the summonses would not compel the taxpayer to do anything, and because individuals do not retain constructive possession of such documents.

Individuals may have expectations of privacy in papers and documents held by their attorneys, but where individuals retain no constructive possession, they have no legitimate claims under the Fifth Amendment. In Fisher the Court reiterated its ruling in United States v. Nobles that the Fifth Amendment protects only against "compelled self-incrimination, not [the disclosure of] private information."[94] Justice White, for the Court, emphasized the rejection of privacy arguments for the amendment:

> The Framers addressed the subject of personal privacy directly in the Fourth Amendment. They struck a balance so that when the State's reason to believe incriminating evidence will be found becomes sufficiently great, the invasion of privacy becomes justified and a warrant to search and seize will issue. They did not seek in still another Amendment—the Fifth—to achieve a general protection of privacy but to deal with the more specific issue of compelled self-incrimination [sic]. . . . We cannot cut the Fifth Amendment completely loose from the moorings of its language, and make it serve as a general protection of privacy—a word not mentioned in its text and a concept directly addressed in the Fourth Amendment.[95]

Fisher, like Couch, underscores the Burger Court's narrow construction of Fifth Amendment-protected privacy. Although the amendment literally suggests safeguards for individuals' privacy expectations in papers, at least where their production would constitutively force individuals to be witnesses against themselves, the Burger Court's strict application of the amendment limits protection to only those situations where an individual orally divulges or produces written materials containing incriminating information. Even when individuals have reasonable expectations of privacy in papers and turn those papers over to their attorneys, they do not retain constructive possession, and the forced production of the papers does not constitute compulsion prohibited by the Fifth Amendment. As Larry Ritchie comments: "The Burger Court's analysis of the application of the privilege to documents and private writings not only reaffirms its literal interpretation of the privilege, but clearly indicates the extent to which that interpretation dilutes the privacy protection that the privilege could afford."96

The Fifth Amendment could afford greater protection for personal privacy than the Burger Court's interpretation recognizes. Couch and Fisher, as Justice Brennan observes, "is but another step in the denigration of privacy principles settled nearly 100 years ago in Boyd v. United States."97 The dissenters maintain, as did Justice Bradley in Boyd, that "the Fourth and Fifth Amendments delineate a 'sphere of privacy' which must be protected against governmental intrusion."98 Indeed, dissenting in Couch, Justice Douglas parted with Justice Brennan, who held that as a precondition of evoking the Fifth Amendment, "reasonable steps" be taken by individuals to secure the privacy of materials not in their possession. Justice Douglas urged that a "Fifth Amendment claim [is] valid even in absence of personal compulsion so long as [the] accused has a reasonable expectation of privacy in articles subpoenaed."99

Justice Marshall's dissenting opinion in Couch remains more helpful in understanding both the significance of the Burger Court's narrow construction and how a broad construction of the amendment could provide extensive safeguards for personal privacy. Justice Marshall began his dissent by pointing out that the Burger Court's reliance on Boyd fails to focus "on the obvious concern of the case, the desire of the author of documents to keep them private."100 Part of the Burger Court's difficulty in addressing safeguards for privacy interests in private papers, Justice Marshall suggested, derived from its interpretation of the interplay between the Fourth and Fifth Amendments:

The Fourth and Fifth Amendments do not speak to totally unrelated concerns. . . . Both involve aspects of a person's right to develop for himself a sphere of personal privacy. Where the amendments "run almost into each other," I

would prohibit the Government from entering. The problem, as I see it, is to develop criteria for determining
whether evidence sought by the Government lies within
the sphere of activities that petitioner attempted to keep
private.[101]

Thereupon, Justice Marshall proposed an analysis of Fifth Amendment-protected privacy similar to that of the Fourth Amendment analysis formulated by Justice Harlan.[102]

Justice Marshall specified four criteria for analyzing claims to
Fifth Amendment-protected privacy. The first criterion is the nature
of the evidence. Justice Marshall observed that "[d]iaries and personal letters . . . lie at the heart of our sense of privacy" and should
receive Fifth Amendment protection, whereas there exists no constitutional bar to the seizure of letters between coconspirators of a
crime. The second consideration lies with the activities of the person to whom the papers were given, and, the third, the purposes for
which the papers were transferred. Finally, Justice Marshall urged
the Court to "take into account the steps that the author took to ensure
the privacy of the records."[103]

According to Justice Marshall, the reasonableness of individuals'
Fifth Amendment claims to informational privacy in papers and records becomes contingent on several factors: the nature of the documents (for example, compare diaries with letters of extortion); what
recipients of personal information do with it (for example, compare
attorneys' use with trustees' use in a bankruptcy); the purposes of
voluntarily relinquishing personal information to another (for example,
compare attorneys' or accountants' use in preparation of individuals'
tax liability with copies of documents for use in blackmailing); and,
the steps that individuals take to secure the privacy of their information (for example, compare placing papers in a safe-deposit box for
years with filing them in a business office or handing them over to an
attorney).

Justice Marshall's analytical framework for Fifth Amendment-
protected privacy bears a family resemblance to Boyd's broad construction of constitutionally protected privacy. Justice Marshall's
analysis, like Boyd and its progeny, provides extensive protection for
personal privacy upon a consideration of the government's need for
evidence of criminal activity and the right of individuals to place limits on their disclosures and access by others to personal information
and engagements. Moreover, the government would be prohibited
from circumventing and, thereby, nullifying the Fifth Amendment's
guarantee "by finding a way [as with administrative summonses to
third parties] to obtain the documents without requiring the owner to
take them in hand and personally present them to the government
agents."[104]

In contrast to a broad construction, the Burger Court significantly limits the contours of the Fifth Amendment and protected privacy. The Court confines Fifth Amendment protection to situations in which an individual is compelled to disclose incriminating information orally or by personally relinquishing private papers or documents. As the Court in <u>Andresen</u> v. <u>Maryland</u> reiterated, "unless incriminating testimony is 'compelled' any invasion of privacy is outside the scope of the Fifth Amendment's protection."[105]

The Distinction between
"Testimonial" and "Real" Evidence

The Burger Court's treatment of privacy claims with regard to private papers and documents disregards the testimonial nature of private papers by drawing a distinction between speech and writing. The amendment "prohibits compelling a person to <u>speak</u> and incriminate himself but it does not prohibit compelled revelation of <u>written</u> thoughts."[106] The Court circumvents claims to informational privacy by holding that the amendment prohibits only governmental compulsion of an individual's oral testimony or production of papers containing testimonial declarations. The amendment affords no protection against third parties' production of written documents, since there exists no "personal compulsion" and the documents are analogous to producing "real" or physical evidence, such as blood, handwriting, or voice samples. The Court's narrow construction of the nature of personal compulsion and Fifth Amendment-protected privacy actually results from extending the doctrine that the amendment protects only "testimonial" but not "real" or physical evidence.

The Burger Court's narrow construction and endorsement of the distinction between testimonial and real evidence is not without considerable precedent. Judicial uncertainties over the breadth of the Fifth Amendment's protection for testimonial evidence arose in the early twentieth century. <u>Boyd</u>'s broad construction implied the extension of the Fifth Amendment's scope, along with the Fourth Amendment's, to any tangible evidence or "any forcible and compulsory extortion of a man's own testimony or of his private papers to be used as evidence to convict him of crime."[107] Judicial policies, nevertheless, subsequently narrowed the contours of the Fifth Amendment by fashioning a distinction between testimonial and real evidence.

In 1910 the Court held that compelling the accused to cooperate physically with police by putting on a blouse, so that it could be established whether it fitted, did not violate the Fifth Amendment. In <u>Holt</u> v. <u>United States</u>, the Court observed that, "the prohibition of compelling a man to be a witness against himself is a prohibition of the physical or moral compulsion to <u>extort communications</u> from him, not an exclusion of his body as evidence when it may be material."[108] Ostensibly the Fifth Amendment protected only against personal compulsion of oral communication. A narrow construction of the nature of personal compulsion, thus, neglected the fact that the government often compels the physical cooperation of the accused, so that it may establish criminal culpability. Furthermore, an individual may suffer personal compulsion either by compelled oral testimony or by compelled cooperation in a process by which identification of physical attributes establishes a "link in a chain" of incriminating evidence.[109]

The distinction between testimonial and real evidence was not further elaborated until the Warren Court's decision in <u>Schmerber</u> v. <u>California</u>.[110] In <u>Schmerber</u>, the petitioner argued that admission into evidence of blood tests, indicating his intoxication at the time of arrest following an automobile accident, violated the Fifth Amendment. The Court, however, held that blood samples are one example of "acts non-communicative in nature as to the person asserting" the amendment. Without clarifying the distinction, the Court observed: "The privilege is a bar against compelling 'communications' in testimony, but that compulsion which makes a subject or accused the source of 'real or physical evidence' does not violate it."[111]

Relying on <u>Schmerber</u>'s distinction, the Court subsequently permitted, over Fifth Amendment claims, compelled handwriting samples, police lineups, and voice samples.[112] The <u>Schmerber</u>-fostered cases, nevertheless, fail to provide a perspicuous discussion of what constitutes a testimonial disclosure. In <u>California</u> v. <u>Byers</u>, for example, the Court dismissed the issue of whether a "hit-and-run" statute constituted a compelled testimonial disclosure by noting that, "A name, linked with a motor vehicle, is no more incriminating than the tax return, linked with the disclosure of income. . . . It identifies but it does not by itself implicate in criminal conduct."[113]

The distinction between testimonial and real evidence promoted by these decisions runs counter to Fifth Amendment privacy claims. Indeed, while the Court discussed in these cases Fourth Amendment issues of personal privacy in obtaining "real" evidence, Fifth Amendment privacy interests were not considered with regard to the compulsion of physical evidence.[114] Consequently, whereas the Court limited protection for informational privacy under the Fourth Amendment because of proprietary concepts, the Court limited Fifth Amendment protection to oral disclosures, excluding the showing of real or physical evidence that may be incriminating. In sum, although the Fifth Amendment provides the principal guarantee against compelled personal disclosures, the Supreme Court has circumscribed the contours of the amendment and protected privacy by its distinction between testimonial and real evidence.

Personal Compulsion and Compelled Disclosures

As another exception to the broad contours of the Fifth Amendment fostered by Boyd and its progeny, the Supreme Court in the early twentieth century developed a doctrine of "required records" that precluded the amendment's protection for personal disclosures and privacy interests.

Dicta in Wilson v. United States first suggested that the Fifth Amendment had no applicability where record keeping was required by law in order to provide information for governmental regulation.[115] The doctrine of required records, however, was not fully articulated until 1948. Shapiro v. United States held that records required to be kept under the regulatory powers of Congress had "public aspects" and, hence, personal information contained therein was not subject to Fifth Amendment protection.[116] Twenty years later, in Grosso v. United States, the Court clarified the doctrine:

> The premises of the doctrine, as it is described in Shapiro, are evidently these: first, the purpose of the United States's inquiry must be essentially regulatory; second, information is to be obtained by requiring the preservation of records of a kind which the regulated party has customarily kept; and third, the records themselves must have issued "public aspects" which render them analogous to public documents.[117]

The required records doctrine was subsequently supported in California v. Byers, where a plurality upheld California's "hit-and-run" statute requiring a driver of a motor vehicle involved in an accident to stop at the scene and give his or her name and address.[118] The Court held that "the disclosure of inherently illegal activity is inherently risky. . . . But disclosures with respect to automobile accidents simply do not entail . . . [a] substantial risk."[119] The Burger Court thus limited Fifth Amendment safeguards for personal privacy by both denying protection for custodians of records and upholding the government's requiring statements concerning criminal activity, as with reporting and registration requirements.[120] Accordingly, many of the Court's commentators found the required records doctrine to "swallow the privilege whole in relation to written documents."[121] As McKay observed, "A government that can roam at will through all records that it may demand to inspect because it may demand that they be kept is not a government that is bound to respect individual privacy."[122]

Certainly, privacy arguments for the privilege can be taken too far; privacy interests can justifiably be invalidated by interests in securing and maintaining civil order, as with accident reports. The Burger Court's construction of the Fifth Amendment, however, appears to dismiss all privacy interests when construing the nature of personal compulsion with regard to required records. Consider, for example, the Court's treatment of the amendment with regard to compelled personal disclosures required in filing tax returns.

Personal income tax returns have long been held to be required records, since the Internal Revenue Service's requirements are part of the government's taxing power. In 1927 in United States v. Sullivan, the Court established that the Fifth Amendment is not a defense against prosecution for failing to file an income tax return. [123] Several years later, the problem posed by illegal income earners and reporting requirements of filing tax returns was again raised, when a taxpayer filed a return claiming certain deductions but refused to answer on Fifth Amendment grounds Internal Revenue Service questions concerning the deudctions; whereupon, he was prosecuted for willful failure to supply the necessary information. [124] The Supreme Court held that even though the taxpayer's claim was invalid, a "good faith" claim of the Fifth Amendment would negate any willfulness of failure to supply information and bar conviction. Nevertheless, pursuant to Sullivan, the government's taxing power appears paramount, outweighing any individual's claim to privacy interests in nondisclosure of financial information.

During the Warren Court some limitations were imposed upon statutes relating to record keeping and required registration. In particular, the Warren Court recognized that obligations of illegal income earners to register and pay occupational and wagering excise taxes created "real and appreciable" hazards of self-incrimination. In Marchetti v. United States the Court struck down a statute requiring gamblers to register and to submit monthly information concerning their wagering activities on the grounds that the information was not customarily kept, the reports had no "public records" aspects, and the requirements were directed at a "select group inherently suspect of criminal activities." [125]

By contrast, the Burger Court strictly interprets the nature of personal compulsion and disregards the forfeiture of privacy interests in compelled disclosures required by filing tax returns. Justice Brennan, dissenting in Beckwith v. United States, observed that the Court's analysis fails to recognize that the "practical compulsion to respond to questions about [an individual's] tax returns is comparable to the psychological pressures described in Miranda." [126] Justice Brennan's criticisms of the Court's narrow construction of personal compulsion is well illustrated by the Court's 1976 decision in Garner v. United States. [127] In Garner, the Court held that taxpayers earning illegal income and not desirous of exposure to criminal charges for failure to file a tax return must claim the Fifth Amendment on their tax returns. If, however, incriminating information is disclosed on the return and the amendment is not asserted, then the taxpayer forfeits any privacy claims and in any future criminal case may not exercise the Fifth Amendment.

Garner epitomizes the Burger Court's literal construction of personal compulsion and how it circumscribes Fifth Amendment-protected privacy. Garner, in filing his federal income tax returns, reported his occupation as a "professional gambler." Subsequently, Garner was indicted for conspiracy involving the use of interstate transportation and communications facilities to "fix" sporting contests and transmit bets. At trial, in order to establish Garner's guilt, the government not only introduced testimony of his coconspirators and telephone toll records but also his tax returns. Garner's objections were overruled and he was eventually convicted. Before the Supreme Court, Garner first relied upon Miranda in arguing that his failure to claim the Fifth Amendment on his tax returns was not a knowing and intelligent waiver. The Court, however, observed that he had prepared his tax returns in the leisure and privacy of his home and, therefore, the Miranda safeguards developed in the context of custodial situations were not applicable. The Court emphasized that "[u]nless a witness objects a government ordinarily may assume that the compulsory processes are not eliciting testimony that [the individual] deems to be incriminating."[128] Second, Garner relied on Mackey v. United States, arguing that his postdisclosure claim provided sufficient protection for his disclosures on his tax returns.[129] Here, Garner's argument failed because Mackey's returns had been directed at persons "inherently suspect of criminal activities," whereas his own were directed toward the general public.

Significantly, the Court disregarded the fact that Garner's disclosures, made for one purpose, filing his income tax return, were being used by the government for another purpose, namely, in a criminal prosecution. Indeed, the Court presumes that such governmental uses of personal information do not threaten the fair state-individual balance reflected in an accusatorial system. "Only the witness knows whether the apparently innocent disclosure sought may incriminate him, and the burden appropriately lies with him to make a timely assertion of the privilege. If, instead, he discloses information sought, then incriminations properly are viewed as not compelled."[130] Garner, thus, underscores other Burger Court rulings, strictly construing the requirement of personal compulsion necessary for enjoying the benefits of the amendment. In United States v. Kordel the Court held that a witness under compulsion to make disclosures who reveals incriminating information instead of claiming Fifth Amendment protection loses the amendment's benefits; in Schneckcloth v. Bustamonte

the Court ruled that individuals may also lose the benefits of the
amendment without making "a knowing and intelligent waiver."[131]

The Burger Court's narrow construction severely contracts the
scope of the Fifth Amendment-protected privacy. An irrebuttable
presumption on the part of the government exists to the effect that
taxpayers may be required to make basic disclosures fundamental to
neutral reporting requirements. Only an individual or a group suspected of criminal activities may not be required to supply information
relating to those activities. Protection of individuals' privacy interests in financial disclosures by claims under the Fifth Amendment will
not bar prosecution, but conviction will not follow, regardless of
whether the claim is valid, if it was asserted in "good faith." If,
however, incriminating information is disclosed on a tax return and
the Fifth Amendment is not claimed, then the taxpayer forfeits any
expectations of privacy and in any future criminal prosecution may
not rely on the amendment.

Contexts and Circumstances of Personal Compulsion

Concomitant with establishing a narrow construction of personal
compulsion, the Burger Court's treatment of the Fifth Amendment restricts the contexts and circumstances in which individuals may enjoy
the benefits of the amendment. The Burger Court has not departed
from the Warren Court's premise in Miranda that "interrogation of
persons suspected or accused of crime contains inherently compelling
pressures which work to undermine the individual's will to resist and
to compel him to speak when he would not otherwise do so freely."[132]
Instead, the Burger Court appears to be reevaluating upon its narrow
construction of the amendment the necessity of full Miranda warnings
in every situation and, by distinguishing Miranda requirements (as
mere "prophylactic rules"[133]) from the Fifth Amendment, sharply defining the contexts and circumstances that require that individuals be
given Miranda warnings.

Prior to Miranda, courts permitted individuals at trials to claim
Fifth Amendment protection and prohibited the introduction of self-incriminating statements obtained through police interrogation only upon
showing "a totality of circumstances evidencing an involuntary . . .
admission of guilt."[134] Five members of the Warren Court enlarged
the Fifth Amendment's scope upon the recognition that, the amendment
"protects the individual from being compelled to incriminate himself
in any way; it does not distinguish degrees of incrimination."[135] The
Court reasoned that the Fifth Amendment's justification in terms of
maintaining a fair state-individual balance requires the government
"to shoulder the entire load" in proving an individual's culpability.

Whereas the Warren Court's evaluation and broad construction fostered procedural guidelines in order to ensure the practical value of the Fifth Amendment, the Burger Court's narrow construction finds Miranda a "procedural (as distinguished from constitutional) ruling," and, thus, permits prosecutory use of an individual's incriminating statements made without full Miranda warnings or a "knowing and intelligent" waiver of Fifth Amendment protection.[136] In Michigan v. Tucker the Court emphasized that the "protective guidelines" of Miranda were designed to "supplement" the amendment, and "these procedural safeguards were not themselves rights protected by the Constitution but were instead measures to ensure that the right against compulsory self-incrimination was protected."[137] Because the Burger Court narrowly construes personal compulsion and views Miranda requirements as not constitutionally mandated, but only procedural safeguards based on policy considerations, law enforcement has considerable flexibility in prosecuting individuals on the basis of their incriminating statements, since deviations from Miranda will not necessarily offend the Fifth Amendment.

Accordingly, in Harris v. New York, the Court held that statements, inadmissible against the defendant in the prosecution's case because of failure to satisfy the procedural guidelines required by Miranda, may, if their trustworthiness satisfies legal standards, be used for impeachment of the defendant's trial testimony.[138] In dissent, Justice Brennan argued that Miranda had settled the issue in holding that: "Statements merely intended to be exculpatory by the defendant are often used to impeach his testimony at trial * * *. These statements are incriminating in any meaningful sense of the word and may not be used without the full warnings and effective waiver required for any other statement."[139] Chief Justice Burger, for the five-member majority, however, was apparently more concerned that "[t]he shield provided by Miranda [would] be perverted into a license to use perjury by way of a defense, free from the risk of confrontation with prior inconsistent utterances."[140] In Oregon v. Hass the Court extended Harris to permit the defendant's impeachment by use of statements obtained while he was in police custody and after he had requested a lawyer, but before the lawyer was present.[141]

The Court further diminished Miranda safeguards in Michigan v. Tucker, ruling that the Fifth Amendment was not violated by the prosecution's use of testimony of a witness discovered as the result of the defendant's statements to police but without Miranda warnings.[142] Again, in the following year, in Michigan v. Mosley, the Court upheld police interrogation, after a two hour interval, of an individual who had earlier exercised his right to remain silent.[143] In Miranda, the majority had held:

Once warnings have been given, the subsequent procedure is clear. If the individual indicates in any manner, at any time prior to or during questioning, that he wishes to remain silent, the interrogation must cease. At this point he has shown that he intends to exercise his Fifth Amendment privilege; any statement taken after the person invokes his privilege cannot be other than the product of compulsion, subtle or otherwise. Without the right to cut off questioning, the setting of in-custody interrogation operates on the individual to overcome free choice in producing a statement after the privilege has been once invoked.[144]

As Justice Brennan pointed out, "Miranda established a virtually irrebuttable presumption of compulsion . . . and that presumption stands strongest where, as in this case, a suspect, having initially determined to remain silent, is subsequently brought to confess his crime."[145] Contrariwise, the majority in Mosley construed the critical Miranda safeguard at issue to require only that police "scrupulously honor" a person's right to cut off questioning. Justice Brennan, dissenting, concluded that Mosley "virtually empties Miranda of principle, for plainly the decision encourages police asked to cease interrogation to continue the suspect's detention until the police station's coercive atmosphere does its work and the suspect responds to resumed questioning."[146]

That the Burger Court's construction entails significant erosion of Miranda safeguards is underscored by its 1977 per curiam ruling in Oregon v. Mathiason.[147] In Mathiason the suspect, a parolee, following a police request, voluntarily went to the police station where, even though he admitted committing a crime, he was informed that he was not under arrest and allowed to leave after the questioning. The Court rejected the Oregon Supreme Court's opinion excluding the confession as having "read Miranda too broadly" and concluded that the suspect was not in "custody" in the police station and, hence, Miranda warnings were not required.

Although the Burger Court has not overturned Miranda per se, it has significantly diluted the practical value of Miranda and the feasibility of Fifth Amendment protection by permitting in Harris and Hass prosecutory use of individuals' self-accusatorial statements and, in Tucker, Mosley, and Mathiason, sanctioning considerable flexibility in police interrogation of criminal suspects. The Burger Court departs from Miranda in part because, as with its treatment of the exclusionary rule and the Fourth Amendment, it views Miranda's requirements as procedural rules based on policy and not constitutional principle.[148] More fundamentally, the Court permits departures from

Miranda because it narrowly defines the nature of personal compulsion necessary for enjoying the benefits of the amendment. The Burger Court's strict construction of the nature of personal compulsion promotes the amendment's protection only when "considering the totality of the circumstances, the free will of the witness is overborne."[149] By contrast, the Warren Court's broad interpretation of the Fifth Amendment led to the imposition of Miranda safeguards not only in station house interrogations but also in any context of "questioning initiated by law enforcement officers after a person has been taken into custody or otherwise deprived of his freedom of action in any significant way."[150] The Burger Court's treatment, thus, signifies a retrenchment, indeed a return to pre-Miranda rulings, so that the Fifth Amendment protects against only police interrogations in contexts in which the "totality of circumstances evidenc[es] an involuntary . . . admission of guilt."[151] Perhaps, because "the Court has taken too literally the maxim that the privilege protects the accused from being convicted on evidence forced 'out of his mouth,'"[152] it fails to consider the psychological pressures that bear upon individuals in police custody, or without full Miranda warnings or a knowing and intelligent waiver of their rights, or after renewed questioning following lengthy periods of detention.

The Burger Court's strict construction fosters not only retrenchment in Fifth Amendment protection for individuals in contexts of custodial interrogation but also the refusal to extend the contours of the amendment to noncustodial interviews and questioning.

In Beckwith v. United States the Court dealt with the issue of whether Internal Revenue Service special agents, investigating criminal income tax violations, must give Miranda warnings in noncustodial interviews with taxpayers.[153] Two Internal Revenue Service special agents visited Beckwith in a private residence in order to question him about his income tax liability and, before beginning their questions, gave him the standard Internal Revenue Service warning (that they could not compel him to answer or submit any incriminating information) rather than informing him that he has a right to remain silent. While Chief Justice Burger, for the majority, agreed that in such instances the taxpayer is already the "focus" of a criminal investigation, he construed Miranda to safeguard only against the compulsion inherent in custodial interrogations, as distinguished from noncustodial interviews as in Beckwith. Narrow construction of the nature of personal compulsion, thus, allowed the Court to avoid serious consideration of whether, in dissenting Justice Brennan's words, "Interrogation under conditions that have the practical consequence of compelling the taxpayer to make disclosures, and interrogation in 'custody' having the same consequences, are . . . peas from the same pod."[154] Hence, in Beckwith, as in Garner, the Court limited the contours of the amendment by its narrow construction of personal compulsion and Miranda's procedural safeguards; it emphasized that, "Proof that some kind of warnings were given or that none were given would be relevant evidence only on the issue of whether the questioning was in fact coercive."[155]

The Court continued to sharply confine the contours of Fifth Amendment protection by further underlining the distinction between custodial and noncustodial interrogations in United States v. Mandujano, United States v. Washington, and United States v. Wong.[156] In Mandujano, Chief Justice Burger, for the Court, held that the Fifth Amendment does not require suppression in perjury prosecution of false statements made to a grand jury by an individual who was not given Miranda warnings when called to testify, even though he was a "putative" or "virtual" defendant. Chief Justice Burger emphasized that individuals have an absolute right to decline to answer questions during an in-custody police interrogation, but before a grand jury (a noncustodial context) have an absolute duty to answer all questions, because of their obligation imposed by taking an oath to testify. Notwithstanding the import of privacy claims in such contexts, the Court added: "Nor can [the amendment] be invoked simply to protect the witness's interests in privacy. Ordinarily, of course, a witness has no right of privacy before the grand jury."[157] In Washington, an individual suspected with others of possible theft was subpoenaed to appear as a witness before a grand jury. While given a series of warnings, including the warning that he had the right to remain silent, he was not informed in advance of his testimony that he was a potential defendant, in danger of indictment and, subsequently, was indicted for theft. Chief Justice Burger, writing for the majority, observed that the Fifth Amendment extends to grand jury proceedings but does not require suppression of an individual's incriminating testimony unless it was obtained by "genuine compulsion." Again reiterating the Court's narrow construction of personal compulsion and Fifth Amendment protection, Chief Justice Burger emphasized "the need for showing overbearing compulsion as a prerequisite to a Fifth Amendment violation."[158] Thus, Washington, as Tucker, Garner, Beckwith, and Mandujano, reaffirmed the Court's strict construction of the protection and benefits of the Fifth Amendment. "The constitutional guarantee is only that the witness be not compelled to give self-incriminating testimony. The test is whether considering the totality of the circumstances the free will of the witness was overborne."[159]

PERSONAL COMPULSION AND PROTECTED PRIVACY

Within the Bill of Rights, the Fifth Amendment provides the principal constitutional safeguard against compelled personal dis-

closures and, thus, the primary guarantee for individuals' interests
in informational privacy. Accordingly, the Supreme Court has extended the amendment's protection beyond a literal interpretation to
provide benefits for both the defendant and witnesses, whether in criminal, civil, legislative, or administrative proceedings, thereby establishing considerable protection for individuals' privacy interests, at
least within these contexts and when personal disclosures would tend
to be incriminating. The potentially broad contours of Fifth Amendment-protected privacy nevertheless have been circumscribed by a
number of judicial policies permitting protection for only an individual's production of incriminating information, but not the production
of incriminating information by third parties, such as individuals'
attorneys, accountants, and banking institutions. The compulsion of
personal disclosures upon grants of immunity as well as the doctrine
of "required records" and the distinction between "testimonial" and
"real" evidence also restrict Fifth Amendment safeguards for personal
privacy.

The Burger Court's strict construction and reevaluation of the
jurisprudential basis for the Fifth Amendment indicates further contraction in the amendment's contours and diminishing protection for
personal privacy. The Court's strict construction and failure to address crucial issues of personal privacy in our information-oriented
society is exemplified by its refusal to consider, in Couch, Fisher,
Andresen, and Garner, the consequences of compelled personal disclosures as well as the practical ways in which an individual may be
compelled to be a "witness against himself." California Bankers Association and Fisher underscore the Court's rejection of privacy arguments and, as with Fourth Amendment privacy claims, its failure
to conceptualize individuals' interests in informational privacy. In
contrast to the Warren Court's extension of the contours of Fifth
Amendment-protected privacy, the Burger Court's strict construction
protects only "compelled self-incrimination, not [the disclosure of]
private information," so that "unless incriminating testimony is 'compelled,' any invasion of privacy is outside the scope of the Fifth
Amendment."160

The diminishing utility of the Fifth Amendment for claims to
constitutionally protected privacy is further promoted by the Court's
reevaluation of the merits of the old woman's rationale and concomitant literal interpretation of personal compulsion requiring a "showing
[of] overbearing compulsion as a prerequisite to a Fifth Amendment
violation."161 Thus, the Burger Court focuses primarily on what
was termed the fox hunter's rationale, namely, the amendment's role
in "the preservation of an adversary system of criminal justice."162
The Court's treatment of the Fifth Amendment guarantee, hence, not
surprisingly curtails protection for individuals' privacy interests with

respect to private papers and required records, condones both police practices that deviate from and thereby dilute Miranda and the prosecutory use of individuals' incriminating statements that result from such police practices, and tolerates "police trickery"[163] in obtaining individuals' self-accusatorial statements.

NOTES

1. For an examination of the maxim and its relation to the Fifth Amendment, see, generally, Leonard Levy, Origins of the Fifth Amendment (New York: Oxford University Press, 1968); and John Wigmore, Evidence, ed. John McNaughton, vol. 8, § 2251 (Boston: Little, Brown, 1961).

2. Levy, Origins of the Fifth Amendment, at 430.

3. See discussion in Chapter 2. See also Slochower v. Board of Education, 350 U.S. 551, 557 (1956); Brown v. Walker, 161 U.S. 519, 610 (1896); Quinn v. United States, 349 U.S. 155, 161-62 (1955).

4. Section 8, Virginia Declaration of Rights, in The Federal and State Constitutions, Colonial Charters, and Other Organic Laws, ed. F. Thorpe (Washington, D.C.: U.S. Government Printing Office, 1909), 3813 (emphasis added).

5. Quoted by Levy, Origins of the Fifth Amendment, at 422 (emphasis added).

6. See, generally, R. Carter Pittman, "The Colonial and Constitutional History of the Privilege against Self-Incrimination in America," 21 Virginia Law Review 763 (1935).

7. The amendments reported by the House Select Committee, July 28, 1789, are printed in 5 Documentary History of the Constitution of the United States of America, at 186-89 (1786-1870).

8. Comment, "The Protection of Privacy by the Privilege against Self-Incrimination: A Doctrine Laid to Rest?" 59 Iowa Law Review 1336, 1343 (1974) (emphasis in original).

9. Leonard Levy, "The Right against Self-Incrimination: History and Judicial History," 84 Journal of Politics 1, 3 n. 9 (1969).

10. Levy, Origins of the Fifth Amendment, at 425-27.

11. Ullmann v. United States, 350 U.S. 422, 438 (1956).

12. See Garrity v. New Jersey, 385 U.S. 493 (1967); Spevack v. Klein, 385 U.S. 511 (1967); Griffin v. California, 380 U.S. 609, 614 (1965).

13. See California v. Byers, 402 U.S. 424, 432 (1971); Mackey v. United States, 401 U.S. 667, 704-5 (1971); Hoffman v. United States, 341 U.S. 479, 486 (1951); Rogers v. United States, 340 U.S. 367, 370 (1951); United States v. Monia, 317 U.S. 424, 437 (1943); and Mason v. United States 244 U.S. 362, 365 (1917).

14. See Hale v. Henkel, 201 U.S. 43 (1906); and Brown v. Walker, 161 U.S. 591 (1896).

15. Emspack v. United States, 349 U.S. 190 (1955), quoting The Queen v. Boyles, 1 B. S. 311, 330-31 (1861).

16. Levy, "Right against Self-Incrimination," at 19.

17. Counselman v. Hitchcock, 142 U.S. 547, 562 (1892).

18. Levy, "Right against Self-Incrimination, at 38.

19. See Escobedo v. Illinois, 378 U.S. 478, 490 (1964), Miranda v. Arizona, 384 U.S. 436 (1966) (police interrogations); Emspack v. United States, 349 U.S. 190 (1955); Quinn v. United States, 349 U.S. 155 (1955) (legislative investigations); ICC v. Brimson, 154 U.S. 447 (1894) (administrative investigations); Lefkowitz v. Cunningham, 429 U.S. 893 (1977); United States v. Kordel, 397 U.S. 1, 6 (1970); Mc-Carthy v. Arndstein, 266 U.S. 34 (1924) (grand jury proceedings).

20. Brown v. Walker, 161 U.S. 519, 631 (1896). See also Ullmann v. United States, 350 U.S. 422, 431 (1956); Kastigar v. United States, 406 U.S. 441 (1972); and United States v. Wilson, 421 U.S. 309 (1975).

21. See Kastigar v. United States, 406 U.S. 441, 444 (1972) (upholding "use" or "testimonial" immunity as authorized by the Organized Crime Control Act of 1970). See also Zicarelli v. New Jersey State Commission of Investigation, 406 U.S. 472 (1972).

22. See Marchetti v. United States, 390 U.S. 39 (1968); Costello v. United States, 383 U.S. 942 (1966); Lewis v. United States, 385 U.S. 206 (1966); Communist Party v. Subversive Activities Control Board, 367 U.S. 1 (1961); United States v. Kahringer, 345 U.S. 22 (1953); Shapiro v. United States, 335 U.S. 1 (1948).

23. See United States v. Dionisio, 410 U.S. 1, 5-7 (1973) (voice samples); United States v. Wade, 388 U.S. 218, 221-23 (1967) (compelled police lineups); Gilbert v. California, 388 U.S. 263, 265-67 (1967) (handwriting samples); Schmerber v. California, 384 U.S. 757, 760-65 (1966) (compulsory blood samples).

24. Murphy v. Waterfront Commission, 378 U.S. 52, 55 (1964).

25. Jeremy Bentham, A Rationale of Judicial Evidence, vol. 5, 238-39 (1827).

26. Miranda v. Arizona, 384 U.S. 436, 460 (1966).

27. Culombe v. Connecticut, 367 U.S. 568, 581-82 (1961). See also United States v. Washington, 431 U.S. 181 (1977); Rogers v. Richmond, 365 U.S. 534 (1961).

28. Miranda v. Arizona, 384 U.S. 436, 460 (1966) (citations omitted).

29. Abe Fortas, "The Fifth Amendment: Nemo Tenetur Prodere Seipsum," 25 Cleveland Bar Association Journal 95, 98-99 (1954).

30. Fortas, "Fifth Amendment," at 95. See also Miranda v. Arizona, 384 U.S. 436, 459-60 (1966).

31. Ibid., at 97.

32. For a survey of arguments offered in support of the Fifth Amendment, see John McNaughton, "The Privilege against Self-Incrimination," 51 Journal of Criminal Law, Criminology, and Police Science 138 (1960).

33. Levy, Origins of the Fifth Amendment, at 266–330; Wigmore, Evidence, at 267–95.

34. See McNaughton, "Privilege against Self-Incrimination," at 145; Erwin Griswold, The Fifth Amendment Today 7–9, 61, 75 (Cambridge, Mass.: Harvard University Press, 1955); Harry Kalven, "Invoking the Fifth Amendment: Some Legal and Impractical Considerations," 9 Bulletin of Atomic Scientists 181, 182–83 (1953).

35. See O. J. Rogge, The First and the Fifth (New York: Da Capo Press, 1971); Barenblatt v. United States, 360 U.S. 109 (1959); Watkins v. United States, 354 U.S. 178 (1957); Sweezy v. New Hampshire, 354 U.S. 234 (1957).

36. See Bernard Meltzer, "Required Records, the McCarran Act, and the Privilege against Self-Incrimination," 13 University of Chicago Law Review 687 (1950–51).

37. See Wilson v. United States, 149 U.S. 60, 66 (1893); Meltzer, "Required Records"; and Wigmore, Evidence.

38. See Escobedo v. Illinois, 378 U.S. 478, 589 (1964); Miranda v. Arizona, 384 U.S. 436, 459–60 (1966); Wigmore, Evidence, at 309; Fortas, "Fifth Amendment," at 97.

39. Robert Gerstein, "Privacy and Self-Incrimination," 80 Ethics 87, 88 (1970).

40. See United States v. Wilson, 421 U.S. 309 (1975).

41. Robert McKay, "Self-Incrimination and the New Privacy," in The Supreme Court Reporter, ed. Philip Kurland (Chicago: University of Chicago Press, 1967) 209, 230.

42. Henry J. Friendly, Benchmarks 271 (Chicago: University of Chicago Press, 1967).

43. Ibid., at 275.

44. Michigan v. Tucker, 417 U.S. 433, 440 (1974).

45. United States v. Washington, 431 U.S. 181 (1977). See also United States v. Monia, 317 U.S. 424 (1943); Garner v. United States, 424 U.S. 648, 654 n. 9 (1976).

46. Ullmann v. United States, 350 U.S. 422, 445–46 (1956) (second emphasis added).

47. Bentham, Rationale of Judicial Evidence, at 231.

48. Quoted by Levy, Origins of the Fifth Amendment, at 177.

49. Pittman, "Colonial and Constitutional History of the Privilege," at 783.

50. Zechariah Chafee, The Blessings of Liberty 188 (Philadelphia: Lippincott, 1956).

51. David Louisell, "Criminal Discovery and Self-Incrimination," 53 California Law Review 89, 95 (1965).

52. See McNaughton, "Privilege against Self-Incrimination," at 147.

53. Louisell, "Criminal Discovery and Self-Incrimination," at 95.

54. Sidney Hook, Common Sense and the Fifth Amendment 73 (Chicago: Henry Regnery, 1963).

55. Friendly, "The Fifth Amendment Tomorrow: The Case for Constitutional Change," 37 Cincinnati Law Review 671, 680 (1968).

56. Leonard Ratner, "The Consequences of Exercising the Privilege against Self-Incrimination," 24 University of Chicago Law Review 472, 488-89 (1957).

57. See Miranda v. Arizona, 384 U.S. 436, 460 (1966); Griswold v. Connecticut, 381 U.S. 479, 484 (1965); Tehan v. United States ex rel. Shott, 382 U.S. 406, 416 (1966); Murphy v. Waterfront Commission, 378 U.S. 52, 55 (1964). See also Boyd v. United States, 116 U.S. 616, 630 (1886); Feldman v. United States, 322 U.S. 487, 489-90 (1944); United States v. White, 322 U.S. 694, 698 (1944).

58. Warden v. Hayden, 387 U.S. 294, 323 (1967).

59. United States v. Grunewald, 233 F.2d 556 (2d Cir. 1956), rev'd, 351 U.S. 391 (1957).

60. United States v. Grunewald, 233 F.2d 556, 581-82 (Frank, J., dis. op.).

61. Tehan v. United States ex rel. Shott, 382 U.S. 406, 446 (1966), denying the retroactivity of Griffin v. California, 380 U.S. 609 (1965).

62. Linkletter v. Walker, 381 U.S. 618 (1965). The exlusionary rule is discussed in Chapter 2.

63. Robert McKay, "Book Review," 35 New York University Law Review 1097, 1100-1 (1960). See Warden v. Hayden, 387 U.S. 294, 302-3 (1967); Mapp v. Ohio, 367 U.S. 643, 656-57 (1961); Cohen v. Hurley, 366 U.S. 117, 154 (1961); Weeks v. United States, 232 U.S. 383, 391-95 (1914); Gouled v. United States, 255 U.S. 298, 311 (1921); Bram v. United States, 168 U.S. 532, 543-44 (1897); Gambino v. United States, 275 U.S. 310, 316 (1927); Boyd v. United States, 116 U.S. 616, 633 (1886).

64. McKay, "Self-Incrimination," at 212.

65. Ibid., at 230.

66. Ibid., at 213-14.

67. Michael Dann, "The Fifth Amendment Privilege against Self-Incrimination: Extorting Evidence from a Suspect," 43 Southern California Law Review 597, 601-2 (1970) (emphasis in original).

68. Comment, "Papers, Privacy, and the Fourth and Fifth Amendments: A Constitutional Analysis," 69 Northwestern Law Review 626, 630-31 (1974).

69. Meltzer, "Required Records," at 687 (emphasis added).

70. Friendly, "The Fifth Amendment Tomorrow," at 688.

71. Ibid., at 689 n. 90.

72. Ibid., at 689.

73. Gerstein, "Privacy and Self-Incrimination," at 89.

74. Charles Fried, "Privacy," 77 Yale Law Journal 475, 482 (1968). Fried's analysis is discussed in Chapter 1.

75. Gerstein, "Privacy and Self-Incrimination," at 89.

76. Ibid., at 90–91.

77. Friendly, "The Fifth Amendment Tomorrow," at 689. See also Robert Ellis, "Vox Populi v. Suprema Lex: A Comment on the Testimonial Privilege of the Fifth Amendment," 55 Iowa Law Review 829 (1970).

78. Gerstein, "Privacy and Self-Incrimination," at 88.

79. Spevack v. Klein, 385 U.S. 511, 522 (1967) (Harlan, J., dis. op.).

80. Boyd v. United States, 116 U.S. 616 (1886). See discussion in Chapter 2.

81. Counselman v. Hitchcock, 142 U.S. 547, 562 (1892).

82. See Escobedo v. Illinois, 378 U.S. 478, 490 (1964), Miranda v. Arizona, 384 U.S. 436 (1966) (police interrogations); Emspack v. United States, 349 U.S. 190 (1955); Quinn v. United States, 349 U.S. 155 (1955) (legislative investigations); ICC v. Brimson, 154 U.S. 447 (1894) (administrative investigations); Lefkowitz v. Cunningham, 429 U.S. 893 (1977); United States v. Kordel, 397 U.S. 1, 6 (1970); McCarthy v. Arndstein, 266 U.S. 34 (1924) (grand jury proceedings).

83. Ellis, "Vox Populi v. Supreme Lex," at 1339.

84. Garner v. United States, 424 U.S. 648, 655 (1976).

85. United States v. Washington, 431 U.S. 181, 188 (1977).

86. See Bellis v. United States, 417 U.S. 85 (1974); McPaul v. United States, 364 U.S. 372 (1960); United States v. Fleishman, 339 U.S. 349 (1950); Oklahoma Press Publishing Co. v. Walling, 327 U.S. 186 (1946); United States v. White, 322 U.S. 694, 701 (1944); Wilson v. United States, 221 U.S. 361 (1911); Hale v. Henkel, 201 U.S. 43 (1906).

87. Perlman v. United States, 247 U.S. 7, 15 (1918), quoted approvingly in Couch v. United States, 409 U.S. 322, 339 (1973).

88. See California Bankers Association v. Shultz, 416 U.S. 21 (1974) (banking institutions); Couch v. United States, 409 U.S. 322 (1973) (accountants); United States v. Miller, 425 U.S. 435 (1976), Fisher v. United States, 425 U.S. 391 (1976) (attorneys).

89. Couch v. United States, 409 U.S. 322, 336 (1973).

90. Idem, at 331.

91. See United States v. White, 322 U.S. 694 (1944).

92. Couch v. United States, 409 U.S. 322, 336 (1973), quoting Perlman v. United States, 247 U.S. 7, 15 (1918).

93. Fisher v. United States, 425 U.S. 391 (1976).
94. United States v. Nobles, 422 U.S. 225, 233 n. 7 (1975).
95. Fisher v. United States, 425 U.S. 391, 400-1 (1976).
96. Larry Ritchie, "Compulsion That Violates the Fifth Amendment: The Burger Court's Definition," 61 Minnesota Law Review 383, 393 (1977).
97. Fisher v. United States, 425 U.S. 391, 414 (1976) (Brennan, J., dis. op.).
98. Couch v. United States, 409 U.S. 322, 339-40 (1973) (Douglas, J., dis. op.).
99. Idem, at 343-44.
100. Idem, at 346.
101. Idem, at 349-50.
102. Katz v. United States, 389 U.S. 347, 360-61 (1967) (Harlan, J., con. op.) is discussed in Chapter 2.
103. Couch v. United States, 409 U.S. 322, 350-51 (1973) (Marshall, J., dis. op.).
104. Idem, at 337 (Brennan, J., dis. op.).
105. Andresen v. Maryland, 427 U.S. 463, 477 (1976).
106. Fisher v. United States, 425 U.S. 391, 405-14 (1976).
107. Boyd v. United States, 116 U.S. 616, 630 (1886).
108. Holt v. United States, 218 U.S. 245, 252-53 (1910).
109. See Hoffman v. United States, 341 U.S. 479, 486 (1951); and Malloy v. Hogan, 378 U.S. 1, 11-12 (1964).
110. Schmerber v. California, 384 U.S. 757 (1966).
111. Idem, at 764.
112. See Gilbert v. California, 388 U.S. 263, 265-67 (1967) (compelled handwriting samples); United States v. Wade, 388 U.S. 218, 221-23 (1967) (police lineups); United States v. Dionisio, 410 U.S. 1, 5-7 (1973) (voice samples).
113. California v. Byers, 402 U.S. 424, 433-34 (1971).
114. See Schmerber v. California, 384 U.S. 757, 761 (1966); United States v. Wade, 388 U.S. 218, 222-33 (1967); Gilbert v. California, 388 U.S. 263, 266 (1967); United States v. Dionisio, 410 U.S. 1, 5-6 (1973).
115. Wilson v. United States, 221 U.S. 361, 380 (1911).
116. Shapiro v. United States, 335 U.S. 1 (1948).
117. Grosso v. United States, 390 U.S. 62, 67-68 (1968).
118. California v. Byers, 402 U.S. 424 (1971).
119. Idem, at 431.
120. See Lewis v. United States, 385 U.S. 206 (1966); United States v. Kahriger, 345 U.S. 22 (1953). But see Marchetti v. United States, 390 U.S. 39 (1968); Grosso v. United States, 390 U.S. 62 (1968); Albertson v. Subversive Activities Control Board, 382 U.S. 70 (1965).

121. McKay, "Self-Incrimination," at 217.

122. Ibid.

123. United States v. Sullivan, 274 U.S. 259, 262-64 (1927).

124. United States v. Murdock, 284 U.S. 141 (1931).

125. Marchetti v. United States, 390 U.S. 39, 47 (1968).

126. Beckwith v. United States, 425 U.S. 341, 349-50 (1976)
(Brennan, J., dis. op.).

127. Garner v. United States, 424 U.S. 648 (1976).

128. Idem, at 655.

129. Mackey v. United States, 401 U.S. 667 (1971).

130. Garner v. United States, 424 U.S. 648, at 655 (1976).

131. United States v. Kordel, 397 U.S. 1 (1970); Schneckcloth
v. Bustamonte, 412 U.S. 218, 222-27, 235-40, 246-47 (1973) (holding that individuals may lose the benefits of the amendment without
asserting "a knowing and intelligent" waiver of their rights).

132. Miranda v. Arizona, 384 U.S. 436, 367 (1966).

133. See Michigan v. Payne, 412 U.S. 47, 53 (1973); and Brown
v. Illinois, 422 U.S. 590, 600 (1974).

134. Haynes v. Washington, 373 U.S. 503, 514 (1962).

135. Miranda v. Arizona, 384 U.S. 436, 476 (1966).

136. See Brewer v. Illinois, 430 U.S. 387 (1977); Oregon v.
Mathiason, 429 U.S. 492 (1977); Michigan v. Mosley, 423 U.S. 96
(1975); Oregon v. Hass, 420 U.S. 714 (1975); Michigan v. Tucker, 417
U.S. 433 (1974); Harris v. New York, 410 U.S. 222 (1971). See also
Doyle v. Ohio, 426 U.S. 610 (1976) (held that due process precludes
use of defendant's silence at time of arrest, after receiving Miranda
warnings, to impeach his exculpatory testimony offered for the first
time at trial); and United States v. Hale, 422 U.S. 171 (1975).

137. Michigan v. Tucker, 417 U.S. 433, 443-44 (1974).

138. Harris v. New York, 401 U.S. 222 (1971).

139. Idem, at 230 (Brennan, J., dis. op.) (emphasis in original).

140. Idem, at 227.

141. Oregon v. Hass, 420 U.S. 714 (1975).

142. Michigan v. Tucker, 417 U.S. 433 (1974).

143. Michigan v. Mosley, 423 U.S. 96 (1975).

144. Miranda v. Arizona, 384 U.S. 436, at 473-74 (1966).

145. Michigan v. Mosley, 423 U.S. 96, 114 (1975) (Brennan, J.,
dis. op.).

146. Idem, at 112 and 118.

147. Oregon v. Mathiason, 429 U.S. 492 (1977).

148. See United States v. Checcolini, 98 S. Ct. 1054 (1978);
United States v. Janis, 428 U.S. 433, 458-59 (1976); United States v.
Calandra, 414 U.S. 338, 348 (1974); Bivens v. Six Unknown Federal
Agents of the Federal Bureau of Narcotics, 403 U.S. 388, 416-17
(1971) (Burger, C.J., dis. op.).

149. United States v. Washington, 431 U.S. 181, 188 (1977).

150. Miranda v. Arizona, 384 U.S. 436, at 444 (1966). See also Mathis v. United States, 391 U.S. 1 (1968); Orozco v. Texas, 394 U.S. 324 (1969).

151. Haynes v. Washington, 373 U.S. 503, 514 (1962).

152. Ritchie, "Compulsion That Violates the Fifth Amendment," at 397, quoting Malloy v. Hogan, 378 U.S. 1, 8, (1964).

153. Beckwith v. United States, 425 U.S. 341 (1976).

154. Idem, at 345–46.

155. Idem, at 350.

156. United States v. Mandujano, 425 U.S. 564 (1976); United States v. Washington, 431 U.S. 181 (1977); United States v. Wong, 431 U.S. 174 (1977).

157. United States v. Mandujano, 425 U.S. 564, at 572–73.

158. United States v. Washington, 431 U.S. 181, 190 (1977).

159. Idem, at 189.

160. United States v. Nobles, 422 U.S. 225, 233 n. 7 (1975); and Andresen v. Maryland, 427 U.S. 463, 477 (1976).

161. United States v. Washington, 431 U.S. 181, 190 (1977).

162. Garner v. United States, 424 U.S. 648, 655 (1976).

163. See Oregon v. Mathiason, 429 U.S. 492 (1977) (police falsely told defendant that his fingerprints were found at scene of a burglary); Michigan v. Mosley, 423 U.S. 96 (1975) (police falsely told defendant that a codefendant had confessed to participation in a homicide but had named the defendant as the one who had shot the victim); Frazier v. Cupp, 394 U.S. 731 (1969) (police falsely told defendant that they had arrested defendant's alibi witness who had confessed to participation in the crime).

4

Preferred Freedoms and the Rights of Conscience

[N]ot one man but a whole nation can become cowed and
frigid. Without privacy the soul of man withers. This
right is the atmosphere of our freedom; it is like the air
we breathe, enveloping invisible, yet sustaining, so long
as it is there. Without it other rights will perish, especially free speech and assembly. What is the right of free
speech and free assembly if Big Brother is listening?

State v. Carluccio

Whereas the Fourth and Fifth Amendments protect personal privacy by regulating the manner in which the government may obtain access to individuals' engagements and information about their activities,
the First Amendment mandates broad protection for individuals against
governmental interference with and regulation of their everyday activities. Indeed, the core of citizens' political ideal of liberty may be
identified with the First Amendment, because First Amendment guarantees, unlike the procedural safeguards of the Fourth and Fifth
Amendments, as Irving Brant observes, "govern a man's normally
day-to-day relations with his fellow men: they also determine his
place in the community and his participation in what we know in America as government of and by the people."[1] Since the First Amendment
guarantees that individuals may define for themselves their beliefs,
activities and associations, the amendment may also be understood as
securing for individuals a "right to be let alone" or freedom from both
governmental and community interference, and, thus, may concomitantly serve as a foundation for constitutionally protected privacy.

FIRST AMENDMENT RIGHTS OF CONSCIENCE

Scholarly discussion and judicial construction of First Amendment-protected privacy invites controversy and paradox. Thomas
Emerson argues that the First Amendment, if not irrelevant, provides no basis for constitutionally protected privacy: "The right of
privacy . . . is essentially the right not to participate in the collective life—the right to shut out the community. A system of privacy
is designed to isolate this area of individual life from various kinds
of interference by the collective."[2] Emerson, as other commentators,
urges that the First Amendment guarantees a "system of freedom of
expression" prohibiting governmental regulation of public discussion.
Contrariwise, privacy interests are generally protected by rules
crosscutting the First Amendment and establishing "a sphere that has
not been dedicated to public use or control."[3] Emerson's analysis
thus associates privacy interests with a "private sphere," wherein the
law of privacy remains primarily that of private tort actions with few,
if any, First Amendment implications, as opposed to a "public sphere,"
wherein the First Amendment governs the activities of the collective.[4]
Only a narrow range of First Amendment privacy claims, those against
disclosures of an embarrassing nature, therefore would be entitled to
protection.

The opposition of a "private" and a "public" sphere, however,
remains ambiguous, because personal privacy denotes limited access
by others to an individual's experiences and engagements. As Katz
recognized, individuals may have expectations of privacy in public
places and expectations of publicity in private places; consequently,
the constitutional law of privacy may not simply rest on a dichotomy
between the private and the public. Judicial construction of the reasonableness of privacy claims, under the Fourth and Fifth Amendments,
relies upon traditionally recognizable private places or, rather, areas
defined in part by proprietary interests. Still, a dichotomy between
the private and the public is simply not an adequate basis for establishing privacy safeguards, let alone for extending First Amendment
protection to individuals' speech and activities in public places while
foreclosing protection for individuals' speech and activities in private
places or areas in which they have proprietary interests.

If personal privacy receives any constitutional protection under
the First Amendment, then the amendment must extend some protection to individuals regardless of whether they are in public or private
places. Overemphasis on the First Amendment's protection of the
public's or collective's interests in maintaining a free flow of information neglects the fact that the amendment governs individuals' everyday activities. As such the amendment guarantees not only the right
to publicly express or distribute in print one's own version of the

truth and the right to adhere to any or no religion, but also the right
to withdraw from public affairs in order to reflect about one's beliefs
and ideas. In other words, the First Amendment embodies a political
ideal not of absolute and unconditional free speech, press, and religious exercise but of limited freedom to speak and act according to
the dictates of one's own conscience.

There was little debate on adopting the First Amendment, because those who feared freedom of speech and press expected the
states to continue common law restrictions on libel and other mischievous publications; furthermore, colonial experiences of both
Whigs and Tories with regard to the abuses of power by the Crown fostered agreement on establishing, what James Madison called, "the
rights of conscience."[5] These "great rights," as Madison referred to
them, were to be secured by the provisions of the First Amendment,
yet its guarantees were not absolute. The First Amendment's symbolic embodiment of the "full and equal rights of conscience" was unconditional, but the amendment's specific provisions were not understood to guarantee unqualified freedom of speech, press, and religious
exercise.

As a matter of legal history, guarantees for free speech, press,
and religious exercise both in common law and as embodied in the
First Amendment were not unlimited. The authors of the First Amendment did not accept an unqualified freedom to speak and publish. The
First Amendment, like the Fourth and Fifth Amendments, incorporated
and gave constitutional effect to traditional common law principles.
As the Supreme Court in 1897 acknowledged: "The law is perfectly
well settled that the first ten amendments to the Constitution, commonly
known as the Bill of Rights, were not intended to lay down any novel
principles of government, but simply to embody certain guarantees and
immunities which we had inherited from our English ancestors."[6]
Accordingly, Leonard Levy argued that the authors of the First Amendment actually bequeathed a "legacy of suppression" insofar as they
accepted and adopted English common law governing the freedom of
speech and press.[7] The legacy of suppression derived from a defer-
ence to Sir William Blackstone's all-too-definitive view of the common
law of free speech and press:

> The liberty of the press is indeed essential to the nature
> of a free state; but this consists in laying no previous re-
> straints upon publications, and not in freedom from cen-
> sure from criminal matter when published. Every free-
> man has an undoubted right to lay what sentiments he
> phrases; but if he publishes what is improper, mischievous
> or illegal, he must take the consequences of his own temer-
> ity.[8]

Blackstone's position implied that the First Amendment protects only against prior restraint and censorship but fails to provide immunity for what, when, and where speakers or publishers may utter or print. Individuals could then be punished for speech or publication that was illegal, improper, or mischievous.

Early U.S. citizens' acceptance of common law principles and practices, aptly characterized by Leonard Levy as "an unbridled passion for a bridled liberty of speech," was manifested with Congress's passage of the Sedition Act of 1789, permitting punishment of individuals who made "any false, scandalous writing" against the government of the United States. More generally, founding fathers such as John Adams, James Madison, and Thomas Jefferson embraced Blackstone's definition of free speech and press, because of their sense of decency and propriety; if a man "publishes what is improper, mischievous or illegal, he must take the consequences of his own temerity."[9] James Wilson, for example, in defending the Constitution at the ratifying convention, argued that "what is meant by the liberty of the press is that there should be no antecedent restraint upon it; but every author is responsible when he attacks the security or welfare of the government, or the safety, character and property of the individual."[10] The political ideal of free speech and press embodied in English common law and the First Amendment was thus limited and conditional.

Similarly, the First Amendment's provision for the free exercise of religion was not unconditional. Thomas Jefferson, for example, in writing the preamble to Virginia's Act for Establishing Religious Freedom, argued:

> Whereas Almighty God hath created the mind free; that all attempts to influence it by temporal punishments or burdens, or by civil incapacitations, tend only to beget habits of hypocrisy and meanness . . . ; that to suffer the civil magistrate to intrude his powers into the field of opinion, and to restrain the profession or propagation of principles on suppression of their ill tendency, is a dangerous fallacy, which at once destroys all liberty, because he being of course judge of that tendency will make his opinions the rule of judgement, and approve or condemn the sentiments of others only as they shall square with or differ from his own; that it is time enough for the rightful purposes of civil government, for its officers to interfere when principles break out into overt acts against peace and good order; and finally, that truth is great and will prevail if left to herself; that she is the proper and sufficient antagonist to error, and has nothing to fear from conflict, unless by human interposition disarmed of her natural weapons, free argument and

debate, errors ceasing to be dangerous when it is permitted freely to contradict them.[11]

Jefferson maintained that the "acts of the body," unlike "the operations of the mind," are "subject to the coercion of the laws" whenever religious "principles break out into overt acts against peace and good order."[12] As common law restrictions on seditious libel and mischievous publications were to be permitted, so too the government might intervene when individuals' exercise of religious freedom led to violence or overt acts against the peace and order of society.

Notwithstanding the view of many contemporary scholars, the First Amendment's broad guarantees are not absolute nor designed primarily to prohibit all governmental regulation. Rather, the amendment was designed to safeguard each individual's "full and equal rights of conscience" and thereby ensure extensive but not unlimited freedom of speech, press, religious exercise, and assembly. The First Amendment rights of conscience, as more generally the political ideal of liberty embodied within the Constitution, were not unqualified nor proved to be unconditional within the practice of rights in the United States.[13] As common law provided, the Supreme Court holds that some speech receives no First Amendment protection:

> There are certain well-defined and narrowly limited classes of speech, the prevention and punishment of which have never been thought to raise any Constitutional problem. These include the lewd and obscene, the profane, the libelous, and the insulting or "fighting" words. . . . It has been well observed that such utterances are no essential part of any exposition of ideas, and are of such slight social value as a step to truth that any benefit that may be derived from them is clearly outweighed by the social interest in order and morality.[14]

The Supreme Court affirmed for over a century that libelous as well as lewd, obscene, and profane language lay outside the purview of the First Amendment, ruling only in 1964 against prosecutions for seditious libel.[15] Still, within the Supreme Court there has never been a generally accepted approach for interpreting the First Amendment; perhaps, best illustrated by Dennis v. United States, where five justices articulated five different theories of First Amendment protection.[16] Instead, judicial approaches range from endorsement of the Blackstonian position, through various techniques of balancing, to advocates of a "preferred position" for First Amendment freedoms, and, finally, to an absolutist-literalist interpretation.[17] The Court nevertheless has developed specific rules for limiting individuals' exercise of freedom of speech and press. Libel, "personal abuse," "fighting words," or language that incites and produces "imminent lawless action," as well as "prurient, patently offensive depiction or description of sexual conduct" fall outside First Amendment protection.[18] Thus, although there are great difficulties in judicial line drawing and discriminating between protected and unprotected speech, the Supreme Court has established that First Amendment freedoms are not absolute and unconditional.

The First Amendment's guarantee of individuals' "full and equal rights of conscience" necessitates judicial line drawing, because the amendment signifies that individuals have an equal right to decide what to say and to whom as well as when, where, and how they will express their ideas. As a correlative right of freedom of speech, religious exercise, and assembly, individuals are also entitled to determine who will hear what, not only about their political and religious beliefs but also about their personal affairs. Thus, under the First Amendment, the Supreme Court inevitably must balance privacy claims against freedom of speech, press, and religious exercise.

PRIVACY AND THE FIRST AMENDMENT

Privacy claims crosscut express First Amendment freedoms in ways that both oppose and complement the amendment's guarantees. Individuals may have privacy interests in not being intruded upon by other citizens' exercise of freedom of speech or expression of religious and political convictions. For example, individuals may have expectations of privacy in their homes that yield privacy claims against door-to-door salesmen's or Jehovah's Witnesses' claims to free speech and religious exercise. In such instances, when and where free speech is exercised becomes crucial, since the Court must balance competing claims to privacy and freedom of speech and religious exercise.

Individuals, however, may have privacy interests that receive protection under the First Amendment's guarantees for free speech and peaceful assembly. When individuals associate for lawful purposes, for example, they may have legitimate First Amendment claims not only to free speech and assembly but also to associational privacy. More specifically, individuals may assert privacy claims against governmental surveillance and requirements for disclosure of personal information concerning their membership and activities in association with others. At least in this respect, individuals' privacy interests and the express freedoms of the First Amendment are not competing but are, rather, complementary.

Finally, individuals may also have privacy expectations against public disclosures and publications of their personal affairs. By contrast with claims to associational privacy, claims against public disclosures require balancing individuals' privacy interests against the public's interests in freedom of the press. Historically, privacy interests were collapsed with those against libel and slander, but as such, constituted legitimate claims against freedom of press and speech. Although privacy interests could not be legitimately asserted as legal claims in English common law in the seventeenth and eighteenth centuries, by the late nineteenth century privacy claims against public disclosures were recognized as independent legal injuries at tort law in the United States.[19] Not until the mid-twentieth century, however, did individuals assert claims to constitutionally protected privacy against public disclosures and publication of personal affairs.

While claims to constitutionally protected privacy often not only compete with but entail limitations upon expressly guaranteed First Amendment freedoms, no principle is easily derived from the text of the amendment so as to demarcate the contours of protected privacy. The scope of First Amendment-protected privacy, like the contours of Fourth and Fifth Amendment-protected privacy thus emerged within the practice of rights as the result of constitutional interpretation. The following section examines the contours of the developing constitutional law of privacy as forged by judicial construction of claims for protection against solicitors, guarantees of associational privacy, and limitations on public disclosures of personal affairs.

JUDICIAL CONSTRUCTION OF
FIRST AMENDMENT-PROTECTED PRIVACY

Personal Privacy, Solicitors, and Offensive Public Displays

In two late-nineteenth century cases the Supreme Court alluded to possible First Amendment protection for personal privacy, but not until 1920 did a member of the Court articulate the view that privacy underlies the guarantees of the First Amendment.[20] In Gilbert v. Minnesota, the majority acknowledged that freedom of speech is not absolute, holding that a state, in exercising its police powers, may enact a statute forbidding the teaching or advocating that men should not enlist in the armed services.[21] In dissent, Justice Brandeis, arguing that the statute was not a wartime enactment and that it was overly broad, concluded that "the statute invades the privacy and freedom of the home. Father and mother may follow the promptings of religious belief, of conscience or of conviction, and teach son or daughter the doctrine of pacificism."[22] Justice Brandeis emphasized that privacy interests relate to individuals' beliefs and receive First

Amendment protection when governmental regulation affects individuals' home lives.

Further development of First Amendment privacy litigation, however, arose in the 1930s with claims against solicitors, door-to-door salesmen, and offensive public exhibitions. In these cases the Supreme Court confronted the difficulty of reconciling two First Amendment claims, a privacy claim not to be intruded upon and claims to free speech and religious exercise. The Court balanced these conflicting First Amendment claims and fashioned a policy toward protected privacy by distinguishing between intrusions made for commercial purposes, as with intrusions by door-to-door salesmen, and intrusions for noncommercial purposes, as with intrusions upon individuals' privacy in their homes by solicitors for religious and political organizations.

Traditionally common law prohibited individuals from going on private property without the owner's consent and forceably expressing their opinions, and lower courts in the United States since 1933 have upheld municipal ordinances prohibiting commercial door-to-door solicitation. In the "Handbills Cases" of 1939, the Supreme Court held that municipalities could not constitutionally prohibit Jehovah's Witnesses or others seeking to engage in religious or political canvassing from doing so. [23] Such ordinances as applied to Jehovah's Witnesses prohibited free exercise of religion and restricted freedom of speech. In Martin v. City of Struthers the Court observed that "the ordinance was designed to protect a legitimate interest, that of privacy in the home, but in balancing the interests, the considerations of free speech and the free exercise of religion out-weighed this interest." [24] Subsequently, the Court forbade owners of a company town and a privately owned shopping center from prohibiting circulation of religious and political literature. [25]

Individuals' privacy claims also yield to claims of freedom of speech and expression of political views. In 1969 in Gregory v. City of Chicago, the Court unanimously reversed the conviction of a group of political picketers, who marched in front of the home of Chicago's Mayor Richard J. Daley, on a charge of disorderly conduct. [26] Concurring, Justices Black and Douglas suggested that in such cases they were ready to subordinate express First Amendment guarantees to their concern for privacy:

> Were the authority of the government so trifling as to permit anyone with a complaint to have the vast power to do anything he pleased, wherever he pleased, and whenever he pleased our customs and our habits of conduct, social, political, economic, ethical, and religious, would all be wiped out. . . . I believe that the homes of men, some-

> times the last citadel of the tired, the weary and the
> sick, can be protected by the government from noisy,
> marching, tramping, threatening picketers and demon-
> strators bent on filling the minds of men, women, and
> children with fears of the unknown.[27]

The majority of the Court nevertheless indicated that it would give
priority to free speech and expression so long as picketing and political protests were peaceful and orderly. The majority reaffirmed
preference for claims to free speech in Organization for a Better Aus-
tin v. Keefe, reversing a lower court injunction designed to protect
privacy interests against picketing and distribution of leaflets in a
residential suburb.[28] Chief Justice Burger's majority opinion found
that "[d]esignating the conduct [picketing] as an invasion of privacy
. . . is not sufficient to support an injunction against peaceful distribution of informational literature."[29]

By contrast, the Supreme Court in Breard v. Alexandria indicated that it would give priority to privacy claims against intrusions
made for commercial purposes.[30] Breard was convicted under an ordinance prohibiting solicitors, peddlers or transient vendors of mer-
chandise from going onto private property without the owner's permission. The Court, upon balancing householders' desires for privacy
and publishers' rights to distribute publications, rejected Breard's
claim that the ordinance was an unconstitutional restriction of freedom of speech. Thus, Breard signifies that free speech may be regulated when its expression is designed primarily for commercial purposes and disturbs the privacy of individuals' activities in their
homes.[31]

Judicial construction of privacy claims against solicitors established that intrusions upon privacy are permissible if prohibitions
would restrict, as in the Jehovah's Witnesses' cases, First Amendment guarantees for freedom of speech and religious exercise. Still,
privacy claims may outweigh claims to free speech, where intrusions
upon private property are for predominantly commercial purposes.
Ostensibly, First Amendment, like Fourth Amendment, privacy claims
are strongest when associated with proprietary interests. Individuals,
however, may have privacy expectations and raise claims against intrusions when they are not in a place, such as their homes, where
they also have proprietary interests. Hence, it is important to consider whether individuals have legitimate privacy interests in areas
where they have no proprietary interests, such as public streets or
in vehicles of public transportation.

In a rather anomalous case in 1932, the Supreme Court accepted
an exceedingly broad construction of First Amendment-protected privacy. In Packer Corporation v. Utah the Court upheld a statute for-

bidding all advertising of tobacco and cigarettes on billboards and streetcar signs, but permitting such ads in newspapers, magazines, or storefront windows.[32] Justice Brandeis, writing for the Court, justified the state's regulation by discussing different modes of communication and their relative intrusiveness on individuals' expectations of privacy:

> Billboards, street car signs, and placards and such are in a class by themselves. . . . [They] are constantly before the eyes of observers on the streets and in street cars to be seen without the exercise of choice or violation on their part. Other forms of advertising are ordinarily seen as a matter of choice on the part of the observer. The young people as well as the adults have the message of the billboard thrust upon them by all the arts and devices that skill can produce. In the case of newspapers and magazines, there must be some seeking by the one who is to see and read the advertisement. The radio can be turned off, but not so the bill board or street car placard.[33]

Justice Brandeis's expansive interpretation of privacy expectations and the intrusiveness of different modes of communication implied that individuals could assert privacy claims against whatever they consider to be offensive signs, billboards, or placards. As such, Justice Brandeis's construction of protected privacy severely restricts First Amendment protection for freedom of speech and leads to an unacceptable political ideal of an unqualified right of privacy.[34]

The Supreme Court traditionally rejected privacy claims such as that raised in Packer. Judicial line drawing nevertheless remains difficult, for when does free speech become so intrusive as to constitute an overbearing intrusion upon interests in personal privacy? Three cases in the late 1940s and early 1950s illustrate the problems of formulating a principle of First Amendment-protected privacy upon an evaluation of the relative intrusiveness of speech upon personal privacy.

In Saia v. New York the Court held unconstitutional as a prior restraint of speech an ordinance prohibiting anyone to operate a loudspeaker casting sound on public streets except where matters of public concern were broadcast and advance permission was obtained from the chief of police.[35] Saia had obtained permission to give lectures on religious subjects, but due to protests from patrons of the park in which he spoke his permit was revoked; Saia nevertheless continued and subsequently was convicted of violating the ordinance. The Court in a five-to-four decision gave priority to the free speech claims. Justice Douglas, writing for the majority, held that loudspeakers and

sound trucks were important means of communication and therefore
any abuses in their use could be controlled only by narrowly drawn
statutes.

By contrast, in the next year the Court in <u>Kovacs</u> v. <u>Cooper</u>
upheld an ordinance forbidding sound trucks from emitting "loud and
raucous noises."[36] The majority distinguished <u>Saia</u> on the ground
that the ordinance provided inadequate standards for issuing permits,
and found, here, "loud and raucous noises" to be a sufficiently definitive guideline for administrative action regulating speech. The Court
argued that intrusions upon privacy by means of loudspeakers and
sound trucks were distinguishable from that presented in the handbills
cases, since individuals need not read the handbills, whereas the intrusiveness of sound trucks is such that "[an individual] is practically
helpless to escape this interference with his privacy by loudspeakers."[37] Thus, the Court recognized legitimate privacy claims against
intrusive means of distributing speech.

Although conflicting in result, <u>Saia</u> and <u>Kovacs</u> denote the Court's
balancing of privacy and freedom of speech claims upon a consideration of the relative intrusiveness of different modes of communication.
City ordinances may place reasonable restrictions on the volume of
sound or the hours during which loudspeakers may be utilized, and,
thereby, provide a modicum of protection for individuals' privacy—
particularly where, as in <u>Kovacs</u>, sound trucks travel along residential streets and their broadcasts may interfere with individuals' privacy in their homes. The Court further elaborated its analysis of the
relative intrusiveness of different modes of communication in <u>Public
Utilities Commission</u> v. <u>Pollak</u>.[38] In <u>Pollak</u>, the Court sustained a
privately owned transit company's use of radio loudspeakers in its
streetcars and buses, for the purpose of providing "music as you
ride" with only a one-minute advertisement every half hour. The
Court rejected privacy claims under the First and Fifth Amendments
because a streetcar constitutes a "public" place and, consequently,
individuals' expectations and claims of privacy are not as great as in
their homes. Justice Burton, announcing the majority's opinion,
stated:

> The Court below has emphasized the claim that the radio
> programs are an invasion of constitutional rights of pri-
> vacy of the passengers. . . . This position wrongly as-
> sumes that the Fifth Amendment secures to each passenger
> on a public vehicle regulated by the Federal Government a
> right of privacy substantially equal to the privacy to which
> he is entitled in his own home. However complete his right
> of privacy may be at home, it is substantially limited by the
> rights of others when its possessor travels on a public
> thoroughfare or rides in a public conveyance.[39]

Justice Burton thereby reaffirmed that First Amendment, like Fourth Amendment, privacy claims are strongest when raised against intrusions upon or interference with individuals' activities in their homes or areas in which they have proprietary interests.

Cohen v. California and Erznoznik v. City of Jacksonville further underscore the Court's reliance on proprietary principles in fashioning the contours of constitutionally protected privacy under both the First and Fourth Amendments.[40] In Cohen, the Court rejected arguments that privacy claims justify a conviction under California's penal code prohibiting malicious disturbing of the peace or quiet of any neighborhood or person by offensive conduct. The offensive conduct, here, was that of a political protest by an individual's wearing of a jacket emblazoned with the words, "Fuck the Draft," in the corridor of a Los Angeles County courthouse. Justice Harlan, speaking for the Court, observed:

> While this Court has recognized that government may properly act in many situations to prohibit intrusion into the privacy of the home . . . we have at the same time consistently stressed that "we are often 'captives' outside the sanctuary of the home and subject to objectionable speech."
> . . . The ability of government, consonant with the Constitution, to shut off discourse solely to protect others from hearing it is, in other words, dependent upon a showing that substantial privacy interests are being invaded in an essentially intolerable manner.[41]

Justice Harlan's opinion reiterated the Court's balancing of First Amendment claims to privacy and freedom of speech not on the basis of the content of the speech (whether some individuals regard certain speech or forms of expression as obscene or indecent), but on the basis of the manner and extent of the intrusion, as well as the locus of individuals claiming privacy. Individuals have no reasonable expectations of privacy in places where they have no assertible proprietary interests and when they may reasonably avoid offensive public displays.

In Erznoznik v. City of Jacksonville, the manager of a drive-in challenged the constitutionality of a city ordinance making it a public nuisance to show any motion picture containing nudity where the screen was visible from a public street. Justice Powell, for the Court, found the ordinance to unconstitutionally discriminate among movies on the basis of their content, adding:

> This discrimination cannot be justified as a means of preventing significant intrusions on privacy. The ordinance seeks to keep these films from being seen from public

streets and places where the offended viewer can avert his
eyes. In short, the screen of a drive-in theater is not "so
unobtrusive as to make it impossible for an unwilling individual to avoid exposure to it." . . . Thus, we conclude that
the limited privacy interest of persons on the public streets
cannot justify this censorship of otherwise protected speech
on the basis of its content. [42]

Over dissenting Chief Justice Burger and Justices Rehnquist and
White, the majority reaffirmed Cohen's holding that individuals have
no legitimate privacy claims against offensive public exhibitions when
a viewer may avoid offensive intrusions by "simply averting [his]
eyes." The majority, however, did not carefully distinguish and consider the relative merits of privacy claims raised by passing motor-
ists and those of resident homeowners located near the drive-in theater. [43]

The Supreme Court's construction of First Amendment privacy
claims, thus, resembles Fourth Amendment-protected privacy in focusing on the manner and extent of intrusions upon individuals' activities. First Amendment privacy claims, however, may be asserted
against both governmental intrusions and private individuals' interference with homeowners' privacy, whereas the Fourth Amendment
safeguards privacy interests only against unreasonable searches and
seizures by the government. Moreover, while judicial construction
of the Fourth Amendment extended the contours of protected privacy
to constitutionally protected areas other than an individual's home,
First Amendment privacy claims are ostensibly legitimate only when
individuals are intruded upon by solicitors whose interests in obtaining access are solely commercial, or when public address systems
unduly disturb residential areas. Still, as Pollak suggests, First
Amendment privacy claims, like those under the Fourth Amendment,
are strongest when raised against intrusions upon or interference
with individuals' activities in their homes. The Court's determination of the reasonableness of privacy claims under either the First
or the Fourth Amendment, indeed, crucially depends upon an individual's assertion of both privacy and proprietary interests.

The Court's treatment of Stanley v. Georgia and its progeny underscores the Court's reliance on proprietary principles in legitimating privacy claims and balancing competing First Amendment claims
to freedom of speech. [44] In Stanley the Court held unconstitutional a
statute prohibiting mere possession of obscene materials even in an
individual's own house. Justice Marshall, announcing the majority's
opinion, argued:

[Stanley] is asserting that right to read or observe what
he pleases—the right to satisfy his intellectual and emo-

tional needs in the privacy of his own home. He is asserting the right to be free from state inquiry into the contents
of his library. Georgia contends that appellant does not
have these rights, that there are certain types of materials
that the individual may not read or even possess. Georgia
justifies this assertion by arguing that the films in the
present case are obscene. But we think that mere categori-
zation of these films as "obscene" is insufficient for such
a drastic invasion of personal liberties guaranteed by the
First and Fourteenth Amendments. Whatever may be the
justifications for other statutes regulating obscenity, we
do not think they reach into the privacy of one's home. If
the First Amendment means anything, it means that a State
has no business telling a man, sitting alone in his own
home, what books he may read or what films he may watch.
Our whole constitutional heritage rebels at the thought of
giving the power to control men's minds. [45]

Justice Marshall emphasizes that there is "something special" about
individuals' activities in their homes, because the crucial factor in
Stanley was that the state attempted to regulate absolutely what individuals read. Justice Marshall therefore focused on the locus of Stanley's activities and the nature and purpose of the intrusion: "[F]un-
damental is the right to be free, except in very limited circumstances,
from unwanted governmental intrusions into one's privacy, . . . Whatever may be the justifications for other statutes regulating obscenity
we do not think they reach into the privacy of one's own home." [46]
    Subsequent decisions reinforce the Court's treatment of privacy
claims by focusing on individuals' activities and proprietary interests
in their homes. On the one hand, the Court rejected individuals' privacy claims when raised outside their homes and where they engaged
in selling obscene materials, in transporting obscene materials by interstate commerce or through international borders, or in viewing
pornographic films in so-called adult theaters. [47] On the other hand,
the Court affirmed the right of householders to request the post office
to order any mailer to stop sending advertisements that the householder
"in his sole discretion believes to be erotically arousing or sexually
provocative." Rowan v. United States Post Office Department held
that "a mailer's right to communicate must stop at the mailbox of an
unreceptive address," [48] recognizing that individuals have legitimate
privacy expectations against intrusions that they consider offensive,
at least with regard to mailings to their homes. As the Court reiterated in Paris Adult Theater I v. Slaton: "[W]e have declined to equate
the privacy of the home relied on in Stanley with a 'zone' of 'privacy'
that follows a distributor or a consumer of obscene materials wherever

he goes. . . . . The idea of a 'privacy' right and a place of public ac-
commodation are, in this context, mutually exclusive."[49]

The Court's framework for constitutionally protected privacy
and balancing of privacy and freedom of speech claims, nevertheless
has been subject to two major criticisms. First, some commentators
argue that the Court's analysis fails to adequately consider the relative intrusiveness of different modes of communication on individuals'
expectations of privacy. Specifically, the Court is criticized for failing to find of any great constitutional significance the difference between aural and visual communications, and thereby neglecting the
respective burdens upon individuals to escape from aural and visual
intrusions. Whereas billboards or drive-in theaters' screens intrude
upon individuals in ways that permit them to turn their heads or physically remove themselves from the area, intrusions by loudspeakers
are such that, as Justice Douglas pointed out in Pollak, all an individual may do is "try not to listen." Zechariah Chafee, however, argued
with regard to door-to-door canvassing that, "A doorbell cannot be disregarded like a handbill. It takes several minutes to ascertain the
purpose of a propagandist and at least several more to get rid of
him."[50] Still, other commentators argue contrariwise: "A doorbell
can be distinguished like a handbill if one does not care any more at
the moment to see who is at the door than he does to look at the handbill."[51] Yet, as Franklyn Haiman observes, "in neither [instance]
is one free to avoid the initial impact, but in both cases one is capable
of shutting out, either physically or mentally, any communication beyond that."[52] Whether individuals in fact can succeed in "shutting out,
either physically or mentally, any communication" nevertheless appears to be contingent upon and relative to each individual.

The dilemma in balancing privacy and free speech claims upon
consideration of the relative intrusiveness of different modes of communication is well illustrated by the Burger Court's 1978 decision in
Federal Communications Commission v. Pacifica Foundation.[53]
Here, the Court accepted the Federal Communications Commission's
finding of George Carlin's monologue, "Filthy Words," a satire about
"words you couldn't say on the public airwaves," as patently offensive
though not necessarily obscene and upheld the commission's power to
ban such indecent broadcasts. Justice Stevens, for the majority, in
reaffirming that the First Amendment does not protect all speech and
that broadcasting, in contrast with other modes of communication, receives the least protection, observed:

> [T]he broadcasting media have established a uniquely per-
> vasive presence in the lives of all Americans. Patently
> offensive indecent material presented over the airwaves
> confronts the citizen, not only in public, but also in the pri-

vacy of the home, where the individual's right to be let
alone plainly outweighs the First Amendment rights of
the intruder. [54]

Justice Stevens continued by adding, "To say that one may avoid further offense by turning off the radio when he hears indecent language
is like saying that the remedy for an assault is to run away after the
first blow. One may hang up on an indecent phone call, but that op-
tion does not give the caller a constitutional immunity or avoid a
harm that has already taken place. "[55] Similarly, Justice Powell observed, "broadcasting—unlike most other forms of communication—
comes directly into the home, the one place where people ordinarily
have the right not to be assaulted by uninvited and offensive sights
and sounds. "[56] By contrast, dissenting Justices Brennan and Marshall argued that the majority misconceived the nature of individuals'
interests both in privacy and listening to public broadcasts: "[t]he
radio can be turned off."

> Although an individual's decision to allow public radio com-
> munications into his home undoubtedly does not abrogate
> all of his privacy interests, the residual privacy interests
> he retains vis-a-vis the communication he voluntarily ad-
> mits into his home are surely no greater than those of the
> people present in the corridor of the Los Angeles court-
> house in Cohen who bore witness to the words "Fuck the
> Draft" emblazoned across Cohen's jacket. Their privacy
> interests were held insufficient to justify punishing Cohen
> for his offensive communication. [57]

The second major criticism levied against the Court's analysis
of privacy claims is that insufficient consideration has been given to
the content of speech considered intrusive. As Stanley, Cohen, and
their progeny indicate, the Court's reliance on proprietary interests
in legitimating privacy claims in part permitted it to avoid evaluating
the content of speech considered intrusive. The Court in general
maintains that "a central tenet of the First Amendment [is] that the
government must remain neutral in the marketplace of ideas, "[58] and,
specifically, in Cohen emphasized that it would not "indulge the facile
assumption that one can forbid particular words without also running
a substantial risk of suppressing ideas in the process. "[59] Nevertheless, as the majority in Pacifica apparently accepted, some scholars
argue that the content of speech should be considered in balancing
claims to privacy and free speech. In Cohen and Pacifica the profanity was unconscionable and individuals had reasonable expectations
not to have to suffer such intrusions upon their moral sensibilities.

Accordingly, Thomas Emerson argues that First Amendment protection should not extend to individuals who thrust allegedly obscene material upon unwilling or captive audiences:

> Ordinarily an individual seeking to exercise the right of
> expression is allowed considerable leeway in obtaining ac-
> cess to other persons, whether or not such persons have
> indicated a desire to receive the communication. . . .
> Why, then, should erotic communication be considered to
> pose any different problem? The answer lies in the inten-
> sity of the psychological forces that pervade our society
> in the area of sex. . . . The notion of a "captive audience,"
> compelled to see or hear erotic communications is intol-
> erable to us. [60]

Likewise, Zechariah Chafee urges that "profanity and indecent talk and pictures, which do not form an essential part of any exposition of ideas, . . . are criminal, not because of the ideas they communicate, but like acts because of their immediate consequences to the five senses."[61]

Such criticisms encourage the Court to import into its privacy analysis what Harry Kalven, Jr., termed the "two level theory" of the First Amendment—namely, that the amendment protects some but not all speech.[62] The First Amendment does not protect obscenity, for example, because of the materials' intrusiveness upon individuals' expectations of privacy, but rather because of the content of obscenity per se. Prior to _Pacifica_, the Supreme Court "never found [individuals'] privacy interests of such moment to warrant the suppression of speech on privacy grounds."[63] Individuals' privacy claims to either possess allegedly obscene and indecent materials, as in _Stanley_, or to secure protection against mailings of offensive materials, as in _Rowan_, were considered apart from the nature of the materials. Individuals' privacy claims were legitimated on the basis of their privacy expectations in their homes, not on the basis of the content of materials considered intrusive or offensive. In holding that the Federal Communications Commission may assert a privacy rationale for banning allegedly offensive broadcasts, the majority in _Pacifica_ collapsed analysis of individuals' privacy expectations with evaluations of the content of speech, thereby permitting governmental regulation of communications media and actions for the enforcement of public morality. As dissenting Justice Brennan observed, "the visage of the censor is all too discernible here"; indeed, _Pacifica_ "permits majoritarian tastes completely to preclude a protected message from entering the homes of a receptive, unoffended minority."[64] The majority in _Pacifica_, moreover, distorts both privacy claims and the constitutional law of privacy insofar as it implies that individuals have an unqualified right to control personal experiences and prohibit offensive intrusions in their homes. Privacy litigation under the First, Fourth, and Fifth Amendments, as well as the political ideal of privacy, establishes that individuals' privacy claims, even in their homes, are conditional and circumscribed by competing claims and rights.

Associational Privacy

The First Amendment's provision for "the right of the people peaceably to assemble" is perhaps the closest approximation to a constitutional guarantee for a right to association and protection for individuals' associational privacy. Yet, a right to association is a logical extension of the First Amendment's guarantees for the "full and equal rights of conscience" and the social practices of citizens. As Alexis de Tocqueville observed in his historic political and social commentary:

> The most natural privilege of a man next to the right of acting for himself, is that of combining his exertions with those of his fellow creatures and of acting in common with them. The right of association therefore appears to be as almost inalienable in its nature as the right of personal liberty. No legislator can attack it without impairing the foundations of society. [65]

Although de Tocqueville found that in "no country in the world has the principle of association been more successfully used or more unsparingly applied to a multitude of different objects, than in America" the authors of the Constitution and the Bill of Rights did not envision, nor did they provide for, an unlimited right to association. [66] Judicial interpretation nevertheless established a First Amendment right of association, including protection for individuals' expectations of associational privacy, as implicit in the founding principles and the guarantees of the First Amendment. As the Court observed in Sweezy v. New Hampshire: "Our form of government is built on the premise that every citizen shall have the right to engage in political expression and association. This right was enshrined in the First Amendment of the Bill of Rights." [67]

Individuals' claims to free association and associational privacy, unlike claims against public intrusions, do not compete with other First Amendment interests such as free speech or religious exercise. Rather, claims to associational privacy logically extend the express rights guaranteed by the First Amendment. Moreover, unlike privacy claims against unwanted intrusions by solicitors that register a concern for the intrinsic worth of personal privacy in one's home, claims to associational privacy may represent interests in both the instrumental and intrinsic value of privacy. Accordingly, in developing constitutional protection for associational privacy, the Supreme Court initially legitimated only a First Amendment right of association, thereby protecting personal privacy as a derivative value. Subsequently, as individuals increasingly asserted a right to nondisclosure of their associational memberships, the Court acknowledged First Amendment protection for associational privacy per se, thus recognizing its intrinsic value.

Actually, the initial claim to the privacy of associations was raised under the Fourteenth Amendment's "due process" clause (see Chapter 5). In 1922 a "service letter" law, requiring every corporation with which the state conducted business to provide a letter explaining the exact reason for an employee's departure from the firm, was challenged as violating a "liberty of silence" under the Fourteenth Amendment. [68] The Supreme Court, however, rejected the argument that any constitutional provision conferred such a right of silence or a right of "privacy upon either person or corporations." Subsequent decisions established that corporations have no constitutional rights to associational privacy, yet individual members of a corporation may have valid claims to associational privacy. [69]

The Supreme Court formally recognized a First Amendment right of associational privacy in 1958 in NAACP v. Alabama; [70] however, the basis for its recognition was laid in the preceding 37 years with judicial enforcement of claims to association regarding religious exercise, where individuals associated for the purpose of forming or supporting political parties, and where employees associated for collective bargaining. [71] In NAACP v. Alabama, Alabama required the National Association for the Advancement of Colored People (NAACP) to produce documents and records, including membership lists, but the NAACP refused to produce its membership lists and was held in contempt of court. The Supreme Court in reversing the contempt citation held that the rights of association and associational privacy are ancillary to express First Amendment freedoms. Justice Harlan, speaking for a unanimous Court, found compulsory disclosure of the NAACP's membership lists a violation of its members' right to lawful association, stating: "Inviolability of privacy in group association may in many circumstances be indispensable to the preservation of freedom of association, particularly where a group espouses dissident beliefs." [72] Two years later, the Court affirmed in Bates v. City of Little Rock and Shelton v. Tucker that compelled disclosures of membership lists diminishes individuals' privacy of association and dilutes their freedom of association under the First Amendment.[73] In <u>Shelton</u> the majority held as overbroad an Arkansas statute requiring as a condition of employment that every teacher file an affidavit listing all organizations in the last five years in which he or she was a member. Justice Stewart, for the majority, pointed out that such mandatory disclosures might bring community pressures to bear on teachers belonging to unpopular organizations and therefore not only diminish their privacy interests but also causally affect their future engagements and activities: "[T]o compel a teacher to disclose his every associational tie is to impair that teacher's right of free association, a right closely allied to freedom of speech, and a right which, like free speech, lies at the foundation of a free society."[74]

The Court in <u>NAACP</u> v. <u>Alabama</u>, however, was forced to distinguish a 1928 decision, <u>Bryant</u> v. <u>Zimmerman</u>, which upheld a New York anti-Klu Klux Klan statute requiring an oath-bound organization to submit membership lists on the basis of the illegal nature of the Klan's activities.[75] Actually, <u>Bryant</u> along with several other decisions in the 1930s provided the basis for the Court's denial of claims to freedom of association and associational privacy whenever individuals' associations were found to manifest unlawful purposes. In <u>De Jonge</u> v. <u>Oregon</u>, for example, the Court reiterated that "[t]he right of peaceable assembly is a right cognate to those of free speech and free press and is equally fundamental," but the right of association may be subject to limitations where associations are used "to incite violence and crime."[76] De Jonge suggested that the principal criterion for constitutionally protected associational privacy was whether individuals associate peaceably for a lawful purpose and refrain from inciting violence and crime.

As Madison had expressed fears over private associations' potential to encourage factionalism and insurrection, so too the Supreme Court through the 1950s in the "subversive activities" cases upheld the government's power to require disclosure of membership lists and activities when individuals associated for "subversive" purposes or engaged in illegal activities. <u>Watkins</u> v. <u>United States</u> illustrates the Court's different evaluation of claims to associational privacy by individuals belonging to allegedly subversive organizations.[77] Watkins, a labor organizer, refused to testify before a congressional investigating committee about former associates who might have been members of the Communist party. The Court upheld Congress's power to compel personal information about individuals' associations, but held that congressional investigations must have a legitimate purpose and any questions asked of an individual must be germane and pertinent to the investigation.[78] Subsequently, the Court upheld state investigating committees' compelled disclosures of membership lists and activities by individuals belonging to allegedly subversive organizations as permissible to ensuring the "self-preservation" of society; "[t]his governmental interest outweighs individual rights in associational privacy which, however real in other circumstances . . . were here tenuous at best."[79] Although in the early 1960s the Court indicated that the balance between governmental demands for personal disclosures and individuals' interests in associational privacy would not always be struck in the favor of the "public interest,"[80] the Court as a matter of policy upheld the government's power to require disclosures of membership lists when investigations had a legitimate purpose and required only pertinent disclosures and a potential danger existed from anonymous memberships in organizations.[81]

The validity of claims to associational privacy thus depended on the nature of an organization's activities and the reasonableness of the required disclosures or restrictions imposed upon an association's members. The Court thereby evolved a policy distinguishing between associations with lawful purposes and activities and those organizations' that were allegedly subversive. Constitutional protection extended to only individuals' associational privacy interests in lawful associations, but not illegal or subversive organizations. The problems inherent with the Court's dichotomy between nonsubversive and subversive organizations, however, became evident in the mid-1960s.

In 1963 <u>Gibson</u> v. <u>Florida Legislative Investigation Committee</u> posed the issue of whether state legislative committees could require a member of a lawful organization, the NAACP, to answer questions relating to infiltration by a subversive organization, the Communist party.[82] Gibson refused to produce NAACP records, arguing that disclosure of membership lists would seriously infringe each member's freedom of association and diminish the practical value of their associational privacy. Justice Goldberg, writing for the Court, distinguished earlier subversive activities cases, which dealt with witnesses' testimony about their past Communist affiliations, and <u>Gibson</u>, in which the object of investigation was not an individual but rather the NAACP as an organization. The Court held that it would not presume the validity of governmental inquiries into associational memberships in legitimate and nonsubversive groups. Instead, the government must establish an "immediate, substantial, and subordinating state interest necessary to sustain its right of inquiry into the membership lists of a nonsubversive organization."[83]

Throughout the 1960s the Warren Court in a number of significant cases further developed the right of association and associational privacy upon the recognition that organizations may have both legal and illegal goals, and thus individual members might be punished for knowing but guiltless behavior.[84] Consequently, individuals have legitimate First Amendment claims to associational privacy when they belong to formal associations or organizations that seek to publicly advance by lawful means religious, political, or economic objectives.

In Griswold v. Connecticut the Court further expanded the contours of associational privacy in order to protect individuals' associations for both public and private purposes, and, thereby, support its denomination of a constitutional right of privacy per se. [85] Justice Douglas, for the majority, argued that the Court had previously "protected forms of 'association' that are not political in the customary sense but pertain to the social, legal and economic benefits of the members," in order to conclude that "[marriage] is an association that promotes a way of life, not causes; a harmony in living, not political faiths; a bilateral loyalty, not commercial or social projects. Yet it is an association for as noble a purpose as any involved in our prior decisions." [86] Griswold thereby extended the contours of constitutional protection afforded religious, political, and economic associations to include protection for individuals' private engagements and activities. Yet, only dicta in Shelton v. Tucker, suggesting that an overbroad statute would require disclosure of every conceivable "associational tie—social, professional, political, avocational or religious," supported the extension of First Amendment-protected associational privacy to solely private engagements. [87]

Griswold's extension of the contours of associational privacy, however, poses several conceptual and constitutional dilemmas. Principally, does a right to associational privacy protect individuals' discrimination in their social relations on the basis of race or religion; and, if so, to what extent may public policies promote antidiscrimination in individuals' social relations? Discrimination is indeed a dimension of personal privacy; as John Plamenatz observed:

> By privacy I mean the opportunity to choose one's company, and above all to avoid uncongenial or unwanted company, which sometimes means all company, or the opportunity to be alone. . . . Except when [privacy] is a claim to solitude, it is essentially a right to discriminate; though, of course, not all discrimination is an exercise of this right. Moreover, a man is not normally held accountable to others for how he exercises it: for example, for inviting some persons and not others into his home. [88]

First Amendment claims to personal and associational privacy reflect individuals' interests in deciding for themselves who they will engage or associate with, as well as what and to whom they will disclose of their personal experiences and activities. Yet, does constitutionally protected associational privacy embrace individuals' interests in discrimination on the basis of race or religion, for example, in private social clubs or schools?

Although Plessy v. Ferguson noted that "social prejudices may [not] be overcome by legislation," [89] twentieth century courts have increasingly legitimated antidiscrimination policies and the protection of "discrete and insular minorities."[90] Moreover, associational rights, including associational privacy, may be circumscribed by governmental regulation of membership requirements, where associations of individuals are forced and where the nature and conduct of the organization is illegal, as well as where associations perpetuate invidious discrimination.[91] The right of association and individuals' expectations of associational privacy do not embrace claims to anonymity, an unqualified liberty of noninterference, but rather claims to an unregulated sphere of lawful activity.

More specifically, the Court has established that constitutional protection for associational privacy is greatest when individuals engage and associate within their homes. First Amendment associational privacy, like Fourth Amendment-protected privacy, thus relies upon an evaluation of the context or locus of individuals' activities and expectations of privacy. Justice Goldberg in Bell v. Maryland, for example, distinguished between restaurants and "private places," such as individuals' homes, in giving protection to the latter, because there exists a "right of every person to close his home or club to any person or to choose his social intimates and business partners solely on the basis of personal prejudice including race."[92] Although the analogy between the home and private social clubs may be subject to criticism, significantly Justice Goldberg focused analysis on the locus of individuals' activities, expectations of privacy, and the nature of governmental regulation imposed upon individuals. Subsequent decisions affirmatively established individuals' claims to association and associational privacy in their homes.[93]

Private associations may be regulated when individuals' activities occur outside their homes, for example, in restaurants, private clubs, or public buildings. "State action" in licensing restaurants and private clubs provides a basis for preventing invidious discrimination by individuals in their private associations. In Garner v. Louisiana concurring Justice Douglas observed: "One can close the doors of his home to anyone he desires. But one who operates an enterprise under a license from a government enjoys a privilege that derives from the people. . . . [T]he necessity of a license shows that the public has rights in respect to those premises. The business is not a matter of mere private concern."[94] Where private clubs serve out-of-state customers, or where food and beverages served or the equipment used are obtained through interstate commerce, the federal government may place restrictions upon discrimination under the "commerce clause."[95] The Thirteenth and Fourteenth Amendments as well as the Civil Rights Act of 1866 also provide constitutional bases for denying individuals' claims to associational privacy with respect to private social clubs and private schools.[96] In 1976 the Court held that Section

1981 of the Civil Rights Act does not violate any constitutionally protected rights of association and privacy when interpreted to forbid ra-
cial discrimination in private schools.[97] The Court reaffirmed the
principle articulated in Norwood v. Harrison: "Invidious private discrimination may be characterized as a form of exercising freedom of
association protected by the First Amendment . . . [yet] it has never
been accorded affirmative constitutional protections."[98] Justice
Stewart, for the Court, emphasized that "the application of § 1981 to
the conduct at issue here—a private school's adherence to a racially
discriminatory admissions policy—does not represent governmental
intrusion into the privacy of the home or a similarly intimate setting."[99]

The Supreme Court, thus, firmly established constitutional protection for associational privacy. Individuals may claim a First
Amendment-protected right of associational privacy, but the government may also intervene when individuals associate for unlawful purposes or engage in illegal activities, whether those activities constitute subversion of the government or invidious discrimination against
other individuals.

Malicious and Mischievous Publications:
"Desperate Hours" for Personal Privacy

Claims to personal privacy against publications of private engagements, unlike claims to associational privacy, compete with
claims to the First Amendment's guarantee of freedom of the press.
Reconciling privacy claims against unwanted publicity with the First
Amendment's provision for freedom of press therefore poses, as
Francis Beytagh points out, the dilemma of determining the limits to
"public disclosures of information about an individual by the news media and the permissible scope of legal protection of that aspect of privacy consistent with the first amendment."[100]

Personal privacy received a modicum of protection in seventeenth and eighteenth century English and colonial common law of
libel, because courts accepted Blackstone's prescription that a man
who "publishes what is improper, mischievous or illegal must suffer
the consequences of his own temerity." Not until the late nineteenth
century were privacy interests distinguished from interests against
defamation, whether by slander or libel, in U.S. tort law.[101] The
Supreme Court, however, refuses to recognize invasions of privacy
by publications as constituting a legal injury apart from the law relating to defamatory statements. Consequently, as traditional common
law relating to publications of what was "improper, mischievous or
illegal" merged interests against defamation and invasion of privacy,

so too in the twentieth century the Supreme Court provides neither a
rule of construction nor legal remedies for constitutionally protected
privacy against unwanted publicity of private engagements.

Individuals' interests in limiting access to and disclosures of
their personal engagements are nevertheless clearly distinguishable
from interests against libelous and slanderous statements. Privacy
claims register individuals' interests in determining for themselves
to whom and what they will disclose of their personal experiences and
engagements. Hence, the truth of a publication should not afford a
legal defense, because the interest protected lies not with any inac-
curacy in disclosure of personal affairs but with the disclosure itself.
As Warren and Brandeis argued, the truth of the publication should
provide no defense in privacy actions, unlike actions for defamation,
because privacy claims are asserted "not merely to prevent inaccurate portrayal of private life, but to prevent its being depicted at all.
. . . The absence of 'malice' in the publisher does not afford a defense."[102] Similarly, Edward Bloustein urged: "The gravamen of
a defamation action is engendering a false opinion about a person,
whether in the mind of one other person or many people. The gravamen in the public disclosure [privacy] cases is degrading a person
by laying his life open to public view."[103] Accordingly, the issue in
privacy cases is whether disclosures of personal engagements are
within "the obvious bounds of propriety and decency" or are sufficiently
"newsworthy" or in the "public interest" to justify an invasion of personal privacy.[104]

By contrast, legal remedies for defamation are afforded because
of the injury done to an individual's reputation; statements are action-
able if they tend "to so harm the reputation of another as to lower him
in the estimation of the community or to deter third persons from associating or dealing with him."[105] The truth of a statement, considered defamatory, therefore provides a complete defense since, at
least theoretically, a true statement will not damage an individual's
reputation in the community. Moreover, the truth of a defamatory
statement affords a defense because of the competing interests in securing and maintaining a free flow of information permitting public
discussion of important issues.

Notwithstanding the different interests and competing values
represented by actions for invasion of privacy and defamation, the
Supreme Court assimilated the two interests in developing the constitutional law of libel. The watershed for constitutional analysis of the
law of libel and its misapplication to privacy claims is the 1964 decision in New York Times v. Sullivan.[106]

Prior to the New York Times ruling it was well established that
defamatory statements "are no essential part of any exposition of
ideas, and are of such slight social value as a step to truth that any

benefit that may be derived from them is clearly outweighed by the social interest in order and morality"; thus, publishers could be prosecuted in the states for defamatory statements according to state statutes and common law.[107] In New York Times, the Court fashioned a federal rule prohibiting public officials from recovering damages for a defamatory statement, unless they could prove that the statement was made with " 'actual malice'—that is, with knowledge that it was false or with reckless disregard of whether it was false or not."[108] Subsequent decisions applied the "actual malice" rule to "public figures,"[109] but the further attempt by a plurality of the Court to apply the rule to private persons, who participated in events of public interest, failed in 1974 with Gertz v. Robert Welch, Inc.[110]

Gertz afforded some protection for privacy interests insofar as the Court held that a lesser standard of proof was permissible for libel of private individuals than for public officials and public figures. Apparently returning to the New York Times rule, the Court held that a defamation plaintiff who is a "public figure" must show that publication was made with knowledge of its falsity or with reckless disregard for the truth, whereas states may impose a lesser standard of liability with regard to private individuals. Although Gertz was a defamation case, the Court's reasons for distinguishing between "public" and "private" persons are crucial for understanding the constitutional law of libel's derivative protection for privacy interests. The Court justified the distinction between "public officials" or "public figures" and private individuals by pointing out that persons in the "public view" have access to the media in order to counter defamatory statements and also assume the risk of such statements by being in the public view. The Court moreover reiterated the necessity for maintaining a free flow of information with regard to matters of public importance, particularly the activities of public officials and public figures. The Court thus adhered to the New York Times doctrine that restrictions upon the freedom of the press must be considered "against the background of a profound national commitment to the principle that debate on public issues should be uninhibited, robust, and wide-open, and that that it may well include vehement, caustic, and sometimes unpleasantly sharp attacks on government and public officers."[111]

Still, the Court's fashioning of a category of public figures remains ambiguous. In an apparent effort to further define the concept of a public figure, the Court in Gertz observed: "In some instances an individual may achieve such pervasive fame or notoriety that he becomes a public figure for all purposes and in all contexts. More commonly an individual voluntarily injects himself or is drawn into a particular public controversy and thereby becomes a public figure for a limited range of issues."[112] The Court affirmed Gertz's claim, since he was a private attorney who was neither a public figure, generally, nor in regard to the specific circumstances of the case. Subsequent decisions by the Burger Court indicate that it will find instances in which private individuals become public figures exceedingly rare. [113]

The Court's treatment of libel and privacy claims results from its rejection of an absolutist interpretation of the First Amendment as well as of ad hoc balancing. [114] Instead, the Court embraces "a balancing process on the definitional rather on litigation or ad hoc basis."[115] Definitional balancing divides "speech into categories: that which is worthy enough to require the application of first amendment protection and that which is beneath first amendment concerns."[116] When applied to privacy issues, definitional balancing requires the development of a rather complex set of crosscutting rules for both distinguishing between two varieties of speech, First Amendment protected and unprotected speech, and two types of individuals, "public" and "private" individuals. In other words, the Supreme Court must define some speech (libelous, obscene, privacy-invading) as laying outside the ambit of First Amendment protection and then superimpose the additional distinction between speech concerning public and private individuals.

The Court's framework for definitional balancing nevertheless mistakenly draws the same boundaries for statements that are defamatory and those that constitute an invasion of privacy. Rather, the Court misapplies its theory of libel to privacy claims. Indeed, in Time Inc. v. Hill, the Court emphasized its reluctance to develop an additional standard for reconciling conflicts between freedom of press and privacy other than that previously drawn with respect to the conflict between freedom of press and libel: "We create a risk of serious impairment of the indispensable service of a free press in a free society if we saddle the press with the impossible burden of verifying to a certainty the facts associated in news articles with a person's name, picture, or portrait, particularly as related to nondefamatory matter."[117]

Time Inc. v. Hill, the first of three privacy cases to reach the Supreme Court, illustrates the Court's endeavor to evade privacy issues by assimilating privacy and defamation interests. The Hills sued Life magazine for a pictorial essay on the opening of a play, The Desperate Hours, in which the play was identified with the Hill family's experiences as hostages of three escaped convicts. The Life account, however, failed to differentiate between the truth and fiction in the play. Hills sued, on a state privacy statute, for invasion of privacy on portrayal of the family in "false-light."[118] The Supreme Court, applying standards relating to defamation, reversed a lower court's award to the Hills on the ground that the opening of the play was a matter of public interest. Not only did the majority refuse to address Hills' privacy claims per se, but Justice Harlan, in a separate opinion, went so far as to say that <u>Hill</u> was "not privacy litigation in its truest sense." In a concurring opinion, Justice Douglas, usually an ardent defender of personal privacy, added: "It seems to me irrelevant to talk of any right of privacy in this context. Here a private person is catapulted into the news by events over which he has no control. He and his activities are then in the public domain. . . . Such privacy as a person has normally ceases."[119] Only dissenting Justice Fortas argued for recognition and protection of privacy against disclosures of personal affairs by publication:

> I do not believe that the First Amendment precludes effective protection of the right of privacy. . . . There are great and important values in our society, none of which is greater than those reflected in the First Amendment, but which are also fundamental and entitled to this Court's careful respect and protection. Among these is the right of privacy, . . . the right to be let alone; to live one's life as one chooses, free from assault, intrusion or invasion except as can be justified by the clear needs of community living under a government of law.[120]

Notwithstanding Justice Fortas's arguments, rather ironically, the Warren Court was singularly unimpressed by Hills' privacy claim in a year, 1967, in which the Court in <u>Katz</u> gave a broad construction to Fourth Amendment-protected privacy.

Seven years later, in another "false-light" privacy case, the Burger Court avoided the privacy-free press issue. In <u>Cantrell</u> v. <u>Forest City Publishing Company</u>, Margaret Cantrell and her children brought an invasion of privacy suit against the Forest City Publishing Company for a follow-up story on the Silver Bridge disaster that claimed the life of her husband.[121] The story inaccurately portrayed the Cantrells as destitute after the bridge collapsed, and Margaret Cantrell claimed that the story invaded her family's privacy and, by misrepresentation, demeaned them. The trial judge instructed the jury that the defendant would be liable only if the statement was made with knowledge of or reckless disregard for the truth (the standard established by <u>New York Times</u> for libel actions). The Court could have elaborated a lesser standard for liability here, following <u>Gertz</u>, and discussed its application to privacy claims.

Instead, the Court, while allowing the Cantrells, unlike the Hills, to prevail, avoided the privacy-free press issue by concluding that the case presented "[n]o occasion to consider whether a state may constitutionally apply a more relaxed standard of liability for a publisher or broadcaster of false statements injurious to a private individual under a false-light theory of invasion of privacy, or whether the constitutional standard announced in Time Inc. v. Hill applies to all false-light cases."[122]

In the next year the Court again evaded the conflict between privacy and freedom of press. Unlike Hill and Cantrell, Cox Broadcasting Corp. v. Cohn raised a public disclosure tort.[123] Cohn, the father of a deceased rape victim, sought damages, under a Georgia statute making it a misdemeanor to name or identify a rape victim, for invasion of his privacy by the Cox Broadcasting Corporation's identification of his daughter as a rape victim during a television broadcast. Justice White, for the Court, did not simply dismiss the privacy claim; he noted that "the century has experienced a strong tide running in favor of the so-called right of privacy" and that state-created rights of privacy possess "impressive credentials." However, he narrowed the issue so as to avoid balancing privacy and freedom of press claims:

> In this sphere of collision between claims of privacy and those of the free press, the interests on both sides are plainly rooted in the traditions and significant concerns of our society. Rather than address the broader questions whether truthful publications may ever be subject to civil or criminal liability consistently with the First and Fourteenth Amendments, . . . it is appropriate to focus on the narrower interface between press and privacy that this case presents, namely, whether the State may impose sanctions on the accurate publication of a rape victim obtained from public records.[124]

Notwithstanding the privacy statute here, Justice White concluded that "by placing the information in the public domain on official court records . . . [Georgia] must be presumed to have concluded that the public interest was thereby being served."[125] Cox thus established that official records and documents must be open to the public, so as to provide basic information about government operations, regardless of any individual's privacy claims to information contained in such records and documents. Although Time Inc. v. Firestone held that publishers may be held liable for inaccurately printing information obtained from public records, the Burger Court continues to deny privacy claims against disclosures of personal affairs gathered from information contained in public records.[126]

The Supreme Court thus avoids formulation of a rule by which to reconcile the conflict between privacy and freedom of press and continues to assimilate privacy and defamation interests. Individuals' nondefamatory privacy claims against publication of personal affairs, therefore, receive no constitutional protection, but they may receive protection where states enact privacy statutes or where privacy interests are conjoined with an action for defamation.[127] Moreover, while both Gertz and Cox indicate that states may enact legislation with regard to defamation and invasion of privacy of private individuals, Justice White's opinion in Cox reflects the Court's approach, since New York Times, of allowing only a narrow application of state-created and common law rights of privacy within the constitutional system of free expression. The Burger Court, for example, upheld governmental publication and circulation of names and photographs of individuals suspected or convicted of criminal activities. Although the Court previously held that local officials could not post notice that sales and gifts of liquor to certain persons were forbidden unless those individuals were given adequate notice and hearing, in Paul v. Davis it permitted police to distribute among local merchants a flyer captioned "Active Shoplifters," containing names and "mug shot" photos of individuals arrested for criminal activities in shopping centers.[128] Justice Rehnquist, for the Court, rejected privacy claims under the First, Fourth, Fifth, Ninth, and Fourteenth Amendments on the ground that "[the privacy] claim is based not upon any challenge to the State's ability to restrict [an individual's] freedom of action in a sphere contended to be 'private,' but instead on a claim that the State may not publicize a record of an official act such as an arrest."[129] Paul, along with Cox, as well as Cohen and Stanley, thus underscore that the controlling considerations in validating privacy claims remain the locus and status of an individual relative to the offensive disclosure or intrusion. Individuals' claims against publications relying on public records as the source of information will not succeed, regardless of individuals' privacy interests, because the information already exists as a matter of public record and, therefore, in a sense is already publicly known. Publications of other defamatory or privacy-invading statements, however, may be regulated by the states, because the status and locus of private individuals, in contrast with public officials or "public figures," within the community afford no effective means of countering defamatory and privacy-invading statements.

PRIVACY AND THE RIGHTS OF CONSCIENCE

Consistent with the First Amendment's guarantees for individuals' rights of conscience, the Supreme Court has extended protection to individuals' claims to associational privacy and freedom from compelled disclosure of associational activities. First Amendment privacy claims, like Fourth Amendment interests, are successful principally where actual intrusions are made on individuals' activities and receive greatest protection when intrusions occur on private property, as with solicitors' intrusions upon the privacy and proprietary interests of homeowners. Individuals' privacy interests in information concerning their activities and associations contained in public records—such as arrest records or documents of judicial proceedings—receive no protection because the information is a matter of public record and, hence, no intrusion upon individuals' activities occurs in obtaining the information. Individuals' privacy claims against public disclosures of personal affairs by the media also fail. Privacy claims against such public disclosures fail both because the Supreme Court assimilates individuals' interests against defamation and invasion of privacy and because historically the Court has been reluctant to consider as constitutionally significant the difference between intrusions upon and disclosures of personal affairs. In this regard, Justice Harlan's opinion in Time Inc. v. Hill remains instructive. Justice Harlan observed: "To me this is not 'privacy' litigation in its truest sense. . . . No claim is made that there was an intrusion upon the Hills' solitude or private affairs in order to obtain information for publication. The power of the state to control and remedy such intrusion for news-gathering purposes cannot be denied."[130] The Court considers as constitutionally significant only intrusions upon but not mere disclosures of personal affairs. Similarly, Justice Rehnquist in Paul v. Davis refused to consider how disclosures of personal information may causally affect individuals' future activities.

The Supreme Court's analysis of First Amendment freedoms, like Fourth and Fifth Amendment procedural safeguards, thus fails to adequately consider the changing nature of individuals' privacy interests in our increasingly information-oriented society. The collection, disclosure, and publication of information relating to individuals' activities apparently is constitutionally permissible, if no actual intrusion takes place in the process of acquiring the information. In California Bankers Association v. Shultz and Laird v. Tatum, the Burger Court expressly refused to consider, respectively, First Amendment claims against the record-keeping and -reporting requirements of the Bank Secrecy Act and the army's collection and maintenance of information on members of activist political groups.[131] In Laird v. Tatum the plaintiffs alleged that army surveillance, data collection, and information storage chilled their exercise of First Amendment freedoms "by invading their privacy, damaging their reputations, adversely affecting their employment and their opportunity for employment, and in other ways" affected their lives. The army had employed surveillance techniques including infiltrating civil rights groups and photographing and electronically monitoring groups' public meetings and demonstrations in order to generate a portfolio of "political activists." The Court nevertheless rejected the plaintiffs' claim because it found no justifiable controversy, since the plaintiffs failed to show any ob-

jective harm or threat of specific future harm. By contrast, in
United States v. United States District Court the Court affirmed that
without prior judicial approval governmental surveillance of individuals' activities by means of wiretaps constitutes an unreasonable intrusion under the Fourth Amendment.[132]

When the factual situations of Laird and United States District
Court are compared, it appears that personal information may receive constitutional protection only when, as in United States District
Court, the government intrudes upon individuals' activities and private
property, but not where, as in Laird, information is gathered solely
from observing and recording—whether photographically or electronically—individuals' activities in public places, such as public streets,
parks, or meeting halls. A property bias thus underlies constitutional
interpretation of First Amendment guarantees for "the full and equal
rights of conscience" insofar as the Supreme Court recognizes privacy
claims against intrusions upon personal affairs but provides little support for claims against disclosures—whether by the mass media or
the government—of individuals' activities. Accordingly, the developing constitutional law of privacy under the First Amendment, like the
Fourth and Fifth Amendments, provides little protection for individuals' interests in informational privacy.

NOTES

1. Irving Brant, The Bill of Rights: Its Origins and Meaning
(New York: Mentor, 1965) 84.
2. Thomas I. Emerson, The System of Freedom of Expression
(New York: Vintage, 1970) 549.
3. Ibid., at 556.
4. See also Edward J. Bloustein, "First Amendment and Privacy: The Supreme Court Justice and the Philosopher," 28 Rutgers
Law Review 41 (1974).
5. See Brant, The Bill of Rights, at 227–31.
6. Robertson v. Baldwin, 165 U.S. 275, 281 (1897).
7. Leonard W. Levy, Legacy of Suppression: Freedom of
Speech and Press in Early American History (Cambridge, Mass.:
Harvard University Press, Belknap Press, 1960).
8. Sir William Blackstone, Commentaries on the Laws of England, book 4 (Oxford: Clarendon Press, 1766) at 151–52.
9. See generally David H. Flaherty, Privacy in Colonial New
England (Charlottesville: University Press of Virginia, 1972).
10. Quoted in Pennsylvania and the Federal Constitution, ed.
J. B. McMaster and F. D. Stone (Philadelphia: Historical Society
of Pennsylvania, 1888) 308.

11. Thomas Jefferson, in The Papers of Thomas Jefferson, ed. Julian P. Boyd (Princeton, N.J.: Princeton University Press, 1950) 545-46 (emphasis added).

12. Thomas Jefferson, "Notes on the State of Virginia," in The Works of Thomas Jefferson, fed. ed., vol. 4 (New York: Putnam, 1904-1905) at 78. See Walter Berns, The First Amendment and the Future of American Democracy (New York: Basic Books, 1976).

13. See James Madison, The Federalist, ed. Clinton Rossiter, no. 10 (New York: New American Library, 1961); and discussion in Chapter 1.

14. Chaplinsky v. New Hampshire, 315 U.S. 568, 571-72 (1942).

15. New York Times v. Sullivan, 376 U.S. 254, 279-80 (1964). See also Robertson v. Baldwin, 165 U.S. 275, 281 (1897); Near v. Minnesota, 283 U.S. 697, 715 (1931); Chaplinsky v. New Hampshire, 315 U.S. 568, 572 (1942); Beauharnais v. Illinois, 343 U.S. 250 (1952); Pennekamp v. Florida, 328 U.S. 331, 349-49 (1946); Roth v. United States, 354 U.S. 476, 486-87 (1957); Times Film Corp. v. City of Chicago, 365 U.S. 43, 48 (1961); Konigsberg v. State Bar of California, 366 U.S. 36, 49 (1961).

16. Dennis v. United States, 341 U.S. 494 (1951).

17. See Robertson v. Baldwin, 165 U.S. 275 (1897), Dennis v. United States, 341 U.S. 494, 524 (1951) (Frankfurter, J., con. op.) (accepted Blackstone's position with regard to First Amendment application); Dennis v. United States 341 U.S. 494 (1951), Gitlow v. New York, 268 U.S. 652 (1925), Whitney v. California, 274 U.S. 357 (1927) (all relied on standard of "reasonableness of legislation" in balancing First Amendment freedoms, but Gitlow and Whitney also utilized a "bad tendency" test for claims to free speech); Schenck v. United States, 249 U.S. 47 (1919), Abrams v. United States, 250 U.S. 616 (1919); Whitney v. California, 274 U.S. 357 (1927) (applied "clear and present danger test" in balancing First Amendment); Palko v. Connecticut, 302 U.S. 319 (1937), Jones v. Opelika, 316 U.S. 584 (1942) (Stone, J.), Murdock v. Pennsylvania, 319 U.S. 105 (1943) (Douglas, J.), Thomas v. Collins, 323 U.S. 516 (1945) (Rutledge, J.) (maintained that First Amendment freedoms have a "preferred position" in our constitutional system); American Communications Association v. Douds, 339 U.S. 382, 452-53 (1950), Dennis v. United States, 341 U.S. 494, 579-81 (1951), Beauharnais v. Illinois, 343 U.S. 250, 268-70 (1952), Barenblatt v. United States, 360 U.S. 109, 140-44 (1959), Konigsberg v. State Bar of California, 366 U.S. 36 (1961) (wherin Justice Black argued for an absolutist-literalist interpretation of the First Amendment).

18. See Chaplinsky v. New Hampshire, 315 U.S. 568, 572 (1942), Lewis v. New Orleans, 415 U.S. 130, 132 (1974) (libel and "fighting

words"); <u>Cantwell</u> v. <u>Connecticut</u>, 310 U.S. 296, 309 (1940) ("personal abuse"); <u>Communist Party</u> v. <u>Whitcomb</u>, 414 U.S. 441, 448 (1974), <u>Brandenberg</u> v. <u>Ohio</u>, 395 U.S. 444, 447 (1969) ("inciting imminent lawless action"); <u>Roth</u> v. <u>United States</u>, 354 U.S. 476 (1957), <u>Miller</u> v. <u>California</u>, 413 U.S. 15, 26 (1973) (obscenity).

    19. See William Prosser, "Privacy," 48 <u>California Law Review</u> 383 (1960).

    20. See <u>Davis</u> v. <u>Beason</u>, 113 U.S. 333 (1890); and <u>Reynolds</u> v. <u>United States</u>, 98 U.S. 145 (1879).

    21. <u>Gilbert</u> v. <u>Minnesota</u>, 254 U.S. 352 (1920).

    22. Idem, at 365 (Brandeis, J., dis. op.).

    23. <u>Schneider</u> v. <u>New Jersey</u>, 308 U.S. 147 (1939).

    24. <u>Martin</u> v. <u>City of Struthers</u>, 319 U.S. 141 (1943).

    25. See <u>Marsh</u> v. <u>Alabama</u>, 326 U.S. 501, 507 (1946); and <u>Amalgamated Food Employees Union</u> v. <u>Logan Valley Plaza</u>, 391 U.S. 308, 316–19 (1968).

    26. <u>Gregory</u> v. <u>City of Chicago</u>, 394 U.S. 111 (1969).

    27. Idem, at 125–26 (Black, J., con. op.).

    28. Organization for a Better Austin v. Keefe, 402 U.S. 415 (1971).

    29. Idem, at 419–20.

    30. <u>Breard</u> v. <u>Alexandria</u>, 341 U.S. 622 (1951).

    31. But see <u>Virginia Pharmacy Board</u> v. <u>Virginia Consumer Council</u>, 425 U.S. 748 (1976) (wherein the Court held that in some respects "commercial speech" will be accorded First Amendment protection). See also <u>Buckley</u> v. <u>Valeo</u>, 424 U.S. 1, 17–18, 44–45 (1976); <u>Bigelow</u> v. <u>Virginia</u>, 421 U.S. 809 (1975); <u>Pittsburg Press Co.</u> v. <u>Pittsburg Commission on Human Relations</u>, 413 U.S. 376 (1973); <u>Valentine</u> v. <u>Chrestensen</u>, 316 U.S. 52 (1942).

    32. <u>Packer Corporation</u> v. <u>Utah</u>, 285 U.S. 105 (1932).

    33. Idem, at 110.

    34. See Chapter 1; and <u>Federal Communications Commission</u> v. <u>Pacifica Foundation</u>, 98 S. Ct. 3026 (1978).

    35. <u>Saia</u> v. <u>New York</u>, 334 U.S. 558 (1948).

    36. <u>Kovacs</u> v. <u>Cooper</u>, 336 U.S. 77 (1949).

    37. Idem, at 86.

    38. <u>Public Utilities Commission</u> v. <u>Pollak</u>, 343 U.S. 451 (1952).

    39. Idem, at 463–65.

    40. <u>Cohen</u> v. <u>California</u>, 403 U.S. 15 (1971); <u>Erznoznik</u> v. <u>City of Jacksonville</u>, 422 U.S. 205 (1975).

    41. <u>Cohen</u> v. <u>California</u>, 403 U.S. 15, at 21 (1971) (footnotes omitted).

    42. <u>Erznoznik</u> v. <u>City of Jacksonville</u>, 422 U.S. 205, at 211–12 (1975).

    43. See also <u>Rabe</u> v. <u>Washington</u>, 405 U.S. 313 (1972) (per curium).

44. Stanley v. Georgia, 394 U.S. 557 (1969). See also Wooley
v. Maynard, 97 S. Ct. 1428, at 4381 (1977), wherein the Court observed that a state may not "constitutionally require an individual to
participate in the dissemination of an ideological message by display-
ing it on his private property in a manner and for the express purpose
that it be observed and read by the public."

45. Stanley v. Georgia, 394 U.S. 557, at 565 (1969).

46. Idem, at 564–65.

47. See United States v. Thirty-Seven Photographs, 402 U.S.
363 (1971), United States v. Reidel, 402 U.S. 351 (1971) (rejected
privacy claims to sell obscene materials); United States v. Orito,
413 U.S. 139 (1973) (transporting obscene materials by interstate
commerce); United States v. Twelve 200-Foot Reels of Super 8mm
Film, 413 U.S. 123 (1973) (transporting obscene materials through
international borders); Paris Adult Theater I v. Slaton, 413 U.S. 49
(1973) (rejected privacy claims extended to adult theaters). But see
Marks v. United States, 97 S. Ct. 990, 996 (1977) (Stevens, J., con-
curred in part and dissented in part), which characterized as "somewhat illogical" the "premise that a person may be prosecuted . . .
for providing another with material he has a constitutional right to
possess."

48. Rowan v. United States Post Office Department, 397 U.S.
728 (1970).

49. Paris Adult Theater I v. Slaton, 413 U.S. 49, at 66–67
(1973).

50. Zechariah Chafee, Jr., Free Speech in the United States
(Cambridge, Mass.: Harvard University Press, 1948) 406.

51. Franklyn Haiman, "Speech v. Privacy: Is There a Right
Not to Be Spoken to?" 67 Northwestern University Law Review 153,
at 178 (1972).

52. Ibid.

53. Federal Communications Commission v. Pacifica Foundation, 98 S. Ct. 3026 (1978).

54. Idem, at 3040.

55. Idem.

56. Idem, at 3045 (Powell, J., con. op.).

57. Idem, at 3049 (Brennan, J., dis. op.), quoting Lehman v.
City of Shaker Heights, 418 U.S. 298, 302 (1974).

58. Idem, at 3038. See also First National Bank v. Bellotti,
98 S. Ct. 1407 (1978).

59. Cohen v. California, 403 U.S. 15, at 26 (1971).

60. Emerson, System of Freedom of Expression, at 500.

61. Chafee, Free Speech, at 150.

62. See Harry Kalven, Jr., "The Metaphysics of the Law of Obscenity," in Supreme Court Review, ed. Philip Kurland (Chicago:

University of Chicago Press, 1960) 1-45. See also Prosser, "Privacy."

63. Federal Communications Commission v. Pacifica Foundation, 98 S. Ct. 3026, at 3049 (Brennan, J., dis. op.).

64. Idem.

65. Alexis de Tocqueville, in Democracy in America, ed. Phillips Bradley, vol. 2 (New York: Vintage Books, 1945) 196.

66. Ibid., at 197. See also The Federalist Papers, ed. Clinton Rossiter, nos. 6, 9, 10, 21, 51, 59, 71 (New York: New American Library, 1961).

67. Sweezy v. New Hampshire, 354 U.S. 234, 250 (1951).

68. Prudential Insurance Company v. Cheek, 259 U.S. 530 (1922).

69. See Hale v. Henkel, 201 U.S. 43 (1906); United States v. White, 322 U.S. 694 (1944); United States v. Morton Salt Co., 338 U.S. 632 (1950) (Fourth Amendment holdings); but see NAACP v. Alabama, 357 U.S. 449 (1958).

70. NAACP v. Alabama, 357 U.S. 449 (1958).

71. See Niemotko v. Maryland, 340 U.S. 268 (1951), West Virginia State Board of Education v. Barnette, 319 U.S. 624 (1943) (recognized religious associations); Smith v. Allwright, 321 U.S. 649 (1944), Terry v. Adams, 345 U.S. 461 (1953) (political associations); the National Labor Relations (Wagner) Act, Ch. 372 1, 49 Stat. 449 and the Labor-Management Relations (Taft-Hartley) Act of 1947, 29 U.S.C. § 151 (1964) codified the right to associate in labor unions (see also Brotherhood of Railroad Trainmen v. Virginia, 377 U.S. 1 [1964]).

72. NAACP v. Alabama, 357 U.S. 449, at 462 (1958).

73. Bates v. City of Little Rock, 361 U.S. 516 (1960); and Shelton v. Tucker, 364 U.S. 479 (1960).

74. Shelton v. Tucker, 364 U.S. 479, at 485-86 (1960).

75. Bryant v. Zimmerman, 278 U.S. 63 (1928).

76. De Jonge v. Oregon, 299 U.S. 353, 364 (1937). See also Stromberg v. California, 283 U.S. 359 (1931); and Herndon v. Lowry, 301 U.S. 242 (1937).

77. Watkins v. United States, 354 U.S. 178 (1957).

78. Idem, at 198-99. See also Sinclair v. United States, 279 U.S. 263 (1929); McGrain v. Dougherty, 273 U.S. 135 (1927); In re Chapman, 166 U.S. 661 (1897); Kilbourn v. Thompson, 103 U.S. 168 (1881).

79. Uphaus v. Wyman, 360 U.S. 72, 81 (1959). See also Barenblatt v. United States, 360 U.S. 109 (1959).

80. See Talley v. California, 362 U.S. 60 (1960) (upholding anonymous handbills).

81. See Scales v. United States, 367 U.S. 203 (1961); Communist Party v. Subversive Activities Control Board, 367 U.S. 1 (1961).

82. Gibson v. Florida Legislative Investigation Committee, 372 U.S. 539 (1963).

83. Idem, at 546. See also Elfbrandt v. Russell, 384 U.S. 11 (1966).

84. See United States v. Robel, 389 U.S. 258 (1967); NAACP v. Button, 371 U.S. 415, 431 (1963); Brotherhood of Railroad Trainmen v. Virginia, 377 U.S. 1 (1964); Baird v. State Bar of Arizona, 401 U.S. 1 (1971); and In re Stolar, 401 U.S. 23 (1971). But see Abood v. Detroit Board of Education, 97 S. Ct. 1782 (1977) (upholding forced union dues for public employees); Law Students Civil Rights Research Council v. Wadmont, 401 U.S. 154 (1971) (upholding "character and general fitness" requirement for admission to bar).

85. Griswold v. Connecticut, 381 U.S. 479, 483 (1965) discussed in Chapter 5.

86. Idem, at 486.

87. Shelton v. Tucker, 364 U.S. 479, at 488 (1960).

88. John Plamenatz, "Privacy and Laws against Discrimination," 4 Rivista Internazionale di Filosofia del Diritto 443, 444 (1974).

89. Plessy v. Ferguson, 163 U.S. 537, 551 (1896).

90. See United States v. Carolene Products Co., 304 U.S. 144, 152 n. 4 (1938) (Stone, J.); and, generally, Walter F. Murphy and C. Herman Pritchett, Courts, Judges and Politics, 2d ed. (New York: Random House, 1974) 661-62.

91. See Smith v. Allwright, 321 U.S. 649 (1944); Terry v. Adams, 345 U.S. 461 (1953); Railway Employees' Department v. Hanson, 351 U.S. 225 (1956); International Association of Machinists v. Street, 367 U.S. 740 (1961); Lathrop v. Donohue, 367 U.S. 820 (1961); Abood v. Detroit Board of Education, 97 S. Ct. 1782 (1977); Bryant v. Zimmerman, 278 U.S. 63 (1928); Watkins v. United States, 354 U.S. 178 (1957); Scales v. United States, 367 U.S. 203 (1961).

92. Bell v. Maryland, 378 U.S. 226, 312-13 (1964).

93. See Department of Agriculture v. Moreno, 413 U.S. 528 (1973); but see also Village of Belle Terre v. Boraas, 416 U.S. 1 (1974).

94. Garner v. Louisiana, 368 U.S. 157, 184-85 (1961).

95. See Daniel v. Paul, 395 U.S. 298, 305, 308 (1969); Heart of Atlanta Motel, Inc. v. United States, 379 U.S. 241, 280 (1964) (Douglas, J., con. op.).

96. See Jones v. Alfred H. Mayer Company, 392 U.S. 409 (1968) (on possible application of Thirteenth Amendment); United States v. Guest, 383 U.S. 745, 761-62 (1966) (Clark, J., con. op.) (suggesting Fourteenth Amendment application to private social clubs); and Sullivan v. Little Hunting Park, 396 U.S. 229 (1969), and Runyon v. McCrary, 96 S. Ct. 2586 (1976) (relying on Civil Rights Act of 1866, 42 U.S.C. § 1981-82 [1969]).

97. <u>Runyon</u> v. <u>McCrary</u>, 96 S. Ct. 2586 (1976).

98. <u>Norwood</u> v. <u>Harrison</u>, 413 U.S. 455, 470 (1973).

99. <u>Runyon</u> v. <u>McCrary</u>, 96 S. Ct. 2586, at 2598 (1976).

100. Francis X. Beytagh, "Privacy and a Free Press: A Contemporary Conflict in Values," 20 <u>New York Law Forum</u> 453, 453 (1975) (emphasis in original).

101. See Prosser, <u>Law of Torts</u>; and Chapter 1 where the four privacy torts are discussed.

102. Samuel D. Warren and Louis B. Brandeis, "The Right to Privacy," 4 <u>Harvard Law Review</u> 193, 205 (1890); their analysis of privacy is discussed in Chapter 1.

103. Edward Bloustein, "Privacy as an Aspect of Human Dignity: An Answer to Dean Prosser," 39 <u>New York University Law Review</u> 962, 981 (1964).

104. See <u>Rosenbloom</u> v. <u>Metromedia, Inc.</u>, 403 U.S. 29 (1971); <u>Time Inc.</u> v. <u>Hill</u>, 385 U.S. 374 (1974); <u>Gertz</u> v. <u>Robert Welch, Inc.</u>, 418 U.S. 323 (1974).

105. Prosser, <u>Law of Torts</u>, at 737.

106. <u>New York Times</u> v. <u>Sullivan</u>, 376 U.S. 254 (1964).

107. See <u>Chaplinsky</u> v. <u>New Hampshire</u>, 315 U.S. 568, 571–72 (1942); <u>Near</u> v. <u>Minnesota</u>, 283 U.S. 697, 715 (1931); <u>Roth</u> v. <u>United States</u>, 354 U.S. 476, 482–83 (1957); <u>Beauharnais</u> v. <u>Illinois</u>, 343 U.S. 250, 256–57 (1952).

108. <u>New York Times</u> v. <u>Sullivan</u>, 376 U.S. 254, at 279–80 (1964).

109. See <u>Curtis Publishing Co.</u> v. <u>Butts</u>, 388 U.S. 130 (1967); <u>Associated Press</u> v. <u>Walker</u>, 388 U.S. 130 (1967); <u>Rosenblatt</u> v. <u>Baer</u>, 383 U.S. 75 (1966); and <u>Garrison</u> v. <u>Louisiana</u>, 379 U.S. 64 (1964).

110. <u>Gertz</u> v. <u>Robert Welch, Inc.</u>, 418 U.S. 323 (1974).

111. <u>New York Times</u> v. <u>Sullivan</u>, 376 U.S. 254, at 270 (1964).

112. <u>Gertz</u> v. <u>Robert Welch, Inc.</u>, 418 U.S. 323, at 351 (1974).

113. See <u>Time Inc.</u> v. <u>Firestone</u>, 424 U.S. 448 (1976).

114. See cases cited in note 17; and Melville B. Nimmer, "The Right to Speak from <u>Time</u> to <u>Time</u>: First Amendment Theory Applied to Libel and Misapplied to Privacy," 56 <u>California Law Review</u> 935 (1968).

115. Nimmer, "Right to Speak from <u>Time</u> to <u>Time</u>," at 942.

116. Kalven, "Metaphysics of the Law of Obscenity," at 217.

117. <u>Time Inc.</u> v. <u>Hill</u>, 385 U.S. 374 (1974).

118. See Prosser, <u>Law of Torts</u>; and Chapter 1.

119. <u>Time Inc.</u> v. <u>Hill</u>, 385 U.S. 374, at 401 (1974).

120. Idem, at 412–13 (Fortas, J., dis. op.).

121. <u>Cantrell</u> v. <u>Forest City Publishing Company</u>, 419 U.S. 245 (1974).

122. Idem, at 249.

123. See Prosser, <u>Law of Torts</u>, discussed in Chapter 1. <u>Cox Broadcasting Corp.</u> v. <u>Cohn</u>, 420 U.S. 469 (1975).

124. Cox Broadcasting Corp. v. Cohn, 420 U.S. 469, at 473 (1975).

125. Idem, at 495.

126. See Time Inc. v. Firestone, 424 U.S. 448 (1976); and Oklahoma Publishing Co. v. District Court, 97 S. Ct. 1045 (1977) (per curium).

127. See Compilation of State and Federal Privacy Laws (Washington, D.C.: Privacy Journal, 1977); "A Summary of Freedom of Information and Privacy Laws of the 50 States," Access Reports (Washington, D.C.: Plus Publications, April 1977).

128. Wisconsin v. Constantineau, 400 U.S. 433 (1971); Doe v. McMillan, 412 U.S. 306 (1973); Paul v. Davis, 424 U.S. 693 (1976).

129. Paul v. Davis, 424 U.S. 693, at 713 (1976). See also Codd v. Velger, 97 S. Ct. 882 (1977) (per curium); Kelley v. Johnson, 425 U.S. 238 (1976); and Quinn v. Muscare, 425 U.S. 560 (1976) (per curium).

130. Time Inc. v. Hill, 385 U.S. 374, at 404 (1974).

131. California Bankers Association v. Shultz, 416 U.S. 21 (1974) (discussed in Chapter 2). Laird v. Tatum, 408 U.S. 1 (1972). But see Whalen v. Roe, 97 S. Ct. 869 (1977), discussed in Chapter 5.

132. United States v. United States District Court, 407 U.S. 297 (1972).

5

A Neglected but
Not Forgotten
Fundamental Right

Why should one assume that the right to privacy is protected
by fundamental law? . . . The answer in a few words must
be that our Constitution and our system of constitutional
government reflect a decision that government is limited in
the powers and in the methods it may use. . . . "Liberty
against government," a phrase used by Professor Corwin,
expresses this idea forcefully. In this sense virtually all
enumerated rights in the Constitution can be described as
contributing to the right to privacy, if by that term is
meant the integrity and freedom of the individual person
and personality.

> William M. Beaney
> "The Constitutional Right to Privacy,"
> Supreme Court Review

Whereas prior to 1965 the Supreme Court legitimated claims to
constirutionally protected privacy under the First, Fourth, and Fifth
Amendments, in Griswold v. Connecticut the Court denominated a
constitutional right of privacy per se.[1] Griswold held as a denial of
individuals' constitutional right of privacy a Connecticut birth control
statute, which prohibited the use of birth control devices as well as
made it a criminal offense for anyone to give information or instruction on their use. In announcing the majority's opinion, Justice Douglas proposed a "penumbra" theory for constitutionally protecting privacy and establishing a constitutional right of privacy.

> [Previous] cases suggest that specific guarantees in the
> Bill of Rights have penumbras formed by emanations from
> those guarantees that help give them life and substance.

. . . Various guarantees create zones of privacy. The
right of association contained in the penumbra of the First
Amendment is one, as we have seen. The Third Amendment in its prohibition against the quartering of soldiers
"in any house" in time of peace without the consent of the
owner is another facet of that privacy. The Fourth Amendment explicitly affirms the "right of the people to be secure
in their persons, houses, papers, and effects, against unreasonable searches and seizures." The Fifth Amendment
in its Self-Incrimination clause enables the citizen to create a zone of privacy which government may not force him
to surrender to his detriment. The Ninth Amendment provides: "The enumeration in the Constitution, of certain
rights, shall not be construed to deny or disparage others
retained by the people."[2]

A constitutional right of privacy thus emerged out of the background of the Constitution and Bill of Rights. Judicial recognition of
a right of privacy was permissible, Justice Douglas maintained, because the Constitution extended protection to individuals' privacy interests as "penumbras" and "emanations" or "shadows"[3] of express
constitutional guarantees. In addition to constitutionally protected
privacy under the First, Fourth, and Fifth Amendments, Justice
Douglas found that privacy interests were also logically related to
the Third Amendment's prohibition against quartering troops in an
individual's home and the Ninth Amendment's recognition of "rights
retained by the people." Although in Griswold Justice Douglas avoided
reliance on the Fourteenth Amendment, in an earlier case challenging
the contraceptive statute, he indicated that a right of privacy was included within the Fourteenth Amendment's provision that no state may
"deprive any person of life, liberty, or property, without due process
of law": "Though I believe that 'due process' as used in the Fourteenth Amendment included all of the first eight amendments, I do not
think it is restricted and confined to them. . . . 'Liberty' is a conception that sometimes gains content from the emanations of other
specific guarantees."[4]
Justice Douglas's penumbra theory purported to forge a jurisprudential basis for a constitutional right of privacy, as well as justify the Court's striking down, what dissenting Justice Stewart called,
"an uncommonly silly law." By design the penumbra theory aimed at
circumventing criticism that a right of privacy, rather than an aspect
of fundamental constitutional law, emerged only as the result of constitutional common law.[5] Judicial construction and enforcement of
unenumerated rights, such as the right of privacy, necessarily raises
serious questions about the limits of judicial power and constitutional

interpretation. As early as 1789 two justices expressed divergent views as to the permissible role of judicial review: Justice Iredell, conceding that a legislative act against natural rights and natural justice must be void per se, argued that no court possesses the power to declare it void; Justice Chase urged that with respect to "certain vital principles . . . [a]n act of the Legislature (for I cannot call it a law) contrary to the great first principles of the social compact, cannot be considered a rightful exercise of legislative authority" and therefore must be declared void.[6] Judicial enforcement of "vital" but implicit principles nevertheless may lead to unprincipled and extraconstitutional decision making. As Justice Black, dissenting in Griswold, cautioned: "Use of any such broad, unbounded judicial authority would make of this Court's members a day-to-day constitutional convention."[7]

Griswold's recognition of a fundamental constitutional right of privacy renewed controversies over substantive due process analysis, associated with the discredited Lochner v. New York,[8] and nationalization, or application to the states, of constitutional guarantees under the Fourteenth Amendment's due process clause.[9] The Supreme Court avoided strict scrutiny of the substance of legislation since the early 1900s, when it was severely criticized for acting like a "super-legislature" in passing judgment on the wisdom, need, and propriety of progressive economic legislation. In reviewing economic regulation at the turn of the century, the Supreme Court interpreted the Fourteenth Amendment's due process clause to protect individuals' "liberty of contract" and, thereupon, voided economic legislation, except where it found a valid legislative purpose in regulating health, welfare, or safety of employees.[10] The Court's construction of a right of privacy thus bears a family resemblance to its earlier substantive due process analysis establishing a liberty of contract. Both the right of privacy and the liberty of contract are unenumerated rights, and both serve to rationalize the Court's examination of the substance of legislation as well as its activist posture toward the exercise of judicial review.

As with the controversy over the doctrine of substantive due process, Griswold also renewed debate over the nationalization of the Bill of Rights. In 1833 Barron v. Baltimore held that the Bill of Rights applied only with regard to the federal government, not the states.[11] In the twentieth century the Supreme Court nevertheless extended to the states guarantees of the first eight amendments by selective "incorporation" or "absorption" within the due process clause of the Fourteenth Amendment.[12] Prior to Griswold, the Court had interpreted the Fourteenth Amendment only to apply to the states' enumerated guarantees that were deemed "fundamental" or "implicit

in the concept of ordered liberty.'"* With the legitimation of a constitutional right of privacy, however, the Court made applicable to
the states under the Fourteenth Amendment an unenumerated right.

   Although Justice Douglas conspicuously omitted reference to the
Fourteenth Amendment, Griswold's denomination of a constitutional
right of privacy inevitably invited controversy over substantive due
process and nationalization of both enumerated and unenumerated
guarantees. [13] Yet, as concurring Justices Harlan and White argued,
the Fourteenth Amendment's due process clause was both pertinent
and necessary to the invalidation of a state statute as an infringement
of personal privacy. [14] Justice Douglas's penumbra theory not only
was more ambiguous than due process formulations but also failed to
indicate the basis for applying the constitutional right of privacy to
the states. Fundamentally, Justice Douglas's penumbra theory failed
to define the right and, thereupon, articulate a principle or standard
for application. Justice Douglas merely listed constitutionally protected privacy interests, which the Court had recognized under various
amendments, and assumed that, collectively, these interests constituted the basis and basic components of a right of privacy. Justice
Douglas, likewise, simply assumed that previous legitimation under
different amendments of constitutionally protected privacy claims dif-
fered only in degree rather than kind of recognition of a constitutional
right of privacy per se. Yet, the Court's legitimation of privacy
claims under the First, Fourth, and Fifth Amendments was not tantamount to establishing a constitutional right of privacy. As dissenting
Justice Black correctly observed: "The Court talks about a constitutional 'right of privacy' as though there is some constitutional provision or provisions forbidding any law even to be passed which might
abridge the 'privacy' of individuals. But there is not. There are, of
course, guarantees in certain specific constitutional provisions which
are designed in part to protect privacy at certain times and places
with respect to certain activities." [15]

   Griswold's declaration of a constitutional right of privacy nevertheless was heralded by some commentators precisely because of its
breadth and loose construction. As one commentator viewed the significance of Griswold:

---

   *By 1976 the Supreme Court had extended to the states under the
Fourteenth Amendment the major guarantees of the Bill of Rights, except for the requirements of a 12-member jury and a unanimous jury;
trial by jury in civil cases; provisions for grand jury indictment; ex-
cessive bail and fines; the right to bear arms; and safeguards against
quartering troops in private homes.

First, it gives broad recognition to the right of privacy, without predicating the right upon any specific constitutional provision. The many diverse opinions help to formulate a right that is implicit in the Constitution. It is found in zones of privacy created by the Bill of Rights; it is found within the "liberty" guaranteed by the due process clause; and it is a right retained by the people in the ninth amendment. . . . Second, the case ignores the technical requirements such as trespass prescribed by the fourth amendment while still retaining the flexibility that is implicit in the due process clause. Third, although the case came before the Court to contest a criminal conviction, the discussion of the right of privacy is divorced from any tint of "preferred position." Finally, while the case deals with the limited facts of marital privacy its reasoning is sufficiently broad to encompass many varied situations. That is, Griswold opens the doors for further development of a protection to personal conduct and thought.[16]

Griswold indeed opened the doors for development of the constitutional law of privacy. Subsequent decisions based on the right of privacy tend to confirm Justice Black's fears that "[o]ne of the most effective ways of diluting or expanding a constitutionally guaranteed right is to substitute for the crucial word or words of a constitutional guarantee another word for the crucial word or words, more or less flexible and more or less restricted in meaning."[17] In post-Griswold cases the Supreme Court expanded the right of privacy but in so doing substituted "privacy" for "liberty" under the Fourteenth Amendment and, also, narrowly construed the range of permissible privacy claims. Consequently, the emerging contours of the constitutional right of privacy are considerably narrower than the scope of constitutionally protected privacy under the First, Fourth, and Fifth Amendments.

The following two sections examine the dynamics of constitutional interpretation and the developing right of privacy under the Ninth and Fourteenth Amendments. The final section compares the Court's treatment of the right of privacy with the constitutional protection afforded personal privacy under the First, Fourth, and Fifth Amendments. The chapter concludes by discussing the scope of constitutionally protected privacy and its implications for further developments in law and public policy.

PRIVACY AS A RIGHT
RETAINED BY THE PEOPLE

Justice Jackson once remarked, "What are those other rights 'retained by the people?' . . . [T]he ninth amendment rights which are not to be disturbed by the federal government are still a mystery to me."[18] Indeed, the role of the Ninth Amendment within the practice of rights in the United States has been particularly unimpressive. Yet in recent years courts and their commentators have endeavored to resurrect the "forgotten" Ninth Amendment in order to support judicial construction of a constitutional right of privacy as well as to supply legitimacy to individuals' claims to protection for their interests in personal privacy.[19] Since 1965 lower courts have been urged to recognize under the Ninth Amendment privacy claims to wear long hair; smoke marijuana; demonstrate and protest; obtain, possess, and sell obscenity and pornography; permit or prohibit sterilizations, abortions, and sex education; as well as affirm the right to die.[20] The wide range of claims to Ninth Amendment-protected privacy thus perpetuates the mystery of the amendment.

Justice Douglas's majority opinion in Griswold was unclear as to the relevance of the Ninth Amendment in supporting a constitutional right of privacy. Subsequently, dissenting in Osborn v. United States, he indicated that "[t]he ninth is simply a rule of construction, applicable to the entire Constitution."[21] Similarly, Justice Goldberg, concurring in Griswold, suggested that the Ninth Amendment provides not an independent source for constitutional rights but only a rule of construction for judicial enforcement of unenumerated rights. The amendment does not constitute an independent source of rights. "Rather, the Ninth Amendment shows a belief of the Constitution's authors that fundamental rights exist that are not expressly enumerated in the first eight amendments and an intent that the list of rights included there not be deemed exhausted."[22] "In sum, the Ninth Amendment simply lends strong support to the view that the 'liberty' protected by the Fifth and Fourteenth Amendments from infringement by the Federal Government or the States is not restricted to rights specifically mentioned in the first eight amendments."[23] Apparently for both Justices Douglas and Goldberg, then, the Ninth Amendment serves as a rule of construction for recognizing and legitimating claims of entitlement to unenumerated rights implicit within contexts of expressly enumerated rights, such as with Fourth Amendment-protected privacy.

As a matter of legal history, the authors of the Constitution and Bill of Rights relied on natural law teachings and, in particular, John Locke's theories of natural rights and a social contract.[24] Accordingly, for the authors, the Bill of Rights did not confer rights upon

individuals but reaffirmed preexisting natural rights. The Ninth
Amendment's provision for "rights retained by the people" registered
in part the authors' acceptance of natural law teachings and the inherent rights of individuals. As Bennett Patterson observed:

> The Ninth Amendment announces and acknowledges in a
> single sentence that (1) the individual, and not the State,
> is the source and basis of our social compact and that
> sovereignty now resides and has always resided in the
> individual; (2) that our Government exists through the
> surrender by the individual of a portion of his naturally
> endowed and inherent rights; (3) that everyone of the peo-
> ple of the United States owns a residue of individual rights
> and liberties which have never been, and which are never
> to be surrendered to the State, but which are still to be
> recognized, protected and secured; and (4) that individual
> liberty and rights are inherent, and that such rights are
> not derived from the Constitution, but belong to the indi-
> vidual by natural endowment.[25]

Indeed, James Madison, author of the Ninth Amendment, argued:

> It has been objected also against a bill of rights, that, by
> enumerating particular exceptions to the grant of power,
> it would disparage those rights which were not placed in
> that enumeration; and it might follow by implication, that
> those rights which were not singled out, were and were
> consequently insecure. This is one of the most plausible
> arguments I have ever heard urged against the admission
> of a bill of rights into this system; but, I conceive, that
> it may be guarded against. I have attempted it, as gentle-
> men may see by turning to the . . . [proposed amend-
> ment].[26]

Ostensibly Madison envisioned the amendment to ensure the "requisite latitude" for express guarantees of the Bill of Rights. As Madison explained in a letter to Thomas Jefferson: "My own opinion has
always been in favor of a bill of rights; provided it be so framed as
not to imply powers not meant to be included in the enumeration. . . .
At the same time I have never thought the omission a material defect,
nor been anxious to supply it even by subsequent amendment, for any
other reason that that it is anxiously desired by others. I have favored
it because I supposed it might be of use, and if properly executed
could not be of disservice. I have not viewed it in an important light

. . . [b]ecause there is great reason to fear that a positive declaration of some of the most essential rights could not be obtained in the
requisite latitude."[27] In response Jefferson wrote: "Your thoughts
on the subject of the Declaration of rights in the letter of Oct. 17
[1788] I have weighed with great satisfaction. Some of them had not
occurred to me before, but were acknoleged [sic] just in the moment
they were presented to my mind. In the arguments in favor of a
declaration of rights, you omit one which has great weight with me,
the legal check which it puts into the hands of the judiciary. This is
a body, which if rendered independent, and kept strictly to their own
department merits great confidence for their learning and integrity."[28]

The Madison-Jefferson correspondence supports the view that
the Ninth Amendment reflects the authors' acceptance of natural law
teachings and their fear that parchment guarantees might not receive
the requisite latitude. The Ninth Amendment also served to counter
Alexander Hamilton's argument that a Bill of Rights would be "not
only unnecessary . . . but would even be dangerous."[29] Jefferson
defended the proposal for a bill of rights against the objection that
"[a] positive declaration of some essential rights could not be obtained in the requisite latitude" by stating that, "Half a loaf is better
than no bread. If we cannot secure all our rights, let's secure what
we can."[30] Both Madison and Jefferson viewed the Bill of Rights as
providing through the judiciary a legal check upon the exercise of
governmental power and, specifically, the Ninth Amendment as providing the judiciary with a rule of construction for ensuring the requisite latitude of individuals' rights, whether enumerated or unenumerated.[31]

Notwithstanding the historical support for Justices Douglas's
and Goldberg's interpretations, Justice Stewart, dissenting in Griswold, accused them of "turn[ing] somersaults with history."[32] According to Justice Stewart the Ninth and Tenth Amendments are correlative provisions that state only truisms. "The Ninth Amendment
like its companion, the Tenth, . . . was . . . simply to make clear
that the adoption of the Bill of Rights did not alter the plan that the
Federal Government was to be a government of express and limited
powers, and that all rights and powers not delegated to it were retained by the people and the individual States."[33] Justice Stewart
maintains that the Ninth and Tenth Amendments were conjoined in
stating only the truism that the federal government may not make in-
cursions into state autonomy, and, therefore, the Ninth Amendment
may not serve (as he interprets Justices Douglas's and Goldberg's
reliance on the amendment) as a source of substantive constitutional
rights.

Neither Justice Douglas nor Justice Goldberg, however, argue
that the Ninth Amendment provides an independent basis for unenum-

erated rights. Instead, consistent with the Madison–Jefferson correspondence, they maintain that the amendment provides an enabling clause, a rule of construction, for ensuring the requisite latitude of the rights secured by the Constitution and Bill of Rights. In several post-<u>Griswold</u> decisions, Justice Douglas indicated that the Ninth Amendment serves only as a rule of construction for enforcing rights explicitly or implicitly protected by other constitutional guarantees. In <u>Palmer</u> v. <u>Thompson</u>, for example, Justice Douglas, dissenting from the majority's decision to allow Jackson, Mississippi to close rather than integrate its public swimming pools, argued: "The 'rights' retained by the people within the meaning of the Ninth Amendment may be related to those 'rights' which are enumerated in the Constitution. . . . [F]reedom from discrimination based on race, creed, or color has become by reason of the Thirteenth, Fourteenth, and Fifteenth Amendments one of the 'unenumerated rights' under the Ninth Amendment that may not be voted up or down."[34]

While Justice Douglas frequently adopted an expansive view of unenumerated rights, he nevertheless rather consistently argued that at least one other amendment-protected right remains a precondition for invocation of the Ninth Amendment.[35] In <u>Doe</u> v. <u>Bolton</u> Justice Douglas emphatically reiterated: "The Ninth Amendment obviously does not create federally enforceable rights. . . . But a catalogue of these rights includes customary, traditional, and time-honored rights, amenities, privileges and immunities. . . . Many of them in my view come within the meaning of the term 'liberty' as used in the Fourteenth Amendment."[36]

The Ninth Amendment as Justices Douglas and Goldberg maintain, and the Madison–Jefferson correspondence confirms, does not limit the power of the federal government. Rather, the amendment constitutes a declaration that the federal government may not exercise its power so as to deprive individuals of their rights, whether those rights are enumerated or unenumerated. As such the Ninth Amendment provides only a rule of construction for judicial enforcement of individuals' claims to constitutionally protected liberties.

The authors of the Ninth Amendment did not intend the amendment to permit arbitrary judicial discretion in enforcing the retained rights of the people. Still, with the amendment exists the potential for abuse of judicial power when legitimating claims to unenumerated rights. In this regard, Justice Black's dissenting opinion in <u>Griswold</u> adds another dimension to criticisms of judicial reliance on the Ninth Amendment by pointing out that employment of the amendment, like the Fourteenth Amendment's due process clause, might well lead to extraconstitutional and unprincipled judicial decision making. Both the Ninth Amendment, as an enabling provision, and due process formulations "require judges to determine what is or is not constitutional

on the basis of their own appraisal of what laws are unwise or unnecessary. The power to make such decisions is of course a legislative
body."[37] According to Justice Black, judicial invocation of the Ninth
Amendment is akin to employing the due process clause in order to
strike down legislation and, consequently, remains vulnerable to the
criticisms levied against the Supreme Court when it went "Lochner-
ing"[38] at the turn of the century.

Justice Goldberg indeed invited Justice Black's criticism by
contending that "judges are not left at large to decide cases in light
of their personal and private notions. Rather, they must look to the
"traditions and conscience of our people' to determine whether a
principle is 'so rooted . . . as to be ranked as fundamental.' "[39] Accordingly, the Supreme Court must determine "whether a right involved is of such a character that it cannot be denied without violating
those 'fundamental principles of liberty and justice which lie at the
base of all our civil and political institutions.' "[40] Justice Goldberg
invites criticisms because he collapses standards for evoking the
Ninth Amendment and the Fourteenth Amendment when legitimating
claims to unenumerated rights.

Anticipating Justice Black's criticism that judicial reliance on
the Ninth Amendment lacks any definite standard for application, Norman Redlich argued:

> When the question of standards is posed within the context
> of the Ninth and Tenth Amendments, rather than in terms
> of due process, a definite pattern starts to emerge. To
> comply with the purposes of these Amendments, the text-
> ual standard should be the entire Constitution. The origi-
> nal Constitution and its amendments project through the
> ages the image of a free and open society. The Ninth and
> Tenth Amendments recognized—at the very outset of our
> national experience—that it was impossible to fill in every
> detail of this image. For that reason certain rights were
> reserved to the people. . . . They were "retained . . . by
> the people" not because they were different from the rights
> specifically mentioned in the Constitution, but because
> words were considered inadequate to define all of the rights
> which man should possess in a free society and because it
> was believed that the enumeration might imply that other
> rights did not exist.[41]

According to Redlich, the Ninth and Tenth Amendments define rights
ancillary to express constitutional rights. The standard for application of the Ninth Amendment is the entire text of the Constitution and,
in particular, the express guarantees of the Bill of Rights.

Griswold's recognition of a constitutional right of privacy supported by the Ninth Amendment therefore need not be viewed as resurrecting Lochner's infamous substantive due process analysis, at least insofar as the amendment only supports recognition of claims to constitutionally protected privacy with regard to explicit guarantees of the Constitution. Moreover, justices need not roam at will like knights-errant, nor need the Supreme Court act like a roving-commission when relying on the Ninth Amendment for recognizing claims to unenumerated rights. The Ninth Amendment provides a rule of construction for safeguarding fundamental liberties not expressly guaranteed in the Bill of Rights. Still, unenumerated liberties, as judicially enforced, must bear a logical connection to express guarantees, demonstrable by reference to the text of the Bill of Rights and borne out by previous constitutional interpretation. As such the Ninth Amendment permits judicial construction and protection of claims to fundamental but unenumerated rights. The Ninth Amendment simply gives strong support to a constitutional background right of privacy and claims to constitutionally protected privacy under the First, Fourth, and Fifth Amendments.

Since Griswold the Supreme Court has minimized the role of the Ninth Amendment in the developing constitutional law of privacy; only dicta suggests the continuing utility of the amendment.[42] Significantly, the Burger Court in Roe v. Wade indicated its preference for basing the right of privacy on the Fourteenth Amendment instead of the Ninth Amendment: "This right of privacy, whether it be found in the Fourteenth Amendment's concept of personal liberty and restrictions upon state action, as we feel it is, or, as the District Court determined, in the Ninth Amendment's reservation of rights to the people, is broad enough to encompass a woman's decision whether or not to terminate her pregnancy."[43]

GRISWOLD'S FUNDAMENTAL
RIGHT OF PRIVACY

In Griswold, Justice Harlan, unlike Justices Douglas and Goldberg, found no aversion to substantive due process and nationalization of unenumerated fundamental rights independent of guarantees of the first eight amendments. As Justice Harlan indicated earlier in Poe v. Ullman: "This 'Liberty' [guaranteed by the Fourteenth Amendment] is not a series of isolated points pricked out in terms of the taking of property; the freedom of speech, press, and religion; the right to keep and bear arms; and so on. It is a rational continuum which, broadly speaking, includes a freedom from all substantial arbitrary impositions and purposeless restraints."[44] Hence, in Griswold, Justice Harlan simply concluded that a right of privacy in family relations stands "on its own" under the due process clause of the Fourteenth Amendment.

Justice Harlan's justification for the right of privacy as a "fundamental right" "implicit in the concept of ordered liberty" escapes the majority's lacuna of failing to distinguish between a constitutional right of privacy and constitutionally protected privacy interests. Moreover, as Justice White, concurring, observed, the contraceptive statute had no rational relation to a valid legislative purpose and appeared unenforceable, short of putting police in couples' bedrooms. Still, Justice Harlan's opinion, like the majority's, failed to specify standards of application necessary to determine the scope of the right and to ensure a measure of predictability in the constitutional law of privacy.

Seven years after Griswold, the Burger Court in 1972 invalidated as a denial of the Fourteenth Amendment's equal protection clause a Massachusetts statute that made it illegal for single persons, but not married persons, to obtain contraceptives. In Eisenstadt v. Baird, Justice Brennan, for the Court, found no rational basis for distinguishing between unmarried and married persons, stating: "If the right of privacy means anything, it is the right of the individual, married or single, to be free from unwanted governmental intrusion into matters so fundamentally affecting a person as the decision whether to bear or beget a child."[45] In extending protection to unmarried individuals' claims to obtain contraceptives, Justice Brennan indicated the expansive power of a constitutional right of privacy. Even concurring Justice Douglas suggested that a narrower basis for the decision was possible on the facts of the case; namely, that Baird's lecture on and distribution of contraceptives was protected by the First Amendment and applicable to the states by the Fourteenth Amendment.

Justice Brennan's expansive application of the right presaged subsequent decisions by not only failing to distinguish between considerations of privacy and liberty but also by assuming a broad connection between individuals' privacy interests and their use of contraceptives, including their obtaining, employing, and selling them. In instances where individuals buy or sell contraceptives (let alone, as in Eisenstadt, where individuals acquire contraceptives at a free public lecture) their expectations of privacy appear minimal, indeed, comparable to cases where the Court denied privacy claims to buy and sell obscenity and pornography (see cases and discussion in Chapter 4). In Eisenstadt, as in later cases, the Court could have reached the same result simply by finding no rational relation between the statute and the activities regulated. The Court thereby would have avoided the conceptual difficulties of justifying the enforcement of privacy claims with regard to buying and selling contraceptives but not

obscenity and pornography. Government regulation of marketing
either contraceptives or obscenity affects individuals' liberty and
may, consequently, causally influence their activities and expectations of privacy. In both instances the issue nevertheless is basically
one of infringing upon individuals' liberty under the Fourteenth Amendment. Hence, by substituting a privacy analysis for that of an evaluation of when and for what purposes the government may regulate individuals' activities, the Court blurred the concepts of privacy and
liberty, as well as circumvented a Fourteenth Amendment due process
and equal protection analysis.

In 1973 the Supreme Court nevertheless concluded that "the
right of personal privacy includes the abortion decision [of a woman;
adding] . . . that this right is not unqualified and must be considered
against important state interests in regulation."[46] Justice Blackmun's
majority opinion in Roe v. Wade noted Griswold's reliance on First,
Fourth, and Fifth Amendment decisions, affirming constitutionally
protected privacy interests, as a foundation for the right of privacy,
but identified the Fourteenth Amendment as the basis for the right's
application. Regulations restricting the fundamental right of privacy
under the Fourteenth Amendment may be justified only by "compelling
state interests" at the end of the first trimester, with regard to protecting the health of the woman, and at the time of viability, with respect to the health of the fetus. Justice Blackmun, however, did little to justify the proposition that the state's interests do not become
compelling until viability. Instead, he simply announced that the
state's goals were insufficient to sustain blanket regulation of abortions.[47]

Roe dramatically extended the right of privacy yet failed to
clarify the nature of privacy and its legal protection. Indeed, the necessity of invalidating the abortion statutes on the basis of a constitutional right of privacy, in contrast to basing the decision on the Fourteenth Amendment's due process clause, remains imperceptible.
Justice Blackmun surveyed constitutionally protected privacy interests
in order to conclude that "only personal rights that can be deemed
'fundamental' or 'implicit in the concept of ordered liberty,' . . . are
included in this guarantee of personal privacy. They also make it
clear that the right has some extension to activities relating to marriage, procreation, contraception, family relationships, and child
rearing and education."[48] Justice Blackmun thereupon asserted that
the right of privacy encompasses a woman's decision to terminate
her pregnancy with little more explanation than that a "pregnant woman cannot be isolated in her privacy."[49]

The majority in Roe failed to heed Justice Black's earlier caution about substituting one crucial word for another and a privacy analysis for interpretation of express constitutional provisions. Ac-

cordingly, Justice Rehnquist, dissenting, correctly observed the "difficulty in concluding, as the Court does, that the right of 'privacy' is involved in this case." Justice Rehnquist objected to both the conceptual and constitutional foundations for and application of the right of privacy:

> Nor is the "privacy" which the Court finds here even a
> distant relative of the freedom from searches and seizures
> protected by the Fourth Amendment. . . . If the Court
> means by the term "privacy" no more than that the claim
> of a person to be free from unwanted state regulation of
> consensual transactions may be a form of "liberty" pro-
> tected by the Fourteenth Amendment, there is no doubt
> that similar claims have been upheld in our earlier deci-
> sions on the basis of that liberty. . . . But that liberty
> is not guaranteed absolutely against deprivation, but only
> against deprivation without due process of law.[50]

Roe like Eisenstadt collapsed interests in personal privacy with interests, more generally, in individual liberty (interests in personal autonomy and self-determination) and attempted to forget the specter of Lochner, which Justice Douglas endeavored to evade in Griswold. Only Justice Stewart, concurring in Roe, accepted in all candor the Court's use of substantive due process in constructing and expanding the constitutional right of privacy.

In two 1976 cases the Burger Court further underscored the expansive nature of the constitutional right of privacy, as well as its unwillingness to address the substantive due process controversy and the assimilation of interests in privacy and liberty under the Fourteenth Amendment's due process clause. Accepting Roe's conceptual and constitutional analysis, the Court in Planned Parenthood of Central Missouri v. Danforth ruled that states may not require a married woman to obtain her husband's consent prior to having an abortion.[51] In Bellotti v. Baird, while referring a parental consent statute for unmarried women under 18 years of age back to a Massachusetts state court for interpretation, the Court indicated that parents do not have an absolute right to determine whether their unmarried daughters may have abortions.[52] Subsequently, in Carey v. Population Services International, the Court extended the Eisenstadt-Roe-Planned Parenthood rationale that the "constitutionally protected right of privacy extends to an individual's liberty to make choices regarding conception."[53] Carey held that since a state may not impose a blanket prohibition, or even a blanket requirement of parental consent, on the choice of a minor to terminate her pregnancy, "the constitutionality of a blanket prohibition of the distribution of contraceptives to minors is <u>a fortiori</u> foreclosed."[54] The conceptual and constitutional differences between protected privacy interests and guarantees for personal liberty were further blurred and the controversy over substantive due process all but forgotten.

Although the Court in <u>Roe</u> relied on <u>Griswold</u>'s penumbra theory as a general justification for denominating a constitutional right of privacy, <u>Roe</u> and its progeny utilize the Fourteenth Amendment as the basis for enforcing the right. The Court's privacy analysis under the Fourteenth Amendment nevertheless fails to distinguish between interests in personal privacy and, more broadly, individual liberty. "[T]he Court has recognized that one aspect of the 'liberty' protected by the Due Process Clause of the Fourteenth Amendment is 'a right of personal privacy,' or a guarantee of certain areas or zones of privacy."[55] Still, the privacy rationale in <u>Eisenstadt</u>, <u>Roe</u>, <u>Planned Parenthood</u>, and <u>Carey</u> appears unnecessary and irrelevant to the invalidation of the contraceptive and abortion statutes. The Court could have avoided the privacy–substantive due process controversy by simply invalidating regulations as an abridgement of due process and deprivation of individual liberty under the Fourteenth Amendment.

The Court's extension of the constitutional right of privacy in <u>Eisenstadt</u>, <u>Roe</u>, <u>Planned Parenthood</u>, and <u>Carey</u>, moreover, severed the right of privacy from <u>Griswold</u>'s recognition of the marital privacy that exists between a husband and wife, so as to principally protect a woman's decision to use contraceptives or terminate her pregnancy. In expanding the constitutional right of privacy, the Supreme Court concomitantly narrowly construed the scope of the right to protect, primarily, individuals' interests in childbearing and child rearing. The Court, however, rejected the broader implication that the constitutional right of privacy establishes protection for individuals' sexual autonomy and freedom from any governmental regulation of private sexual activities.[56] In 1977 Justice Brennan emphasized the narrow scope of interests embraced by the right of privacy, observing: "This right of personal privacy includes 'the interest in independence in making certain kinds of important decisions.' While the outer limits of this aspect of privacy have not been marked by the Court, it is clear that among the decisions that an individual may make without unjustified government interference are personal decisions relating to marriage, procreation, contraception, family relations, and child rearing and education."[57]

THE SUPREME COURT, CONSTITUTIONALLY PROTECTED PRIVACY, AND THE RIGHT OF PRIVACY

The Supreme Court's denomination of a constitutional right of privacy in <u>Griswold</u> and its extension in <u>Roe</u> and its progeny provide

protection for only a narrow range of individuals' privacy interests.
By contrast to the political ideal of a constitutional background right
of privacy and judicial construction of constitutionally protected privacy interests under the First, Fourth, and Fifth Amendments, the
Court's treatment of the right of privacy appears circumscribed and
limited. Whereas individuals' claims to the privacy of their engagements and experiences receive more or less extensive protection
with judicial enforcement of the guarantees of these amendments,
the Burger Court's restrictive, albeit activist, application of the right
of privacy primarily encompasses matters relating to procreation
and the personal intimacies of motherhood, marriage, the family,
and the home. In other words, while other privacy interests may still
receive constitutional protection when the Court discerns a connection
between a privacy claim and an express constitutional guarantee, the
scope of the right of privacy itself has been significantly narrowed to
matters relating to individuals' sexual activities.

Because the Supreme Court interprets the constitutional right
of privacy to principally protect individuals' intimate relationships
and basic decisions over family life, its articulated rationale often
remains irrelevant and inapplicable to areas where individuals raise
privacy claims under specific guarantees of the Bill of Rights. For
example, consider issues of informational privacy, whether they
arise with respect to electronic surveillance, compelled personal disclosures, or claims against intrusions upon and interference with individuals' activities and associations. The Court's acknowledgment
of the constitutional right of privacy as "fundamental" or "implicit in
the concept of ordered liberty" notwithstanding, the right of privacy
appears to afford little protection beyond safeguarding individuals
against "unwarranted government intrusions into matters so fundamentally affecting a person as the decision whether to bear or beget
a child."[58] The Court in a number of post-Roe decisions emphasized
that privacy interests receive constitutional protection and recognition
under a general right of privacy, not because of the intimacies of
family life per se but rather because of the nature of individuals' decisions regarding their sexual activities. Several decisions since
1965 nevertheless refused to recognize First, Fourth, and Fifth
Amendment claims to informational privacy, even though individuals
asserted that their decisions and engagements relating to economic,
political, and religious matters were no less fundamental than those
relating to their sexual activities.[59]

In 1977 the Supreme Court, however, dealt specifically with issues of informational privacy and suggested the possibility that the
constitutional right of privacy encompassed more than individuals'
interests in matters of procreation and sexual activities. In Whalen
v. Roe, physicians and patients challenged the constitutionality of New

York statutes designed to control the distribution of dangerous drugs
by requiring that the state be provided with copies of prescriptions
for certain drugs.[60] The statutes also provided security measures
for the information gathered, confined access to a limited number of
health officials and investigating personnel, prohibited public disclosure of patients' identities, and limited the state's maintenance of
the records to a five-year period. Justice Stevens, writing for a
unanimous Court, addressed the privacy claims by observing:

> The cases sometimes characterized as protecting "privacy"
> have in fact involved at least two different kinds of inter-
> ests. One is the individual interest in avoiding disclosure
> of personal matters, and another is the interest in indepen-
> dence in making certain kinds of important decisions. . . .
> The mere existence in readily available form of informa-
> tion about patients' use of . . . drugs creates a genuine
> concern that information will become publicly known and
> it will adversely affect their reputations. . . . Thus, the
> statute threatens to impair both their interest in the non-
> disclosure of private information and also their interest
> in making important decisions independently.[61]

The Court nonetheless was not persuaded that the New York program
posed a sufficient threat to either privacy interest. Justice Stevens,
noting "the threat to privacy implicit in the accumulation of vast
amounts of personal information in computerized data banks or other
massive government files," emphasized that "[t]he right to collect
and use such data for public purposes is typically accompanied by a
concomitant statutory or regulatory duty to avoid unwarranted disclosures."[62] The majority rejected the lower court's view of the
statutes as too broad, thereby infringing the privacy of the physician-
patient relationship and holding that the state must demonstrate the
necessity of its regulation. Justice Stevens observed: "The holding
in Lochner has been implicitly rejected many times. State legislation
which has some effect on individual liberty or privacy may not be
held unconstitutional simply because a court finds it unnecessary, in
whole or in part."[63] Here, the Court found the New York statute to
be a reasonable exercise of the states' broad police power, finding
no basis for assuming that security measures would be improperly
administered or for showing that the regulations would either deprive
the public of access to drugs or physicians of their right to practice
medicine free from unwarranted state interference.

While Whalen suggests that individuals may have legitimate
claims to informational privacy, states have broad latitude in collecting and maintaining personalized information. The Court will presume

a rational relation between the legislative purpose and establishment of computerized information systems, particularly where the state provides security provisions for the collection, maintenance, and dissemination of information. Although the majority failed to specify any constitutional limitations on states' information gathering, Justice Brennan, concurring, suggested that the Constitution, and, in particular, the Fourth Amendment, places some limits on the type of information collected and the means by which states may gather or disseminate personal information.

Within historical perspective, the Supreme Court generally has been less than receptive to recognition and protection of interests in informational privacy, considering either the Court's denomination and elaboration of the constitutional right of privacy, or its construction of First, Fourth, and Fifth Amendment-protected privacy. As Justice Stewart, concurring in Whalen, stated: "Whatever the ratio decidendi of Griswold, it does not recognize a general interest in freedom from disclosure of private information."[64]

Albeit Katz recognized that the Fourth Amendment protects people, not places, the Court continues to rely on analysis of constitutionally protected areas and proprietary concepts when validating claims to Fourth Amendment-protected privacy. Accordingly, with the exception of cases dealing with warrantless wiretaps and electronic surveillance, Fourth Amendment safeguards have been narrowly applied to claims to informational privacy. Similarly, the potentially broad contours of Fifth Amendment-protected privacy were circumscribed with respect to claims to informational privacy asserted against third-party disclosures. A number of judicial policies, including acceptance of common law principles of ownership and possession of property, limited the amendment's applicability to circumstances where an individual was personally compelled to disclose incriminating information, but not where incriminating information was produced by a third party. Judicial construction of First Amendment guarantees legitimated interests in informational privacy when conjoined with interests in associational privacy, but failed to recognize privacy interests against the public disclosure of personal affairs. The apparent property bias within the developing constitutional law of privacy results, in part, from the difficulty of evaluating and formulating standards for legitimating individuals' claims to informational privacy. Thus, while the Supreme Court affirmed in constitutional litigation the broad political ideal of privacy embedded within the Constitution and Bill of Rights, it also left issues in safeguarding informational privacy to the states, Congress, and, more generally, political and administrative policy-making processes.

NOTES

1. <u>Griswold</u> v. <u>Connecticut</u>, 381 U.S. 479 (1965).
2. Idem, at 482-84.
3. <u>Whalen</u> v. <u>Roe</u>, 97 S. Ct. 869, 876 n. 23 (1977).
4. <u>Poe</u> v. <u>Ullman</u>, 367 U.S. 497, 516-17 (1961).
5. See Harry M. Wellington, "Common Law Rules and Constitutional Double Standards: Some Notes on Adjudication," 83 <u>Yale Law Journal</u> 222 (1973). See also Henry Monaghan, "The Supreme Court, 1974 Term—Foreword: Constitutional Common Law," 89 <u>Harvard Law Review</u> 1 (1975); and Thomas S. Schrock and Robert C. Welsh, "Reconsidering the Constitutional Common Law," 91 <u>Harvard Law Review</u> 1117 (1978).
6. <u>Calder</u> v. <u>Bull</u>, 3 U.S. 386, 388, 399 (1798).
7. <u>Griswold</u> v. <u>Connecticut</u>, 381 U.S. 479, at 520 (1965) (Black, J., dis. op.).
8. Between 1897 and 1937 the Supreme Court invalidated congressional and state economic regulation on the assumption that the Fourteenth Amendment's provision that "No state shall . . . deprive any person of life, liberty, or property, without due process of law" guaranteed individuals' economic liberty or freedom from government regulation to strike a bargain in a free market. See <u>Allgeyer</u> v. <u>Louisiana</u>, 165 U.S. 578 (1897); <u>Chicago, M. & St. P. R. Co.</u> v. <u>Minnesota</u>, 134 U.S. 418 (1890); <u>United States</u> v. <u>E. C. Knight</u>, 156 U.S. 1 (1895); <u>Lochner</u> v. <u>New York</u>, 198 U.S. 45 (1905); <u>Adair</u> v. <u>United States</u>, 208 U.S. 161 (1908); <u>Coppage</u> v. <u>Kansas</u>, 236 U.S. 1 (1915); <u>Adkins</u> v. <u>Children's Hospital</u>, 261 U.S. 525 (1923). Because of criticisms of the Court's invalidation of New Deal legislation and construction of a "liberty of contract," after 1937 the Court abandoned the doctrine of substantive due process and its review of economic legislation. See <u>Home Building and Loan Assn.</u> v. <u>New York</u>, 290 U.S. 398 (1934); <u>Nebbia</u> v. <u>New York</u>, 291 U.S. 502 (1934); <u>West Coast Hotel</u> v. <u>Parrish</u>, 300 U.S. 379 (1937); <u>Olsen</u> v. <u>Nebraska</u>, 313 U.S. 236 (1941); and <u>City of Pittsburgh</u> v. <u>Alco Parking Corp.</u>, 417 U.S. 369 (1974). See, generally, Robert McCloskey, "Economic Due Process and the Supreme Court: An Exhumation and Reburial," in <u>Supreme Court Review</u>, ed. Philip Kurland (Chicago: University of Chicago Press, 1962).
9. <u>Barron</u> v. <u>Baltimore</u>, 7 Pet. 243 (1833) held the Bill of Rights inapplicable to the states; the guarantees protected only against infringements by the national government. Consequently, basic civil liberties at the state level were protected only by provisions of individual state constitutions. The Fourteenth Amendment, ratified in 1868, however, provided in part that, "No State shall . . . deprive any person of life, liberty or property without the due process of law."

In the twentieth century the Supreme Court interpreted the Fourteenth Amendment's due process clause to embrace certain substantive national rights and extended them to the states.

10. See Powell v. Pennsylvania, 127 U.S. 678 (1888); Jacobson
v. Massachusetts, 197 U.S. 11 (1905); Mugler v. Kansas, 123 U.S.
623 (1887); and Euclid v. Ambler Realty Co., 272 U.S. 365 (1926).

11. Barron v. Baltimore, 7 Pet. 243 (1833).

12. The Supreme Court never agreed on a single theory for na-
tionalizing the guarantees of the Bill of Rights. Instead, four theories
have been advanced: (1) "incorporation" of all the guarantees of the
Bill of Rights, Hurtado v. California, 110 U.S. 516 (1884) (Harlan,
Sr., J.); (2) "selective incorporation" or "absorption" of those freedoms of the first eight amendments that are "implicit in the concept
of ordered liberty," Palko v. Connecticut, 302 U.S. 319 (1937) (Car-
dozo, J.); (3) case-by-case approach to specific freedoms, Adamson
v. California, 332 U.S. 46 (1947) (Frankfurter, J.); and (4) "total
incorporation plus other fundamental liberties," Adamson v. California, 332 U.S. 46 (1947) (Murphy, J.; and Rutledge, J.).

13. See, generally, Thomas I. Emerson, "Nine Justices in
Search of a Doctrine," 64 Michigan Law Review 219 (1965); Ernest
Katin, "Griswold v. Connecticut: The Justices and Connecticut's
'Uncommonly Silly Law,'" 42 Notre Dame Lawyer 680 (1967); Paul
G. Kauper, "Penumbras, Peripheries, Emanations, Things Funda-
mental and Things Forgotten: The Griswold Case," 64 Michigan Law
Review 235 (1965).

14. Griswold v. Connecticut, 381 U.S. 479, 499-502 (1965)
(Harlan, J., con. op.) and 502-7 (White, J., con. op.).

15. Idem, at 508-9 (Black, J., dis. op.).

16. Note, "Privacy after Griswold: Constitutional or Natural
Right?" 60 Northwestern University Law Review 813, 828 (1966).

17. Griswold v. Connecticut, 381 U.S. 479, at 508 (1965) (Black,
J., dis. op.).

18. Robert H. Jackson, The Supreme Court in the American
System of Government (New York: Harper & Row, 1963) 74-75.

19. See Bennett B. Patterson, The Forgotten Ninth Amendment
(Indianapolis: Bobbs-Merrill, 1955); and William O. Bertelsman,
"Ninth Amendment and Due Process of Law—Foreword: A Viable
Theory of Unenumerated Rights," 37 University of Cincinnati Law Re-
view 777 (1968); and R. H. Clark, "The Ninth Amendment and Consti-
tutional Privacy," 5 University of Toledo Law Review 83 (1973).

20. See, generally, Lyman Rhoades and Rodney R. Patula,
"The Ninth Amendment: A Survey of Theory and Practice in the Federal Courts since Griswold v. Connecticut," 50 Denver Law Review
153 (1973).

21. Osborn v. United States, 385 U.S. 323, at 352-53 (1966)
(Douglas, J., dis. op.).

22. Griswold v. Connecticut, 381 U.S. 479, at 492 (1965) (Goldberg, J., con. op.).

23. Idem, at 498.

24. See, generally, John Locke, in Two Treatises of Government, ed. Peter Laslett (New York: New American Library, 1960); and Morton White, The Philosophy of the American Revolution (New York: Oxford University Press, 1977).

25. Patterson, The Forgotten Ninth Amendment, at 1-2.

26. Letter of James Madison to Thomas Jefferson (October 17, 1788), Julian Boyd, ed., The Papers of Thomas Jefferson, vol. 14 (Princeton, N.J.: Princeton University Press, 1958) 16, 18.

27. Ibid.

28. Letter of Thomas Jefferson to James Madison (March 15, 1789), Boyd, The Papers of Thomas Jefferson, 659.

29. See Clinton Rossiter, ed., The Federalist Papers, no. 84 (New York: New American Library, 1961).

30. Boyd, The Papers of Thomas Jefferson, at 660.

31. See Joseph Story, Commentaries on the Constitution of the United States, 5th ed. (Boston: Little, Brown, 1891) 651.

32. Griswold v. Connecticut, 381 U.S. 479, at 529 (1965) (Stewart, J., dis. op.).

33. Idem, at 529-30.

34. Palmer v. Thompson, 403 U.S. 217, 233 (1971) (Douglas, J., dis. op.).

35. See, for example, Poe v. Ullman, 367 U.S. 497, 516-17 (1961) (Douglas, J., dis. op.); Freeman v. Flake, 405 U.S. 1032 (1972) (Douglas, J., dis. op.).

36. Doe v. Bolton, 410 U.S. 179, 210 (1973) (Douglas, J., con. op.).

37. Griswold v. Connecticut 381 U.S. 479, at 511-12 (1965) (Black, J., dis. op.).

38. John Hart Ely, "The Wages of Crying Wolf," 82 Yale Law Journal 920, 944 (1973).

39. Griswold v. Connecticut, 381 U.S. 479, at 493 (1965), quoting Snyder v. Massachusetts, 291 U.S. 97, 105 (1934) (Goldberg, J., con. op.).

40. Idem, quoting Powell v. Alabama, 287 U.S. 45, 67 (1932).

41. Norman Redlich, "Are There 'Certain Rights . . . Retained by the People?'" 37 New York University Law Review 787, 810-11 (1962).

42. See Stanley v. Illinois, 405 U.S. 645 (1972) ("the integrity of the family unit has found protection . . . [in] the Ninth Amendment," idem at 651); Law Students Civil Rights Research Council v. Wadmond, 401 U.S. 154 (1971). Prior to Griswold, the Court had dealt with the Ninth Amendment in Brown v. New Jersey, 175 U.S. 174

(1899); <u>McCurdy</u> v. <u>United States</u>, 246 U.S. 263 (1918); <u>Ashwander</u>
v. <u>Tennessee Valley Authority</u>, 297 U.S. 288, 330-31 (1936); <u>Tennes-</u>
<u>see Electric Power Co.</u> v. <u>T.V.A.</u>, 306 U.S. 118, 143 (1939); <u>United</u>
<u>Public Workers of America</u> v. <u>Mitchell</u>, 330 U.S. 75 (1947); and
<u>Roth</u> v. <u>United States</u>, 354 U.S. 476 (1957).

43. <u>Roe</u> v. <u>Wade</u>, 410 U.S. 113, 153 (1973).

44. <u>Poe</u> v. <u>Ullman</u>, 367 U.S. 497, at 503 (1961).

45. <u>Eisenstadt</u> v. <u>Baird</u>, 405 U.S. 438, 464 (1972).

46. <u>Roe</u> v. <u>Wade</u>, 410 U.S. 113, at 154 (1973). See also <u>Doe</u> v.
<u>Bolton</u>, 410 U.S. 179 (1973).

47. See, generally, Lawrence H. Tribe, "Forword: Toward a
Model of Roles in the Due Process of Life and Law," 87 <u>Harvard Law</u>
<u>Review</u> 1 (1973); Cyril C. Means, Jr., "The Phoenix of Abortional
Freedom: Is a Penumbral or Ninth Amendment Right about to Arise
from the Nineteenth-Century Legislative Ashes of a Fourteenth-Cen-
tury Common Law Liberty?" 17 <u>New York Law Forum</u> 335 (1971);
Ely, "The Wages of Crying Wolf"; Wellington, "Common Law Rules
and Constitutional Double Standards"; and Michael J. Perry, "Abortion, the Public Morals, and the Police Power: The Ethical Function
of Substantive Due Process," 23 <u>U.C.L.A. Law Review</u> 689 (1976).

48. <u>Roe</u> v. <u>Wade</u>, 410 U.S. 113, at 152-53 (1973) (citations
omitted). The Court cited in support of its privacy analysis, <u>Loving</u>
v. <u>Virginia</u>, 388 U.S. 1, 12 (1967) (activities relating to marriage);
<u>Skinner</u> v. <u>Oklahoma</u>, 316 U.S. 535, 541-42 (1942) (procreation);
<u>Eisenstadt</u> v. <u>Baird</u>, 405 U.S. 438, 453-54 (1972) (contraception);
<u>Prince</u> v. <u>Massachusetts</u>, 321 U.S. 158, 166 (1944) (family relation-
ships); <u>Pierce</u> v. <u>Society of Sisters</u>, 268 U.S. 510, 535 (1925), <u>Meyer</u>
v. <u>Nebraska</u>, 262 U.S. 390, 399 (1923) (child rearing and education);
and <u>Union Pacific Ry. Co.</u> v. <u>Botsford</u>, 141 U.S. 250, 251 (1891).

49. <u>Roe</u> v. <u>Wade</u>, 410 U.S. 113, at 159 (1973).

50. Idem, at 172-73 (Rehnquist, J., dis. op.).

51. <u>Planned Parenthood of Central Missouri</u> v. <u>Danforth</u>, 96 S.
Ct. 2831 (1976).

52. <u>Bellotti</u> v. <u>Baird</u>, 96 S. Ct. 2857 (1976).

53. <u>Carey</u> v. <u>Population Services International</u>, 97 S. Ct. 2010,
2017 (1977).

54. Idem, at 2020-21.

55. Idem, at 2016.

56. See <u>Roe</u> v. <u>Wade</u>, 410 U.S. 113, at 154 (1973); <u>Jacobson</u> v.
<u>Massachusetts</u>, 197 U.S. 11 (1905) (upholding compulsory vaccinations
for smallpox); <u>Buck</u> v. <u>Bell</u>, 274 U.S. 200 (1972) (upholding compulsory sterilizations). See also <u>Doe</u> v. <u>Commonwealth's Attorney</u>, 425
U.S. 901 (1976), wherein the Court affirmed a lower court's refusal
to grant relief from the enforcement of a criminal sodomy statute;
but see also <u>Buchanan</u> v. <u>Batchelor</u>, 401 U.S. 989 (1971) (vacated and

remanded to lower courts on grounds that Griswold rendered a Texas sodomy statute overbroad insofar as it sought to regulate the nature of marital intimacies).

57. Carey v. Population Services International, 97 S. Ct. 2010, at 2016 (1977).

58. Eisenstadt v. Baird, 405 U.S. 438, 564 (1972).

59. See, for example, California Bankers Association v. Shultz, 416 U.S. 21 (1974); Laird v. Tatum, 408 U.S. 1 (1972).

60. Whalen v. Roe, 97 S. Ct. 869 (1977).

61. Idem, at 876-77.

62. Idem, at 879.

63. Idem, at 875.

64. Idem, at 881 (Stewart, J., con. op.).

PART III

PRIVACY AND
PUBLIC POLICY

6

Personal Privacy
as an Issue of
Public Policy

As every man goes through life he fills in a number of
forms for the record, each containing a number of questions. . . . . There are thus hundreds of little threads in
all. If these threads were suddenly to become visible,
the whole sky would look like a spider's web, and if they
materialized as rubber bands, buses, trams and even
people would lose the ability to move, the wind would be
unable to carry torn-up newspapers or autumn leaves
along the streets of the city. They are not invisible,
they are not material, but every man is constantly aware
of their existence.

> Aleksandr Solzhenitsyn
> The Cancer Ward

Personal privacy, particularly informational privacy, emerged
in the 1970s as an issue of public policy, partly because judicial policies and constitutional interpretation failed to promote legal recognition of and protection for individuals' claims that their right of privacy
entails safeguards against abuse of personal information collected,
maintained, and utilized by the government. Development of public
policies relating to personal information and, more generally, to information control within the federal government, are partially a response to the Court's failure to legally recognize individuals' privacy
interests and claims with regard to personalized information held by
third parties, in both the public and private sector. As the Privacy
Protection Study Commission, in its two-year study, concluded:

> Current law is neither strong enough nor specific enough to
> solve the problems that now exist. In some cases, changes

in record-keeping practice have already made even recent
legal protections obsolete. As record-keeping systems
come to be used to preclude action by the individual, a
recent trend in the credit and financial areas, it is important that the individual also be given preventive protections to supplement the after-the-fact protections he sometimes has today. . . . The law as it now stands simply
ignores the strong interest many people have in records
about them. [1]

The developing constitutional law of privacy and its limited protection for individuals' claims to informational privacy (as in California Bankers Association v. Shultz, United States v. Miller, Fisher
v. United States, and Laird v. Tatum) provide both an appropriate
background and focus for examining public policies designed to address "[t]he imbalance in the relationship between individuals and
record-keeping institutions."[2] Privacy protection policies may be
viewed as designed to ensure citizens' political ideal of privacy by
legislative enactments that compensate for the circumscribed contours
of constitutionally protected privacy. The scope of judicial construction of the right of privacy itself and of First, Fourth, and Fifth
Amendment-protected privacy falls short of an adequate conceptualization of interests in informational privacy, and, consequently, fails
to provide the necessary principles for determining what, if any, restrictions may be imposed on government collection, storage, and
transmittal of personal information. In other words, judicial policies
failed to foster a framework for and legal safeguards for ensuring
privacy interests with respect to mandatory nonassociational and non-
incriminatory disclosures of personal information, governmental access to personal information held by third parties, and governmental
storage and disclosure of personal information.

PRIVACY AS AN ISSUE OF PUBLIC POLICY

Both judicial and legislative recognition of the salience of issues
of informational privacy reflect broad public concern over the impact
of computer technology on society. Since the 1930s the exponential
increase in the volume of information that may be processed by computers has greatly minimized time and distance constraints upon communications—thereby, promoting greater dependence upon information
and communications services and increasing interdependence among
institutions in both the public and private sectors, as well as among
levels of government. Developments over the last 40 years in information and communication technology have been characterized as

ushering in a "post-industrial society" and a "knowledge economy." The impact of computer technology will not only change individuals' expectations of personal privacy but also basic economic and social practices in the United States. By 1980 the estimated percentage of the work force involved in information collection, maintenance, and processing will approximately equal the percentage of workers both in service and industry. [3]

Perhaps the best illustration of the impact of information technology on citizens' lives is the increase in the federal government's collection and dissemination of personal information. In 1975, for example, governmental expenditures for federal agencies' information systems amounted to $3.2 billion, and in the last ten years federal agencies acquired 6,000 computer terminals so that over 9,260 computers are currently used by the federal government. While not all of these computers process personal information, federal agency reports, in compliance with the Privacy Act of 1974, indicate that the executive branch presently maintains 6,723 record systems containing more than 3.8 billion records on individuals, and over 58 percent of the information maintained is held by three departments, the Department of Defense, the Treasury, and Health, Education and Welfare. [4]

At the national level of government, issues of informational privacy arise within the broader context of policies designed to secure information control within the federal bureaucracy. Although developments in information and communications technology posed important issues for public policy makers for over 40 years, only in the last decade have Congress and the president endeavored to directly address these issues. Somewhere between 10,000 and 25,000 federal statutes authorize the executive branch to collect and maintain information, yet there exists no comprehensive framework for resolving conflicting interests with regard to federal agencies' information practices. [5] Historically, agencies have developed their own guidelines with little direction from the president. In 1970 the president ordered the Office of Management and Budget and the General Services Administration to initiate a 10 percent reduction in federal reporting requirements, and in 1974, President Ford ordered another 5 percent reduction by July 1976. Perhaps most noticeable has been the proliferation of commissions to study specific aspects of information policies—for example, the National Commission for Review of Federal and State Laws on Wiretapping and Electronic Surveillance, the National Commission on Records and Documents of Federal Officials, the Commission on Federal Paperwork, the Domestic Council on the Right of Privacy, and the Privacy Protection Study Commission.

Still, no comprehensive or coordinated policy framework has been developed for reconciling competing interests in personal privacy, the public's right to know, and administrative confidentiality. Indeed, national information policies are often crosscutting and occasionally conflicting. The pillars of federal information policy are the Freedom of Information Act, the Privacy Act, the Federal Register, the Federal Advisory Committee Act, and Federal Sunshine legislation. While these policies may appear to attain "a point of equilibrium in the field of information practices,"[6] their crosscutting nature makes administrative compliance and the practical value of informational privacy uncertain. That is, legislation such as the Privacy Act requires agencies to maintain the confidentiality of personal information, whereas legislation such as the Freedom of Information Act requires agencies to permit access to government-held information. Thus, historically, besides the complexity of issues and the difficulties of conceptualizing individuals' expectations of privacy in order to develop adequate procedural safeguards, a major obstacle has been the piecemeal approach to information practices by Congress, the president, and federal bureaucracy.[7]

Personal privacy has become an increasingly salient and controversial issue for policy makers because developments in information and communications technology threaten to diminish the practical value of personal privacy; because constitutional interpretation of the guarantees of the First, Fourth, and Fifth Amendments, focusing as it does on common law principles and proprietary concepts, failed to promote legal recognition and protection for interests in informational privacy; and, finally, because current information policies at times are crosscutting and conflicting, rendering safeguards for interests in personal information ineffectual within administrative contexts. The objectives of privacy protection policies therefore lie with promoting legal recognition of individuals' interests in informational privacy and establishing procedural requirements for governmental acquisition, maintenance, and dissemination of personal information. As the Privacy Protection Study Commission emphasized: "[N]either law or technology now gives an individual the tools he needs to protect his legitimate interests in the records organizations keep about him."[8] Accordingly, the Commission isolated three concurrent objectives for effective privacy protection policies:

> to create a proper balance between what an individual is expected to divulge to a record-keeping organization and what he seeks in return (to minimize intrusiveness);

> to open up record-keeping operations in ways that will minimize the extent to which recorded information about an individual is itself a course of unfairness in any decision about him made on the basis of it (to maximize fairness); and

to create and define obligations with respect to the uses and disclosures that will be made of recorded information about an individual (to create legitimate, enforceable expectations of confidentiality).[9]

These objectives both subsume and conceptually augment the underlying principles of the Privacy Act of 1974 in focusing attention on the problems involved in formulating and implementing privacy protection policies, as well as providing a basis for future privacy legislation.

PRINCIPLES AND PROVISIONS FOR INFORMATIONAL PRIVACY

The Privacy Act of 1974

While the Fair Credit Reporting Act of 1970 (regulating consumer reports), the Crime Control Act of 1973 (regulating access to individuals' criminal records), and the Family Educational Rights and Privacy Act of 1974 (regulating access to student educational records) dealt with specific kinds of interests in informational privacy, the Privacy Act of 1974 embodies the principal legislative affirmation that "the right of privacy is a personal and fundamental right protected by the Constitution of the United States."[10] In adopting the act, Congress recognized that "the opportunities for an individual to secure employment, insurance, and credit, and his right to due process, and other legal protections are endangered by the misuse of certain information systems" of the federal government.[11] The Privacy Act institutionalized individuals' interests in personal privacy by requiring safeguards on what information federal agencies may legitimately collect and how they may utilize the information maintained. Still, as Harold Relyea observes: "The Act does not protect the privacy of individuals in the sense of a 'right to be let along.' Rather it provides a federal 'Code of Fair Information Practice' that secures to individuals a legal right to exercise some measure of control over the information collected about them by the government."[12] The distinction between recognizing a right of privacy (that would entail prohibition of access to some kinds of personal information per se) and a right to fair information practices (that entails only procedural safeguards to ensure the confidentiality of personal information) underscores the fact that the Privacy Act regulates only the processes and procedures by which federal agencies acquire, store, and disseminate information.

The basic principles for privacy protection were initially developed in a 1973 report by the Department of Health, Education and Welfare Secretary's Advisory Committee on Automated Personal Data

Systems. The Secretary's Advisory Committee recommended five principles for guiding information policy, which subsequently furnished the analytical framework for the Privacy Act:

    1. There must be no personal data record-keeping systems whose very existence is secret.

    2. There must be a way for an individual to find out what information about him is in a record and how it is used.

    3. There must be a way for an individual to prevent information about him that was obtained for one purpose from being used or made available for other purposes without his consent.

    4. There must be a way for an individual to correct or amend a record of identifiable information about him.

    5. Any organization creating, maintaining, using, or disseminating records of identifiable personal data must assure the reliability of the data for their intended use and must take precautions to prevent misuse of the data. [13]

    The Privacy Protection Study Commission, in its study of agency operations under the Privacy Act, further elaborated eight principles as underlying one or more of the act's provisions. [14] An openness principle requires that no personal-data record-keeping systems be secret, and, more generally, that agencies establish a policy of openness about their record-keeping policies, practices, and systems. An individual access principle permits an individual about whom information is maintained in individually identifiable form to see and copy that information, and an individual participation principle grants individuals the right to correct or amend the substance of privileged information maintained. In terms of establishing information control, a collection limitation principle prescribes limits on the type of and manner by which information may be collected from an individual. Moreover, a use limitation principle places limits on the internal uses of personal information within a record-keeping organization, whereas a disclosure limitation principle limits external disclosures of privileged information. Further, an information management principle requires agencies to bear an affirmative responsibility for establishing reasonable and proper information management policies and practices, thereby assuring that agencies' collection, maintenance, and dissemination of information about individuals is necessary and lawful, as well as current and accurate. Finally, the act embodies an accountability principle inasmuch as agencies are accountable for their personal-data record-keeping policies and practices.

The Privacy Act establishes "a right of access for individuals to their files, a right to correct mistakes contained in those files, and a responsibility on the part of the Government to protect personal information from misuse and disclosure which constitute[s] an invasion of privacy of the subject of that information."[15] The act governs only information systems containing records from which information is retrieved by the name of the individual, or some other individual identifier of the federal government; state, local, and private information systems are exempt. Because the "systems of records" definition is the main threshold requirement for the act's other provisions, and since an "attribute search," in contrast to a name or index search, of information falls outside the scope of the act, some records containing personal information may still not be accessible to an individual.

Only individuals, not corporations, are granted rights of access to information contained in such systems. Individuals' rights of access to personal information depend upon effective implementation of the openness and individual access principles. The act's basic provisions for ensuring the principle of openness to governmental information are, first, the requirement that every agency annually publish notices of its record systems in the Federal Register, and second, that each agency provide a "Privacy Act Statement" whenever requests are made of individuals for individually identifiable personal information. In general, both of these requirements make a "significant step" toward ensuring agencies' accountability for privileged information. Yet, because current statements of record systems and uses, in both the Federal Register and Privacy Act Statements, are often too vague, annual notices should provide more detail, especially with regard to distinguishing between systems and subsystems, and more accurate descriptions of the "context and manner" of agencies' "routine uses" of information.[16]

The individual access principle underlies requirements that an agency, upon request, must respond by informing individuals whether a system of records contains personal information about them, permit the individuals to review any records pertaining to them, as well as make copies of such records at reasonable costs. Prior to the Privacy Act, some agencies did make certain records accessible (for example, the armed services permitted servicemen access to personnel, medical, and performance records) but in general the basic statutory authority for permitting individuals' access was the Freedom of Information Act. Individuals may use the Freedom of Information Act to obtain access to personal files as well as any record maintained by the federal government, except where a record falls within one of nine exemptions to the act. Individuals' reliance on the Freedom of Information Act however has several shortcomings. For example, an

agency may decline to disclose information it regards as part of its
internal deliberative process, and, ironically, agencies often refuse
to release personnel and medical records to individuals on the ground
that it constitutes an invasion of the individuals' privacy. [17] The Privacy Act, thus, may be viewed as a clarification of the Freedom of
Information Act's establishment of rights of access insofar as individuals' access to personalized information is refined and embellished.

Individuals having gained access to their records may request
amendment of what they consider to be erroneous information and,
further, if the request is refused by an agency, review is available.
The Privacy Act, thereby, establishes a principle of individual participation permitting "the individual . . . to keep some measure of
control (although not absolute control) over the substance of what he
himself reveals to an agency, as well as to check on what the agency
collects about him from other sources."[18] The principle's application, nevertheless, remains circumscribed with respect to perhaps
the most crucial files, namely, those agency records that are exempt
from the access requirement and consequently not subject to provisions for correction or amendment.

The Privacy Act's exemptions are permissive, not mandatory,
and apply to "systems of records" rather than to specific requests for
access to information. Consequently, agencies must invoke an exemption when publishing its systems of records and, hence, may in-
appropriately exclude records from the scope of the act, as well as
deny, in some cases, individuals' legitimate claims to access to personal information.

There are two types of exemptions, general and specific. General exemptions are extremely broad in order to reflect the complex-
ities of problems of national security and criminal law enforcement.
Although there are legitimate reasons for denial of access in these
areas, agencies may exercise discretion so as to deny individuals'
right of access to records, the right to know who has had access to
the records, the right to amend the records, and the right to bring
civil action for damages for violation of the act. Accordingly, agencies may well frustrate the act's underlying principles of openness,
individual access and participation, and, potentially, accountability
for information management. Indeed, under the general exemptions
agencies need not comply with all statutory provisions governing the
collection and maintenance of personal records.[19] Thus, while some
provisions still apply for information management, in the areas of national security and criminal justice the permissible discretion allowed
to agencies in deciding whether to grant or deny access remains such
as to leave open some of the very problems of information control that
the act was designed to solve.

By contrast, the specific exemptions are more narrowly drawn
and allow exemption of information systems only from certain pro-

visions. There are seven kinds of specific exemptions: classified materials and records covered by the foreign policy and national defense provision of the Freedom of Information Act; investigatory material compiled for law enforcement purposes; records of the Secret Service; statistical records; federal testing or examination material used solely to determine individual qualifications for appointment and promotion; investigatory material used to determine "suitability, eligibility, or qualifications" for federal employment, contracts, or access to classified material; and, finally, evaluation material used solely to determine potential for promotion in the military.[20] Administration under these exemptions is more accountable than under the general exemptions since they allow for civil remedies.

The breadth of the exemptions and their applicability to systems of records, rather than specific requests for access, creates the potential for serious dilution of individuals' rights and remedies under the act. Moreover, the Privacy Act, as Harold Relyea observes, "exempts precisely those agencies and kinds of record systems the abuses of which generated much of the very concern that led to passage of the Act. Subjects of investigations conducted in the name of law enforcement and national security are not given the right to see what is in their files."[21] Although both congressional committee reports indicated that the broad exemptions for law enforcement agencies did not permit carte blanche withholding of all personal information, the act's exemptions when implemented allow for considerable retrenchment by agencies from the principles of openness and systematic management of information practices.[22] In this regard, the Privacy Protection Study Commission concluded that present limitations on individuals' access to their records encourages "individuals [to] continue to rely on pre-existing laws and practices [those established by the Freedom of Information Act] when they want access to agency records about themselves."[23] There are several advantages for individuals seeking to claim access to personal information under the Freedom of Information Act rather than the Privacy Act. For example, the Freedom of Information Act's exemptions relate to specific requests rather than systems of records, and it contains specific time limits for agencies' responses to requests for disclosures. Accordingly, the Commission recommended that, "the Privacy Act should parallel the approach of the Freedom of Information Act in that an individual should be required to make a request which reasonably describes the record to which he desires access."[24] Such a revision of the Privacy Act would promote coordination of information practices by decreasing the present uncertainty for agencies implementing both acts.

Individuals' interests in privileged information and maintaining a modicum of informational privacy are primarily safeguarded by provisions governing collection and maintenance of personal information.

The collection limitation principle embraces the act's requirements that agencies collect only information that is relevant and necessary to accomplish a lawful purpose; collect information whenever practicably possible directly from the individual concerned; provide the individual with a Privacy Act Statement; and collect no information about an individual's exercise of First Amendment rights, as well as refrain from collecting and identifying individuals by their Social Security numbers.

These provisions indicate three criteria for evaluating federal agencies' collection and use of privileged information. First, agencies must have in their records only "relevant and necessary" information. Second, administrative needs for information must be legitimate; agencies cannot maintain information except for an agency purpose "required to be accomplished by statute or by executive order of the President." Third, the information collected must indeed be necessary and not simply relevant. Agencies' information needs are dictated when the "goals of the program cannot reasonably be met through alternative means."[25] While determination of need ultimately rests with each agency, the act significantly structures agencies' discretion in determining their needs and collection procedures. Furthermore, by encouraging agencies to gather information directly from the individuals concerned, and providing individuals with a Privacy Act Statement, agencies are required to evaluate their needs for personal information, the accuracy of the information is enhanced, and individuals may assess the burdens and benefits of their disclosures.

Whereas these provisions govern agencies' collection and maintenance of privileged information, provisions embodying principles of use and disclosure limitation regulate agencies' uses and dissemination of information. A principal difficulty with implementation of the use and disclosure limitation principles, however, appears to be that agencies often disclose more information than they are asked for "simply as a matter of convenience and economy."[26]

On the one hand, the act permits routine disclosures within an agency of privileged information to only officers and employees who have "a need for the record in the performance of their duties." Yet, "need" and "duties" remain sufficiently indefinite so as to perpetuate problems fostered by the act's definition of "agency," predicated of departments, such as the Department of Health, Education and Welfare. Since the relation between the individual and the government changes with intraagency disclosures, routine dissemination may often constitute an abuse of privileged information, because agencies utilize the information for purposes not compatible with its collection. In recognition of the potential for abuse of privileged information, the Privacy Commission recommended that, "the routine-use provision, which forbids disclosures that are not compatible with the purpose for which the information was originally collected, should be applied to internal agency uses."27

On the other hand, the disclosure limitation principle places limits on external dissemination of privileged information. While the act permits external disclosures without an individual's consent in ten categories, again the greatest potential for abuse of privileged information lies with agencies' practice of routine transfers of information to other agencies and institutions. In this regard, the Privacy Commission, observing that "disclosure provisions of the Privacy Act must allow for a certain amount of agency discretion, since, in an omnibus statute, it is impossible to enumerate all of the necessary conditions of disclosure," recommended amendment of the act, so that routine interagency exchanges of privileged information would be permissible only where the dissemination was compatible and consistent with the initial purposes of collecting the information.28

Collectively these principles and provisions encourage information management and accountability by regulating agencies' practices and procedures of collection, maintenance, use, and dissemination of privileged information. The Privacy Commission, however, found that the act's requirements that privileged information must be accurate, timely, complete, and relevant had had little impact on the kind of information collected and maintained by agencies:

> Most agencies, to the extent they have a position, stand by their prior record maintenance practices [as developed under the Freedom of Information Act]. They contend that they have always attempted to achieve accuracy, and that the terms "timely, complete, and relevant" are meaningful only in the context of a specific record or record-keeping situation—which is true. Nonetheless, interviews with operating personnel suggest that, although some accuracy standards have been tightened and retention periods for documents have been re-examined, agencies continue to maintain a substantial amount of information that is not as accurate, timely, complete, and relevant as it should be. The fact is that there are few if any formal mechanisms to review existing records and there is seldom if ever, enough time to do so.
>
> Because no specific, consistently applied criteria have been established for determining when an agency is in compliance with the Act's information management principles, they are not being adequately implemented.29

If, as the Privacy Commission suggests, no established criteria exist for determining compliance with information management principles, then it becomes difficult to determine the practical feasibility of provisions for safeguarding personal privacy.

Agencies' operations, moreover, demonstrate considerable confusion over implementing the Privacy Act concurrently with the Freedom of Information Act (for example, often the Privacy Act is cited improperly as a basis for withholding information requested under the Freedom of Information Act) and, thereby, mirror the failure to resolve basic inconsistencies in provisions for information management at the congressional level. As a House Report indicates, "the most difficult task in drafting Federal privacy legislation was that of determining the proper balance between the public's right to know about the conduct of their government and their equally important right to have information which is personal to them maintained with the greatest degree of confidence by Federal agencies."[30] Agencies may well adhere to prior information practices because they must comply with information management principles and provisions of both the Privacy Act and the Freedom of Information Act. Indeed, the Privacy Act's regulation of privileged information does not supersede the principles and provisions of the Freedom of Information Act. Instead, legislative history of the Privacy Act shows that the statute was "designed to preserve the status quo interpreted by the courts regarding disclosure of personal information under" the Freedom of Information Act.[31]

Although the Privacy Act may be understood as embellishing the privacy exemption of the Freedom of Information Act, in practice the crosscutting nature of these two acts leads to confusion, frustrating the principles of privacy protection and, more generally, diminishing the effectiveness of information control.[32] Because requirements for ensuring interests in personal privacy and access to governmental information are in many ways discordant, "neither privacy nor access can ever be considered alone; both must be considered in relation to other needs and in relation to each other."[33] Furthermore, because the Privacy Act was enacted against the background of the Freedom of Information Act and because agencies must simultaneously comply with the principles and provisions of both acts, the objectives and practical feasibility of privacy protections must be considered within the context of other information control policies and practices, particularly those established by the Freedom of Information Act.

Privileged Information and Freedom of Information

The Freedom of Information Act of 1966, premised on the principle that the public has a right to know about basic workings of its government, established a policy of governmental openness by pro-

viding the basic authority and procedure for individuals to petition the
executive branch for unreleased documents and records. The act resulted from 11 years of investigative hearings by the House Government Operations Committee's former Special Government Information
Subcommittee (1955–62) and, later, the Foreign Operations and Government Information Subcommittee, as well as a series of studies and
legislative proceedings conducted simultaneously by subcommittees of
the Senate Judiciary Committee. [34]

Previously, under the Administrative Procedure Act, federal
agencies effectively thwarted the public's right to know by denying
legitimate information to the public. Often, information was "withheld
in order to cover up embarrassing mistakes or irregularities and the
withholding justified by such phrases in Section 3 of the Administrative
Procedure Act as—'requiring secrecy in the public interest, ' or 'required for good cause to be held confidential. '"[35] Even when no good
cause could be found for withholding information, agencies were allowed to release information selectively to individuals "legitimately
and properly concerned." Consequently, the right of the public to
know about governmental activities was frequently "reduced by the
'right—or duty, or responsibility—of the Government to withhold' in
the public interest."[36]

The purpose of the Freedom of Information Act was to confine
agencies' discretion in deciding whether to grant or deny access to information by eliminating the ambiguous phrases of the Administrative
Procedure Act and, thereby, establish "a general philosophy of full
agency disclosure unless information is exempt under the delineated
statutory language and to provide a court procedure by which citizens
and the press may obtain information wrongfully withheld."[37] Access
to government information is not limited to those persons with particular reasons for seeking disclosure. Instead material is available to
"any person." Courts, moreover, are precluded from considering
the needs of the party seeking access, unless the information sought
falls within one of nine statutory exemptions.

Initial administrative compliance with the Freedom of Information Act was not particularly impressive. In 1972 the House Government Operations Subcommittee on Foreign Operations and Government
Information found that the act had been "hindered by five years of foot-
dragging" by agencies and recommended further legislative and administrative remedies. Two years later, after overriding a presi-
dential veto, Congress reiterated support for a policy of governmental
openness by strengthening provisions of the act with amendments and
further regulating administrative discretion in permitting or denying
access to government information. [38]

In enacting the Privacy Act and amending the Freedom of Information Act in 1974, Congress endeavored to attain "a proper balance

between the protection of the individual's right of privacy and the preservation of the public's right to Government information by excluding
those files the disclosure of which might harm the individual."[39] In
other words, Congress attempted to balance interests in nondisclosure
and disclosure by regulating administrative discretion, which often
led to disregard for both individuals' privacy interests in privileged
information and the public's interest in freedom of information. On
at least one level, then, the Privacy and Freedom of Information Acts
are complementary in regulating information practices and procedures
by providing specific rights and remedies for individuals' access to
information, both about their own activities collected and maintained
by federal agencies and about the basic operations of the government.

The crosscutting provisions of the two acts nonetheless render
the practical feasibility of ensuring either privacy interests in privileged information or the public's interests in freedom of information
uncertain. In this regard, the Privacy Commission concluded: "The
Privacy Act and the Freedom of Information Act mesh well. There
are no statutory conflicts. Recent court decisions have also better defined the balances that must be struck between the competing interests.
Nonetheless, there do appear to be some practical problems in the
implementation of these two Acts."[40] There are indeed some "practical problems in the implementation of these two laws," but they arise
precisely because the two acts do not in fact "mesh well." There are
actually several statutory conflicts that frustrate agencies' implementation of the concurrent policies.

Ironically, one of the most serious problems for ensuring safeguards for personal privacy arises from the overlap of the Privacy
Act and the Freedom of Information Act's exemption from disclosure
of information that would constitute "a clearly unwarranted invasion
of personal privacy." Although administrators implementing both
acts have found considerable confusion to exist over these crosscutting
provisions, the Privacy Commission suggested:

> To understand the meshing of these requirements, it is use-
> ful to consider first the situation prior to the passage of the
> Privacy Act. The exemptions on access to information in
> the Freedom of Information Act are discretionary, not man-
> datory. Thus, under the FOIA (prior to the passage of the
> Privacy Act), an agency could withhold information, the
> disclosure of which would, in the agency's opinion, con-
> stitute a "clearly unwarranted invasion of personal pri-
> vacy," but the agency was not required to do so. Today,
> after the passage of the Privacy Act, an agency is still
> required, by the Freedom of Information Act, to disclose
> information that would not constitute a "clearly unwarranted

invasion of personal privacy," but now an agency no longer
has the discretion to disclose information it believes would
constitute such a clearly unwarranted invasion. [41]

While the Privacy Commission found that "confusion, widely differing
implementation, and occasional frustration of the intent of both laws
[had] resulted," it concluded that problems arise because "agency operating personnel responsible for the day-to-day implementation of the
two Acts have not been clearly enough appraised of how the laws mesh,
of the applicable interpretations and court decisions, and of an agency's
corresponding responsibilities under them. "[42]
     The Privacy Commission's conclusions notwithstanding, the
Privacy and the Freedom of Information Acts do not mesh well. There
are several statutory conflicts, and considerable confusion exists over
the role of the Privacy Act vis-à-vis the Freedom of Information Act's
privacy exemption. In general, the Freedom of Information Act encourages agencies to err on the side of disclosure by not forbidding
disclosures and by neglecting to provide incentives to safeguard personal privacy; while the Privacy Act permits disclosures only when
required, it does not supersede the Freedom of Information Act.
Moreover, administrative compliance is uncertain, if not impossible,
because of conflicting requirements of the acts. The acts are inconsistent with respect to their provisions for time limits on agencies'
determinations to grant or deny access to records, on the fees charged
for materials, in their notice provisions that individuals, upon denial
of access to records, may appeal the decision within the agency, and
in administrative remedies for denial of materials. Also, the leader-
ship role for ensuring compliance with each act is assigned to two different departments, the Department of Justice and the Office of Management of the Budget. [43]
     More important, administrators encounter difficulties in their
discretionary determinations as to whether disclosures of personal
information are prohibited by the Privacy Act or required under the
Freedom of Information Act. Major problems arise with reconciling
the Privacy Act and the Freedom of Information Act's exemption for
disclosures constituting "a clearly unwarranted invasion of personal
privacy." In some instances, personal information covered by the
Privacy Act, but not required to be disclosed under the Freedom of
Information Act, may be disclosed under the Privacy Act for "routine
uses" or with prior written consent of the subject of the records.
Still, more troublesome is the fact that the Privacy Act allows for
disclosures in the public interest of only certain kinds of information,
while the Freedom of Information Act allows for disclosures of privileged information if a public need is established. Because the Privacy
Act does not supersede the Freedom of Information Act, which permits

the release of privileged information unless it constitutes "a clearly unwarranted invasion of personal privacy," there are insufficient safeguards against the arbitrary exercise of administrative discretion and possible abuse of privileged information.

The proper exercise of administrative discretion in responding to third-party requests for privileged information is also difficult to determine, since administrators are confronted with two conflicting standards. The Privacy Act protects all individually identifiable information, whereas the Freedom of Information Act permits agencies' nondisclosures of only information constituting "a clearly unwarranted invasion of personal privacy." Disclosures under the Freedom of Information Act, therefore, might violate the Privacy Act. Thus, administrators face a dilemma of refusing to disclose information and risking a lawsuit under the Freedom of Information Act by the party denied access, or disclosing the information and risking litigation under the Privacy Act by the individual whose file was released. Administrative difficulties in determining whether to grant or deny access to third-party requests for individually identifiable information are compounded by the language of the Freedom of Information Act's privacy exemption. Some administrators may well find an inconsistency between the right of privacy and the permissibility of disclosures of privileged information under the Freedom of Information Act, which may be deemed an unwarranted disclosure but not "a clearly unwarranted invasion of personal privacy."

Administrators' uncertainties in complying with the crosscutting provisions of the Privacy and Freedom of Information Acts diminish the practical feasibility of safeguards for informational privacy. Administrative uncertainties, however, result from the failure to resolve basic inconsistencies in the acts at the congressional level. During committee hearings on the Freedom of Information Act, several agencies argued that the words "clearly unwarranted" should be omitted so as to assure more stringent safeguards for personal privacy. In rejecting proposals for more stringent safeguards, Congress indicated a preference for balancing interests in privileged information and governmental openness. In particular, the Senate Report discussed the meaning of the phrase "clearly unwarranted invasion of personal privacy":

> It is believed that the scope of exemption is held within bounds by the use of the limitation of "a clearly unwarranted invasion of personal privacy." The phrase . . . enunciates a policy that will involve a balancing of interests between the protection of an individual's private affairs from unnecessary public scrutiny, and the preservation of the public's right to government information.[44]

According to the Senate Report the privacy exemption establishes a policy for agencies to balance opposing interests. Administrators, in deciding whether to grant or deny access, should balance interests in privacy and access not only as recognized by the Privacy Act and the Freedom of Information Act but also under the privacy exemption of the Freedom of Information Act. Yet, the House Report suggests contrariwise that the privacy exemption itself balances the respective interests: "The limitation of a 'clearly unwarranted invasion of personal privacy' provides a proper balance between the protection of an individual's right of privacy and the preservation of the public's right to Government information by excluding those kinds of files the disclosure of which might harm the individual."[45]

Thus, with conflicting committee reports, agencies are left with no clear guidelines or processes by which to reach a reconciliation of interests in personal privacy and governmental openness.

PRIVACY, ACCESS, AND PUBLIC POLICY

Conceptualizing Privacy and Access

The crosscutting nature of the Privacy and Freedom of Information Acts may well suggest to administrators that the respective interests in privacy and freedom of information are incompatible, if not contradictory, and, thus, privacy safeguards and information control policies are destined to failure. One of the greatest difficulties in formulating a comprehensive information policy that would ensure within administrative contexts interests in both privacy and access is the ambiguous nature of privacy. Legislative history provides no specific definition of privacy, and traditional approaches to the concept confuse it with a right of privacy, thereby prejudging the problems of information control. Furthermore, the precise relationship between rights of privacy and access remains ill-defined.

Analysis of the concept of privacy in Chapter 1 suggested that privacy underlies a broad range of interests in limiting access to an individual's experiences and engagements. Individuals do not have a single interest in privacy; nor do they value privacy only for either its intrinsic worth or instrumental value.

> For any individual, privacy, as a value, is not absolute or constant: its significance can vary with time, place, age and other circumstances. There is even more variability among groups of individuals. As a social value, furthermore, privacy can easily collide with others, most notably free speech, freedom of the press, and the public's "right to know."[46]

Although the normative importance of privacy may not be constant for all of an individual's activities, nor the same for an entire population, protection of personal privacy is necessary because intrusions upon or disclosures of individuals' affairs diminish not only the particular value they attach to privacy but, more important, their liberty and personal autonomy in defining their activities.

Legislative and judicial acknowledgments of a right of privacy legitimate individuals' interests in their own privacy and in their liberty to control and define their lives. In particular, congressional recognition of the right to informational privacy was designed to safeguard against potential abuses of personal information. Fundamentally, privacy-protection legislation acknowledges that individuals in a free society have a right to self-determination and control over their engagements.

Contrary to the assumption of some proponents of privacy protection and advocates of information control, interests in privacy and access are not contradictory. They are, rather, complementary. Legislation safeguarding informational privacy registers the concern that privacy is in important ways related to individuals' decisions as to their self-government. Alternatively, legislation supporting the public's right to know through legal rights of access acknowledges that in a free society citizens must be informed about their government's decisions and practices. Therefore, the rights of privacy and access are actually political correlates; both involve the right of individuals to control information important to their self-government. This self-government is viewed in terms of both their freedom to determine their everyday activities and, in the broader political sense, their freedom to collectively determine the direction of their government's activities.

The interrelationship between rights of informational privacy and access to information held by the government thus appears as two sides of a coin. Interests in informational privacy found protection with judicially enforced rights of privacy and institutionalization in the Privacy Act, requiring nondisclosure of personal information; while the right of the people to know about the basic workings of their government receives support in the principles of free government and the guarantees of access to government information established by the Freedom of Information Act, requiring disclosure of government records and documents. Although informational privacy and access to governmental information appear contrary and point in opposite directions, they are conceptually complementary, and the nexus between the two is information flow. As the Privacy Protection Study Commission recognized, privacy protection policies fundamentally involve the regulation of the "free flow of information" among federal agencies.

The flow of information to and from the individual and the government therefore becomes important in analyzing issues of privacy,

FIGURE 1

Framework for Studying Information Flow within Administrative
Contexts

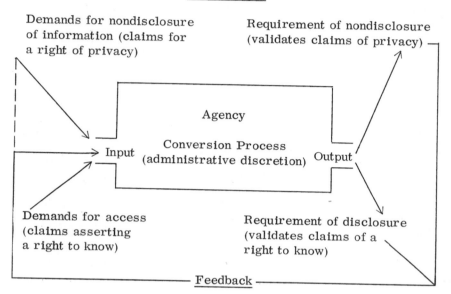

Source: Compiled by the author.

access, and information control. The notion of information flow suggests as a heuristic device a framework for illuminating claims to informational privacy and access. This framework is schematically
represented in Figure 1.

Models inevitably oversimplify. This one, however, illuminates
the formal relationship between claims to informational privacy and
access within administrative contexts. On the input side, interests
in informational privacy are represented in the statutory provisions
of the Freedom of Information and Privacy Acts, as well as by individuals' demands for nondisclosure. Alternatively, demands for access may represent either the claim of individuals under the Privacy
Act to know what information about them is held by an agency, or the
assertion of the people's right to know, guaranteed by the Freedom of
Information Act. Agencies, then, must process these demands and,
on the output side, either validate or invalidate them. Demands for
nondisclosure may be either validated under the Privacy Act or by an

exemption of the Freedom of Information Act, or invalidated according to some other provision of the Privacy Act or Freedom of Information Act. Similarly, demands for disclosure may be either ratified by an agency, according to provisions of the Freedom of Information Act or, in instances where individuals claim access to their own personal records, the Privacy Act. They may also be rejected by an agency according to one of the nine exemptions of the Freedom of Information Act.

The principal merits of conceptualizing the relationship between interests in privacy and access in terms of information flow are twofold. First, although the framework illuminates only the formal relationship between privacy and access, it indicates why balancing these interests has been so difficult in policy making and administration. Far from being monolithic, the interests represented are extremely fluid. Disputes among individuals, groups, and agencies under the acts often result from generalizing the specific values of privacy, access, and administrative needs that underlie information transfers. Second, the framework suggests the relationship between the variables of disclosure, that is, interests in and demands for informational privacy and access, and the conversion process by which agencies ratify or reject demands for nondisclosure or disclosure. The conversion process refers to an agency's decision-making structures and development of plans, guidelines, policy statements, rules, and regulations governing its nondisclosure or disclosure of information. The crucial element in attaining the policy objectives sought through information control, therefore, appears to lie in regulating the administrative discretion inherent in agencies' disclosure practices and procedures.

Balancing Acts and Gauging Administrative Discretion

The discretion inherent in administrative implementation of policies in general, and the decision-making structures establishing disclosures procedures in particular, is necessary but subject to abuse. Administrative discretion is essential because of the hard cases that require individualized evaluation of interests in personal privacy, disclosure, and agency needs. Yet, administrative discretion often leads to abuses in agencies' collection and maintenance of personal information. Also, this discretion promotes syndromes of bureaucratic secrecy, such as those permitted by the Administrative Procedure Act.

In this regard, the Freedom of Information and Privacy Acts regulate agencies' information practices by not only providing for external restraints on the exercise of administrative discretion but also by requiring agencies to constrain their discretion internally by confining, structuring, and checking their disclosure procedures, thereby insuring a modicum of information control.[47]

The Freedom of Information Act in establishing rights of access and a policy of governmental openness, confined agencies' discretion by requiring the following: publication of the organization, place, officers, and method by which access to information may be requested; development of procedures for responding to requests; and limiting nondisclosures to nine specific categories.[48] More important perhaps, the act structures agencies' practices by requiring that they develop and publish rules governing disclosure, final opinions, statements of policy, staff manuals, and so on.[49] Finally, the act checks agencies' procedures and practices by providing for judicial review and annual reports to Congress on information transfers.[50]

The Privacy Act institutionalized interests in personal privacy by restricting the collection, maintenance, and dissemination of individually identifiable information. The act confines discretion and encourages agencies to evaluate their information needs through its provisions governing collection, maintenance, and disclosure of personal information; it requires that agencies maintain only necessary information and specifies both general and specific exemptions from the act.[51] Agencies' information practices are significantly structured by requirements governing disclosure, access to records, rules relating to requests for personal information, procedures for reviewing requests, fees charged for materials released, and the reporting of all new record systems.[52] Like the Freedom of Information Act, the Privacy Act provides checks for abuse of discretion by mandating that agencies account for all their disclosures and that they establish processes by which individuals may amend and appeal the information contained in their records. In addition, it provides for civil remedies and criminal penalties for unwarranted disclosures of personal information.[53]

Although provisions of each act significantly regulate administrative discretion, together the acts do not "mesh well," nor do they supply adequate guidelines for reconciling interests in both privacy and access. Basically, the Privacy Commission's view of the two acts remains too simplistic:

> When the two Acts are read together any disclosure of a record about an individual in a system of records as defined by the Privacy Act to any member of the public other than the individual to whom the record pertains is forbidden if the disclosure would constitute a "clearly unwarranted invasion of personal privacy." The reverse obligation also holds: even though a record is about an

individual, it cannot be withheld from any member of the
public who requests it if the disclosure would not constitute
a clearly unwarranted invasion of personal privacy. The
courts are the final arbiters of which disclosures do or do
not meet the unwarranted-invasion test and over the years
they have established certain types of recorded information which must be disclosed without question.[54]

Because the Privacy and Freedom of Information Acts are crosscutting
and in many ways inconsistent, they fail to provide adequate safeguards
for individual's privacy interests and to promote a comprehensive information policy. Agencies, moreover, may not expect definitive
guidance from the courts; indeed, reliance on the judiciary may well
prove costly and not always conclusive. Lower courts disagree as to
what constitutes "a clearly unwarranted invasion of personal privacy.[55] The Supreme Court also promises little by way of clarification, having stated only that, "Exemption six [constitutes a clearly unwarranted invasion of personal privacy] does not protect against disclosure of every incidental invasion of privacy—only such disclosures
as constitute 'clearly unwarranted' invasions of personal privacy."[56]

PROPOSALS AND PROSPECTS

The Privacy Act significantly contributes to the recognition and
protection of individuals' interests in personal privacy, and, in particular, informational privacy. Still, the incremental approach of the
Privacy and Freedom of Information Acts to federal agencies' information management fostered inconsistencies between the acts and resulted in the failure to provide clear standards and mechanisms for
reconciling the policy objectives of privacy protection and freedom of
information. Indeed, the acts confront agencies and the courts with
what appears to be "a 'split-personality' legislative reaction, by the
conflict between a seeming passion for privacy and a comparable passion for needless invasions of privacy."[57] The crosscutting nature
of present information policies promotes in some instances ad hoc
decision making and costly and not always conclusive litigation, and,
therefore, leaves open the possibility for agencies' abuse of privileged
information and denial of reasonable requests for access to government-held information.

The prospects for ensuring privacy safeguards within administrative contexts, and reconciling interests in personal privacy and
the public's right to know, depend upon the development of information
policy that simultaneously treats interests in privacy and access. Interests in personal privacy and the public's right to know are not nec-

essarily incompatible. Rather they are complementary and political
correlates. Privacy protection and information management within
the federal bureaucracy presuppose the acknowledgment of both interests in personal privacy and public access and requires a comprehensive policy framework through which information issues may be resolved. Only a comprehensive information policy establishing clear
and consistent guidelines for agencies and appropriate mechanisms
for implementing them will increase the practical feasibility of privacy safeguards, the reconciliation of interests in privacy and access,
and promote agencies' accountability for their information practices.

The Privacy Protection Study Commission's recommendations,
if adopted, would achieve greater parity between the Privacy Act and
the Freedom of Information Act. [58] In particular, the conflict between
the Privacy Act and the Freedom of Information Act's privacy exemption needs to be resolved so as to eliminate the agencies' dilemmas
and possible discretionary injustice in determining whether to disclose
or not to disclose personal information that might constitute an invasion of personal privacy. More generally, in order to facilitate coordination of information practices, the Privacy Commission proposed:

> [C]ertain of the specific exemptions in the Freedom of In-
> formation Act should actually be duplicated in the Privacy
> Act. These include the Freedom of Information Act ex-
> emptions dealing with information specifically authorized
> to be kept secret in the interest of national defense and
> foreign policy, certain investigative information compiled
> for law enforcement purposes, and operating reports used
> by an agency responsible for the supervision of financial
> institutions. [59]

Amendment of the act would promote greater parity between the grants
of access under the Freedom of Information Act and the Privacy Act
and minimize discretionary injustice in agencies' reliance on the exemptions of either act to deny individuals' requests for disclosures of
personal information. Individuals' interests in personal privacy are
enhanced by allowing them to know what information the government
collects and maintains on them, as well as by permitting them to request correction of information they believe to be inaccurate.

The strongest protection for individuals' privacy interests entails express prohibitions on agencies' collection of certain types of
information. In this regard, the Privacy Commission refused to rec-
ommend revision, except with respect to medical records, of either
the Privacy Act or the Freedom of Information Act so as to forbid in
some cases collection and disclosure of personal information per se.
The Commission concluded:

Quite simply, there is no vehicle for answering the question: "Should a particular record-keeping policy, practice, or system exist at all?" While the Act takes an important step in establishing a framework by which an individual may obtain and question the contents of his record, it does not purport to establish ethical standards or set limits to collection or use of certain types of information. Without such standards, however, the principal threat of proliferating records systems is not addressed. Nowhere, other than in the ineffective section requiring the preparation and review of new system notices, does the Act address the question of who is to decide what and how information should be collected, and how it may be used. To deal with this situation, the Congress and the Executive Branch will have to take action. [60]

Although presently the Privacy Act forbids collection of information describing individuals' exercise of First Amendment freedoms, the act does not go far enough in prohibiting collection of other kinds of personal information. Moreover, "a true act to protect privacy would neither have authorized release of information required to be disclosed under the FOIA, nor have allowed the exemption in the FOIA [clearly unwarranted invasion of personal privacy] to be modified by the inclusion of 'clearly.'"[61]

In addition to legislation designed to achieve greater statutory parity between the Privacy and Freedom of Information Acts and clarification or prohibition of agencies' collection of personal information, the objectives of privacy protection would be furthered by the establishment of institutional mechanisms for overseeing the implementation of information policies and reconciling in hard cases conflicts between interests in privacy and access. As one remedy for the difficulties in attaining compliance with privacy safeguards, federal agencies could adopt the present policy of some agencies, with regard to both the Privacy and Freedom of Information Acts, of designating officials to oversee the implementation of the agencies' information procedures and practices. As the Privacy Commission observed, designation of a Privacy Act officer would provide an internal incentive for more effective management and accountability of agencies' disclosure practices:

Strengthening the individual agency enforcement mechanisms in the Privacy Act by the appointment of a Privacy Act officer in each agency is not intended to relieve the agency's operating personnel of their responsibilities under the Act. Rather, it is intended to make their jobs easier by providing a mechanism for guidance, instruction, and interpretation. A "reasonableness" test in the law is important for a court, but it does little to provide insight and guidance for those charged with the day-to-day implementation of the law.

By the same token, creation within an agency of an enforcement mechanism will serve to hold agency employees accountable in a way that no external entity or individual record subject can. This is as it should be, for ultimately the record-keeping agency must bear the burden for assuring that its record-keeping practices are fair. [62]

While a Privacy Act officer would promote within an agency compliance with privacy safeguards, the establishment of an independent Federal Privacy Board, or "Federal Information Practices Board," [63] would enhance privacy protection legislation by establishing a mechanism for minimizing discrepancies in information practices among federal agencies. The Privacy Commission recommended an independent Federal Privacy Board to monitor and evaluate implementation of privacy policies, and "research, study, and investigate areas of privacy concern," as well as issue "interpretative rules" for guiding agencies' information practices and procedures. [64] The Privacy Commission's recommended board, however, would have only enforcement power "in connection with the implementation by Federal agencies of the Privacy Act itself." Unlike an earlier proposal by the Domestic Council Committee on the Right of Privacy for an Office of Information Policy, the Privacy Commission's proposal permits only the narrower focus on privacy protection policies, and, thus, while promoting agencies' compliance with privacy safeguards, would not foster the necessary coordination of information policies. [65] Establishment of a Federal Privacy Board would at least provide an institutional mechanism for resolving inconsistencies between the Privacy Act and the Freedom of Information Act and among agencies' implementation of the acts.

NOTES

1. U.S., The Privacy Protection Study Commission, Report of the Privacy Protection Study Commission, Privacy in an Information Society (1977) 10-11.
2. Ibid., at 6.
3. U.S., Domestic Council Committee on the Right of Privacy, Report to the President of the United States, National Information Policy, (1976) at 5. See also Arthur R. Miller, The Assault on Privacy (Ann Arbor: University of Michigan Press, 1971); Daniel Bell,

The Coming of Post-Industrial Society (New York: Basic Books, 1976); and Peter Drucker, The Age of Discontinuity (New York: Harper & Row, 1969).

4. See U.S., National Bureau of Standards, Information Technology Division, Computers in the Federal Government (1976); National Information Policy at 23; and U.S., Office of Management and Budget, First Annual Report to President, Federal Personal Data Systems Subject to the Privacy Act of 1974 (1975) 2-3.

5. U.S., Estimate of the Congressional Research Service for the Commission on Federal Paperwork, A Report of the Commission on Federal Paperwork, Confidentiality and Privacy (1977).

6. Francis Rourke, Secrecy and Publicity (Baltimore: Johns Hopkins Press, 1966), p. 16.

7. See National Information Policy, at 9-19.

8. Privacy in an Information Society, at 8 (emphasis in original).

9. Ibid., at 14-15 (emphasis in original).

10. The Privacy Act, Pub. Law. 93-579, 5 U.S.C. § 552 (a) (1974).

11. Statement of one of the congressional findings prefacing the act. 5 U.S.C. § 552 (a) (3).

12. Jerome J. Hanus and Harold C. Relyea, "A Policy Assessment of the Privacy Act of 1974," 25 American University Law Review 555, 573 (1976).

13. U.S., Department of Health, Education and Welfare, Report of the Secretary's Advisory Committee on Automated Personal Data Systems, Records, Computers, and the Rights of Citizens (1973), at 41.

14. Privacy in an Information Society, at 501-2.

15. Senator Edward Kennedy, "Freedom of Information and the Privacy Act," Congressional Record, S. 18144-45, 18144 (daily ed., Oct. 9, 1975).

16. See 5 U.S.C. § 552 (a) (e) (3), and Privacy in an Information Society, 506, 517-20.

17. Privacy in an Information Society, at 508.

18. Ibid., at 512. See also, 5 U.S.C. § 552 (a) (d) (3), (g) (1) (A), (j)-(k).

19. See 5 U.S.C. § 552 (a) (j).

20. See 5 U.S.C. § 552 (a) (k) (1)-(7).

21. Hanus and Relyea, "Policy Assessment," at 586.

22. H. Rept. 1416, 93d Cong., 2d sess. (1974) 19.

23. Privacy in an Information Society, at 509.

24. Ibid., at 510 (emphasis in original).

25. S. Rept. 1183, 93d Cong., 2d sess. (1974) 46.

26. Privacy in an Information Society, at 19.

27. Ibid., at 516.

28. Ibid., at 517-21.

29. Ibid., at 522.

30. H. Rept. 1497, 89th Cong., 2d sess. (1966), reprinted in United States Code Congressional and Administrative News 2418 (89th Cong., 2d sess., 1966).

31. Analysis of House and Senate Compromise Amendments to the Federal Privacy Act, 120 Congressional Record 12243 (daily ed., Dec. 17, 1974).

32. The Freedom of Information Act, 5 U.S.C. § 552 (b) (6), provides an exemption for disclosures "which would constitute a clearly unwarranted invasion of personal privacy."

33. Mary Hulett, "Privacy and the Freedom of Information Act," 27 Administrative Law Review 275 (1975).

34. See, generally, U.S. Congress, Senate, Committee on the Judiciary, subcommittee on Administrative Practice and Procedure of the Committee of the Judiciary, Freedom of Information Source Book: Legislative Materials, Cases, Articles, 93d Cong., 2d sess. (1974).

35. See, H. Rept. 1497; and S. Rept. 813, 89th Cong., 1st sess. (1965).

36. Louis Henkin, "The Right to Know," 120 Pennsylvania Law Review 271, 275 (1971).

37. S. Rept. 813, at 3.

38. See, generally, U.S., Congress, House Committee on Government Operations and Senate Committee on Judiciary, Freedom of Information Act and Amendments of 1974, 94th Cong., 1st sess. (1975).

39. See, U.S., Library of Congress, Congressional Research Sercice, The Administration of the Freedom of Information Act: A Brief Overview of Executive Annual Reports for 1975, by Harold Relyea (September 2, 1976).

40. Privacy in an Information Society, at 530.

41. Ibid., at 520 (emphasis in original).

42. Ibid., at 521.

43. Compare 5 U.S.C. § 552a (4) with 5 U.S.C. § 552 (a) (f) (5) and (q) (5); 5 U.S.C. § 552a (6) (A) (i) with 5 U.S.C. § 552 (a) (d) (i); and, see Congressional Record, S. 18144 (daily ed., Oct. 9, 1975).

44. See, S. Rept. 813, at 9.

45. H. Rept. 1497, at 2428 (emphasis added).

46. Records, Computers, and the Rights of Citizens, at 38.

47. The framework for discussing administrative discretion in terms of "confining, structuring, and checking" discretionary injustice is derived from Kenneth Culp Davis's book Discretionary Justice (Urbana, Ill.: University of Chicago Press, 1969).

48. 5 U.S.C. § 552a (1) (A)-(E), (b) (1)-(9).

49. 5 U.S.C. § 552a (2), (3), (4) (A).

230 / PRIVACY, LAW, AND PUBLIC POLICY

50. 5 U.S.C. § 552a (d) (1)-(7).

51. 5 U.S.C. § 552 (a) (b) (1)-(11), (N), (e) (1) and (1) (1)-(2), (k).

52. 5 U.S.C. § 552 (a) (b), (d), (f), (o).

53. 5 U.S.C. § 552 (a) (c), (d) (i)-(ii), (d) (3), (g) (1), (i) (1), and (p).

54. Privacy in an Information Society, at 25 (emphasis in original).

55. Compare Getman v. NRLB, 45 F.2d 670 (D.C. Cir. 1971) and Wine Hobby U.S.A., Inc. v. IRS, 502 F.2d 133 (3d Cir. 1974) (requiring balancing within the Exemption) with Robles v. EPA, 484 F.2d 843 (4th Cir. 1973) (interpreting the exemption itself to balance competing interests and to safeguard "intimate details of highly personalized nature"), and Rural Housing Alliance v. Department of Agriculture, 498 F.2d 73 (D.C. Cir. 1971).

56. Department of Air Force v. Rose, 96 S. Ct. 1592, 1608 (1976).

57. Idem, at 1610 (Burger, C. J., dis. op.).

58. Several bills were introduced in Congress as a result of the Privacy Commission's recommendations. See, H.R. 10076, 95th Cong., 1st sess. (Nov. 11, 1977) and H.R. 9986, 95th Cong., 1st sess. (Nov. 3, 1977) (amending the Privacy Act and establishing a Federal Information Practices Board); H.R. 8279 (amending Privacy Act), H.R. 8280 (restricting access to consumer reports), H.R. 8281 and 8282 (amending Fair Credit Reporting Act), H.R. 8283 (amending Social Security Act), H.R. 8284 (restricting use of Social Security numbers), H.R. 8285 (amending Fair Credit Reporting Act), H.R. 8286 (to assure privacy of certain public assistance records), H.R. 8287 (amending the Internal Revenue Code), H.R. 8288 (amending the Fair Credit Reporting Act), 95th Cong., 1st sess. (July 13, 1977).

59. Privacy in an Information Society, at 512 (emphasis in original).

60. Idem, at 536. See, also, generally, Alan F. Westin, Computers, Health Records, and Citizen Rights (Washington, D.C.: National Bureau of Standards Monograph 157, 1976).

61. Hanus and Relyea, "Policy Assessment," at 590.

62. Privacy in an Information Society, at 523.

63. See H. R. 10076.

64. Privacy in an Information Society, at 510.

65. See National Information Policy.

7

Conclusion: Law, Policy, and the Political Ideal of Privacy

An American has no sense of privacy. He does not know what it means. There is no such thing in the country.

George Bernard Shaw
<u>Speech</u>

Citizens in the United States, as the always perceptive Alexis de Tocqueville observed, tend to translate moral and social concerns into legal and political issues. As though to confirm de Tocqueville's observation, since the turn of the century they have extensively litigated and legislated protections for matters of personal privacy. Moreover, although Shaw, as an Englishman, may not value or may simply reject an American's sense of privacy, Americans historically have understood personal privacy to involve a "right to be let alone." Both the extent of litigation over and the common understanding of privacy as a "right to be let alone" exemplify the "American way of life" and the vision of liberalism, or, rather, dedication to individualism, the rule of law, and freedom from unwarranted governmental intrusions into citizens' private affairs.

The particular fascination with and understanding of privacy and the practice of rights of U.S. citizens fostered, in the twentieth century, increasing litigation over and legislation of safeguards for individuals' privacy interests. The salience and symbolic appeal of a political ideal of privacy, however, is a measure of both the growing concern and confusion over privacy and its legal protection. Scholarly treatment, no less than the common understanding, of a "right to be let alone" tends to idealize privacy politically, in the sense of an unqualified liberty or right. Such a broad political ideal of privacy animates, indeed, invites litigation and legislation at the cost of obscuring the nature of personal privacy and its relationship to freedom, liberty, and the practice of rights.

Privacy is fundamentally a nonlegal, even parapolitical, concept. Privacy basically denotes an existential condition of limited access to individuals' life experiences and engagements. Consequently, individuals may have a wide range of privacy interests and expectations with respect to their activities. Individuals' privacy interests also may diverge in terms of interpretative privacy, or informational privacy, and causal privacy, or limitations on physical intrusions upon personal affairs (such as those accompanying solicitors, loud and raucous noise, or government searches and seizures). Hence, individuals may have many different kinds of privacy interests with respect to either interpretative or causal access. For example, individuals may have interests in limiting access to personal information concerning their finances, religious or political affiliations, as well as in preventing physical intrusions upon their activities in their homes, apartments, or automobiles.

Perhaps precisely because privacy so intimately and inwardly touches individuals' lives, individuals tend to presume a "right to be let alone" and fail not only to examine the nature of privacy and its legal protection but also to appreciate the sources and extent of nonlegal protection for personal privacy (such as the customs, traditions, and social practices respecting individualism and private property in the United States). Contemporary controversies over the nature and scope of a constitutional right of privacy, moreover, tend to overshadow the sources of legal protection for privacy in tort law, legislation and, most broadly, public policy. Still, individuals' claims to a right of privacy, whether in constitutional or tort law or with respect to statutory provisions, involve the assertion of entitlement to protection for specific privacy interests, unless there are overriding legal, moral, or political considerations. The legal right of privacy and the extent of its protection depends upon the kinds of privacy interests individuals litigate or promote through legislation, and in turn, which of those claims to legal protection are recognized and enforced through judicial interpretation or legislative enactments. Thus, by comparison with the wide range of individuals' privacy interests and innumerable nonlegal safeguards, the political ideal of privacy as a legal right remains considerably more circumscribed than a "right to be let alone" in the sense of individuals' freedom, even liberty, from unqualified noninterference.

For almost a century the Supreme Court has been instrumental in the legitimation of individuals' claims to the legal recognition and protection of personal privacy. The political ideal of a constitutional right of privacy exists as a background right of the fundamental law of the Constitution, supported by the principles of constitutionally limited government and the guarantees of the Bill of Rights. The absence

of any explicit constitutional provision for a right of privacy necessitated that privacy interests lay dormant until either constitutional interpretation acknowledged their connection with express guarantees
of the Constitution or judicial creativity fashioned a constitutional
right of privacy. Within the developing law of constitutionally protected privacy, the Supreme Court forged extensive protection for a
wide range of privacy interests under the First, Fourth, Fifth, Ninth,
and Fourteenth Amendments, and ultimately, with the denomination
of a constitutional right of privacy.

Personal privacy attains its principal constitutional protection
and the closest approximation of express recognition in the Fourth
Amendment. Privacy interests receive broad protection under the
Fourth Amendment's proscription of unreasonable governmental
searches and seizures of individuals' homes and other constitutionally
protected areas. The Supreme Court's construction and application
of Fourth Amendment safeguards to privacy claims varied, with reliance upon common law property principles, from Boyd's liberal construction and application, through Olmstead's strict construction and
application, to Katz and its progeny's liberal construction of Fourth
Amendment-protected privacy but strict application of the amendment.
With varying degrees of enforcement, liberal construction of Fourth
Amendment safeguards for "the sanctities of a man's home and the
privacies of life" underscores the fact that the amendment gives constitutional effect to the common law maxim "a man's house is his
castle," and thereby serves to protect the core of individuals' private
activities and expectations of privacy.

Individuals' privacy interests receive broad protection conso-
nant with the underlying principles of the Fourth Amendment. Yet
because the Supreme Court approaches issues of constitutionally protected privacy in terms of property concepts and the locus of individuals' activities, it precludes protection for claims to informational
privacy. Rather, what protection has been accorded interests in informational privacy derives from judicial construction of the underlying property principles of the Fourth Amendment. Although Katz
recognized that the amendment protects people, not places, the Court
never abandoned its spatial and proprietary analysis of the reasonableness of individuals' expectations of privacy. The Burger Court's
renewed emphasis upon proprietary concepts not only forecloses protection for claims to informational privacy, as in California Bankers
Association and United States v. Miller, but also narrows the contours
of constitutionally protected areas and Fourth Amendment-protected
privacy, as in Santana and Rakas. The contemporary Court, like the
Taft Court, by reemphasizing proprietary concepts, therefore, fails
to conceptualize Fourth Amendment interests more appropriate to the
technological changes that threaten to diminish personal privacy in an
increasingly information-oriented society.

By comparison with Fourth Amendment-protected privacy, a narrower range of privacy interests are embraced by the Fifth Amendment's provision that no person "shall be compelled in any criminal case to be a witness against himself." The Fifth Amendment nonetheless provides the principal constitutional guarantee for informational privacy, because it proscribes the government from coercing and compelling individuals to divulge personal information. The Supreme Court extended the benefits of the amendment beyond a strict construction to protect both defendants and witnesses in criminal, civil, and legislative or administrative proceedings, thereby establishing protection for privacy interests within these contexts and when personal disclosures would be incriminating. A privacy rationale for the Fifth Amendment, however, failed to attain wide acceptance, because historically the Court primarily focused on policy considerations of the amendment's role in the preservation of our adversary system of criminal justice. The Court limited the scope of the amendment and protected privacy by a number of judicial policies permitting the compulsion of personal disclosures upon grants of immunity, with respect to "required records" and the distinction between testimonial and real evidence. In particular, the Burger Court's narrow construction of personal compulsion and its emphasis upon the possession of incriminating evidence protects only an individual's compelled production of incriminating information but not the disclosure of such information by third parties, such as an individual's attorney, accountant, or banking institution. Thus, the Court refuses to address crucial issues of informational privacy by failing to consider, as in Couch, Fisher, Andresen, and Garner, the consequences of compelled disclosures of personal information and the practical ways in which individuals may be compelled to bear witness against themselves.

Whereas the Fourth and Fifth Amendments safeguard privacy interests by regulating the manner by which the government may obtain access to evidence or information about individuals' activities, the First Amendment guarantees citizens' liberty against governmental interference with and regulation of their everyday activities. Although privacy claims and First Amendment freedoms are at times conflicting, constitutional interpretation extended the amendment's guarantees to individual's interests in associational privacy. The Court also carved out areas of First Amendment-protected privacy with regard to intrusions upon individuals' activities in their homes by solicitors, whose interests in obtaining access are solely commercial, and where public address systems unduly disturb residential areas. The Court's treatment of First Amendment privacy interests against intrusions upon personal affairs imports, from Fourth Amendment privacy analysis, consideration of the locus and proprietary interests of individuals relative to the intrusiveness of different modes of communication, such as handbills, public address systems, radio, and television. Traditionally, consideration of the relative intrusiveness of different modes of communication and reliance on proprietary principles in balancing privacy and free speech claims permitted the Court to safeguard homeowners' privacy without significantly curtailing freedom of speech or evaluating the content of the speech considered intrusive. In _Pacifica_, the Court nevertheless held that the FCC may assert a privacy rationale for banning allegedly indecent broadcasts. The Court thereby collapsed its privacy analysis with an evaluation of First Amendment-protected and unprotected speech, inviting further privacy litigation and government regulation of the mass media.

By contrast, individuals' interests against public disclosure of private affairs have not been recognized as independent, constitutionally protected interests. Privacy interests against unwanted publicity receive protection only derivatively, as in seventeenth and eighteenth century common law, by assimilation with actions for defamation. The Supreme Court fails to formulate a rule by which to reconcile the conflict between privacy and freedom of press; instead it misapplies its theory of libel to privacy claims. Publication of defamatory or privacy-invading statements of private individuals, however, may be regulated by the states, because the status and locus of private individuals, in contrast to public officials and "public figures," within the community affords no effective means of countering defamatory and privacy-invading statements. More generally, because of the Court's spatial and proprietary analysis of personal privacy, it has been reluctant to consider as constitutionally significant the difference between intrusions upon and disclosures of personal affairs, and, thus, has evaded important issues of informational privacy. The Court tends to avoid the policy issues raised by privacy claims against federal and state governments' computerized data banks and systems of records. Governmental collection, maintenance, and dissemination of information concerning individuals' activities, except their exercise of First Amendment freedoms, is constitutionally permissible if no actual intrusion takes place in the process of acquiring the information, and information systems include reasonable security provisions for access to privileged information.

Individuals' interests in personal privacy receive broad protection with the procedural safeguards of the Fourth and Fifth Amendments and the basic freedoms guaranteed by the First Amendment. Together these amendments, along with the Ninth and Fourteenth Amendments, promote extensive protection for personal privacy and support the denomination of a constitutional right of privacy. Within the developing constitutional law of privacy, the Ninth Amendment does not provide an independent source of protected privacy. Rather it serves to augment judicial construction of protected privacy interests under other amendments as well as lends support to the recognition of a constitutional right of privacy. The Fourteenth Amendment serves as a vehicle for applying to the states constitutionally protected privacy under the First, Fourth, and Fifth Amendments and as the principal basis for the Court's elaboration of a constitutional right of privacy.

In fashioning the scope of constitutionally protected privacy under the First, Fourth, and Fifth Amendments, the Supreme Court acknowledged the political ideal of a constitutional background right of privacy and fulfilled its historic role of ensuring the "requisite latitude" of the guarantees of the Bill of Rights. As James Madison and Thomas Jefferson envisioned, the Bill of Rights provided the Supreme Court with a legal check upon political power so that it might become "in a peculiar manner the guardian of those rights . . . against every assumption of power in the Legislature or Executive." In developing constitutional protections for personal privacy, the Supreme Court proved to be a guardian of both enumerated and unenumerated rights.

To the extent that constitutional interpretation of the guarantees of the Bill of Rights limits the exercise of governmental power, the Supreme Court sits as a superlegislature. The Court's denomination of a constitutional right of privacy in Griswold, however, significantly departs from the developing constitutional law of privacy under the First, Fourth, and Fifth Amendments. The differences between legitimating constitutionally protected privacy interests under enumerated guarantees and denominating a constitutional right of privacy are not simply matters of the degree but rather differences in the kind of judicial activism and creativity employed in constitutional interpretation. Moreover, the Court's construction and application of the constitutional right of privacy in Griswold, Roe, and their progeny primarily encompass matters relating to procreation and the intimacies of motherhood, marriage, and family life. The Court's analysis of and rationale for a constitutional right of privacy not only collapses issues of protected privacy and personal liberty under the Fourteenth Amendment but also often remains irrelevant and inapplicable to privacy claims under specific guarantees of the Bill of Rights. The emerging contours of the constitutional right of privacy are therefore considerably narrower than the scope of constitutionally protected privacy interests under the First, Fourth, and Fifth Amendments.

Although Roe and its progeny transcend the threshold of judicial propriety and prudence by invalidating on privacy grounds state regulations, the Supreme Court more generally did not forsake the "passive virtues" of judicial review in recognizing constitutionally protected privacy interests. The developing constitutional law of privacy emerged incrementally, constrained by the Court's spatial analysis of privacy and its interpretation of the underlying common law principles of the First, Fourth, and Fifth Amendments. By focusing on the locus and proprietary interests of individuals relative to the nature and extent of intrusions upon their privacy expectations, the Court construed enumerated guarantees to protect personal privacy, yet avoided the complex issues of safeguarding informational privacy. The Court's framework for and property bias in constitutionally protected privacy, instead of manifesting so much a lack of judicial creativity or even a conservative reaction to changing technology and new privacy issues, may rather constitute the proper response to the difficulties of conceptualizing and formulating standards for individuals' interests in informational privacy. In other words, while the Supreme Court affirmed the political ideal of a constitutional background right of privacy in almost a century of constitutional interpretation, it also appropriately left the complicated issues of safeguarding informational privacy to the states, Congress, and, more generally, political and administrative policy-making processes.

Developments in information and communications technology posed important issues for policy makers for the last 40 years. Yet only in the last decade have Congress and the federal bureaucracy endeavored to address issues of the use and abuse of personal information collected, maintained, and disseminated by the government. Legislation designed to protect personal privacy was partially a response to the inadequate protection afforded informational privacy within the developing constitutional law of privacy and a consequence of growing public demands for greater information management by federal agencies. Privacy protection policies thus aim at compensating for existing law's inadequate protection for interests in informational privacy and complementing other policies designed to achieve information control within the federal bureaucracy.

The Privacy Act of 1974 symbolizes congressional affirmation of individuals' fundamental right of privacy and embodies the principal privacy safeguards for personal information collected and utilized by the federal government. Although significantly contributing to the protection of personal privacy, the act fails both to address crucial issues of prohibiting collection of some kinds of personal information per se and to adequately regulate the dissemination of privileged information within and among federal agencies. The practical feasibility of ensuring privacy interests in privileged information, moreover, remains difficult because of crosscutting and occasionally conflicting legislation, such as the Freedom of Information Act, designed to ensure public access to government-held information. The policy objectives of securing both personal privacy and the public's right to know, however, are not mutually exclusive; indeed, both values are complementary political ideals. Nonetheless, because the Privacy Act and the Freedom of Information Act are crosscutting and in many ways inconsistent, administrators frequently encounter the dilemma of deciding whether to disclose information that may constitute an invasion of personal privacy. The prospects for guaranteeing privacy interests in privileged information depend upon future policy developments establishing greater parity between the Privacy and Freedom of Information Acts, clarification or prohibition of agencies' collection of personal information, and appropriate institutional mechanisms for reconciling in hard cases conflicts between interests in privacy and access.

The salience of personal privacy and its legal protection reflects U.S. citizens' historical dedication to individualism and freedom from governmental intrusions into their lives. Likewise, the sources and scope of protections for personal privacy in constitutional law and public policy reflect individuals' commitment to the practice of rights as well as the capacity of governmental institutions to respond, albeit at times slowly, to challenges of a rapidly changing society. Although the founders of the Constitution failed to recognize privacy as an important political value, they designed a constitutional system in which individuals could vindicate their interests. In particular, the Supreme Court historically proved instrumental to the legitimation of privacy interests in both constitutional law and public policy. Still, as the United States becomes more economically, socially, and politically information-oriented, personal privacy promises to become a matter of increasing litigation, legislation, and political concern. Indeed, the political ideal of privacy is destined to increase rather than lessen in importance within the polity.

Selected Bibliography

BOOKS

Berns, Walter. The First Amendment and the Future of American Democracy. New York: Basic Books, 1976.

Brant, Irving. The Bill of Rights: Its Origins and Meaning. New York: Mentor, 1965.

Brenton, Myron. The Privacy Invaders. New York: Coward-McCann, 1964.

Carroll, John Miller. Confidential Information Sources, Public and Private. Los Angeles: Security World, 1975.

Compilation of State and Federal Privacy Laws. Washington, D.C.: Privacy Journal, 1977.

Emerson, Thomas I. The System of Freedom of Expression. New York: Vintage, 1970.

Ernst, Morris L., and Alan V. Schwartz. Privacy: The Right to Be Let Alone. New York: Macmillan, 1962.

Flaherty, David H. Privacy in Colonial New England. Charlottesville: University Press of Virginia, 1972.

Fried, Charles. An Anatomy of Values. Cambridge, Mass.: Harvard University Press, 1970.

Gross, Hyman. Privacy—Its Legal Protection. New York: Oceana, 1964.

Landynsky, Jacob W. Search and Seizure and the Supreme Court. Baltimore: Johns Hopkins Press, 1966.

Lasson, Nelson B. The History and Development of the Fourth Amendment to the United States Constitution. Baltimore: Johns Hopkins Press, 1937.

Levy, Leonard. Legacy of Suppression: Freedom of Speech and Press in Early American History. Cambridge, Mass.: Harvard University Press, Belknap Press, 1960.

_____. Origins of the Fifth Amendment. New York: Oxford University Press, 1968.

Long, Edward V. The Intruders. New York: Frederick A. Praeger, 1966.

Marwick, Christine M., ed. Litigation under the Amended Federal Freedom of Information Act. 4th ed. Washington, D.C.: Project on National Security and Civil Liberties, 1978.

Meiklejohn, Alexander. Political Freedom. New York: Oxford University Press, 1965.

Miller, Arthur R. The Assault on Privacy. Ann Arbor: University of Michigan Press, 1971.

Packard, Vance. The Naked Society. New York: David McKay, 1964.

Patterson, Bennett B. The Forgotten Ninth Amendment. Indianapolis: Bobbs-Merrill, 1955.

Pember, Don R. Privacy and the Press. Seattle: University of Washington Press, 1972.

Pennock, J. Roland, and John W. Chapman, eds. Privacy, Nomos XIII. New York: Atherton Press, 1971.

Records, Computers and the Rights of Citizens. Report of the Secretary's Advisory Committee on Automated Personal Data Systems, U.S. Department of Health, Education and Welfare. Cambridge: Massachusetts Institute of Technology, 1973.

Robertson, A. H. Privacy and Human Rights. Reports and Communications Presented at the Third International Colloquy about the European Convention on Human Rights, Organized by the Belgian Universities and the Council of Europe, with the Support of the Belgian Government, Brussels, September 30–October 3, 1970. Manchester: Manchester University Press, 1973.

Slough, M. C. Privacy, Freedom and Responsibility. Springfield, Ill.: Charles C. Thomas, 1969.

Westin, Alan F. Privacy and Freedom. New York: Atheneum, 1970.

Westin, Alan F., and Michael A. Baker. Data Banks in a Free Society. New York: Quadrangle/New York Times, 1972.

Young, J. B., ed. Privacy. New York: John Wiley & Sons, 1978.

ARTICLES

Alschuler, Albert W. "A Different View of Privacy." 49 Texas Law Review 872-80 (1971).

Altman, Irwin. "Privacy: A Conceptual Analysis." 8 Environment and Behavior 7-29 (1976).

Aynes, Richard L. "Katz and the Fourth Amendment: A Reasonable Expectation of Privacy or a Man's Home Is His Fort." 23 Cleveland State Law Review 63-89 (1974).

Beaney, William M. "The Constitutional Right to Privacy." In Supreme Court Review, 1962, edited by Philip Kurland, 212-51. Chicago: University of Chicago Press, 1963.

_____. "Griswold Case (85 Sup. Ct. 1678) and the Expanding Right to Privacy." Wisconsin Law Review 976-95 (1966).

_____. "The Right to Privacy and American Law." 31 Law and Contemporary Problems 253-71 (1966).

Bertelsman, William O. "The First Amendment and Protection of Reputation and Privacy: New York Times v. Sullivan and How It Grew." 56 Kentucky Law Journal 718-56 (1967/68).

_____. "Ninth Amendment and Due Process of Law—"Foreword: A Viable Theory of Unenumerated Rights." 37 University of Cincinnati Law Review 777-96 (1968).

Beytagh, Francis X. "Privacy and a Free Press: A Contemporary Conflict in Values." 20 New York Law Forum 453-514 (1975).

Bloustein, Edward J. "First Amendment and Privacy: The Supreme Court Justice and the Philosopher." 28 Rutgers Law Review 41-95 (1974).

_____. "Privacy as an Aspect of Human Dignity: An Answer to Dean Prosser." 39 New York University Law Review 962-1007 (1964).

_____. "Privacy, Tort Law, and the Constitution: Is Warren and Brandeis's Tort Petty and Unconstitutional as Well?" 46 Texas Law Review 611-29 (1968).

Bogomolny, Robert L. "The Right to Nondisclosure." 5 Human Rights 153-75 (1976).

Clark, R. H. "Constitution Sources of the Penumbra Right to Privacy." 19 Villanova Law Review 833-84 (1974).

_____. "The Ninth Amendment and Constitutional Privacy." 5 University of Toledo Law Review 83-110 (1973).

Comment. "Discrimination in Private Social Clubs: Freedom of Association and Right to Privacy." Duke Law Journal 1181-222 (1970).

Comment. "Government Access to Bank Records." 83 Yale Law Journal 1439-74 (1974).

Comment. "Papers, Privacy and the Fourth and Fifth Amendments: A Constitutional Analysis." 69 Northwestern University Law Review 626-52 (1974).

Comment. "The Protection of Privacy by the Privilege against Self-Incrimination: A Doctrine Laid to Rest?" 59 Iowa Law Review 1336-50 (1974).

Countryman, Vern. "The Diminishing Right of Privacy: The Personal Dossier and the Computer." 49 Texas Law Review 837-71 (1971).

Davis, Frederick. "What Do We Mean by 'Right to Privacy'?" 4 South Dakota Law Review 1-24 (1959).

Dixon, Robert G. "The Griswold Penumbra: Constitutional Charter for an Expanded Law of Privacy?" 64 Michigan Law Review 197-218 (1965).

Doss, Arden, Jr., and Diane Kay Doss. "On Morals, Privacy, and the Constitution." 25 University of Miami Law Review 395-419 (1971).

Dworkin, Gerald. "The Common Law Protection of Privacy." 2 University of Tasmania Law Review 418-45 (1967).

Dworkin, Ronald. "Hard Cases." 88 Harvard Law Review 1057-109 (1975).

Ely, John Hart. "The Wages of Crying Wolf: A Comment on Roe v. Wade." 82 Yale Law Journal 920-50 (1973).

Emerson, Thomas I. "Nine Justices in Search of a Doctrine." 64 Michigan Law Review 219-34 (1965).

Epstein, Richard A. "Substantive Due Process by Any Other Name: The Abortion Cases." In Supreme Court Review, 1973, edited by Philip Kurland, 159-85. Chicago: University of Chicago Press, 1973.

Ervin, Sam J. "Privacy and the Constitution." 50 North Carolina Law Review 1016-37 (1972).

Franklin, Marc A. "Constitutional Problem in Privacy Protection: Legal Inhibitions on Reporting of Fact." 16 Stanford Law Review 107-48 (1963).

Fried, Charles. "Privacy." 77 Yale Law Journal 475-93 (1968).

Garrett, Roland. "The Nature of Privacy." 18 Philosophy Today 263-84 (1974).

Gerber, D. "Types of Property Seizable under the Fourth Amendment." 23 U.C.L.A. Law Review 963-87 (1976).

Gerety, Tom. "Redefining Privacy." 12 Harvard Civil Rights-Civil Liberties Law Review 233-96 (1977).

Gerstein, Robert S. "Privacy and Self-Incrimination." 80 Ethics 87-101 (1970).

Greenwalt, Kent. "Privacy and Its Legal Protections." 2 Hastings Center Studies 45-68 (1974).

Griswold, Erwin N. "The Right to Be Let Alone." 55 Northwestern Law Review 216-26 (1960).

Gross, Hyman. "The Concept of Privacy." 42 New York University Law Review 34-54 (1967).

Haiman, Franklyn S. "Speech v. Privacy: Is There a Right Not to Be Spoken to?" 67 Northwestern University Law Review 153-99 (1972).

Henkins, Louis. "Privacy and Autonomy." 74 Columbia Law Review 1410-33 (1974).

Hill, Alfred. "Defamation and Privacy under the First Amendment." 76 Columbia Law Review 1206-1313 (1976).

Kalven, Harry, Jr. "Privacy in Tort Law—Were Warren and Brandeis Wrong?" 31 Law and Contemporary Problems 326-41 (1966).

Katz, Alan. "Privacy and Pornography: Stanley v. Georgia (89 Sup. Ct. 1243)." In Supreme Court Review, 1969, edited by Philip Kurland, 203-16. Chicago: University of Chicago Press, 1969.

Kauper, Paul G. "Penumbra, Peripheries, Emanations, Things Fundamental and Things Forgotten." 64 Michigan Law Review 235-59 (1965).

Kurland, Philip B. "The Private I." 69 University of Chicago Magazine 7-10 (1976).

Leigh, Lawrence J. "Informational Privacy: Constitutional Challenges to the Collection and Dissemination of Personal Information by Government Agencies." 3 Hastings Constitutional Law Quarterly 229-59 (1976).

Lusky, Louis. "Invasion of Privacy: A Clarification of Concepts." 72 Columbia Law Review 693-710 (1972).

McCloskey, H. J. "The Political Ideal of Privacy." 21 Philosophical Quarterly 303-14 (1971).

McKay, Robert B. "Mapp v. Ohio, the Exclusionary Rule and the Right of Privacy." 15 Arizona Law Review 327-41 (1973).

_____. "The Right of Privacy: Emanations and Innovations." 64 Michigan Law Review 259-82 (1965).

Miller, Arthur R. "Computers, Data Banks and Individual Privacy: An Overview." 4 Columbia Human Rights Law Review 1-265 (Winter 1972).

Miller, Arthur S. "Privacy in the Corporate State: A Constitutional Value of Dwindling Significance." 75 Administrative Law Review 231-64 (1973).

Nimmer, Melville B. "The Right to Speak from Time to Time: First Amendment Theory Applied to Libel and Misapplied to Privacy." 56 California Law Review 935-67 (1968).

Note. "Formalism, Legal Realism, and Constitutionally Protected Privacy under the Fourth and Fifth Amendments." 90 Harvard Law Review 945-91 (1977).

Note. "Privacy and the First Amendment." 82 Yale Law Journal 1462-81 (1973).

Note. "Toward a Constitutional Theory of Individuality: The Privacy Opinions of Justice Douglas." 87 Yale Law Journal 1579-1600 (1977).

O'Brien, David M. "The Fifth Amendment: Fox Hunters, Old Women, Hermits, and the Burger Court." 54 Notre Dame Lawyer 26-72 (1978).

_____. "Privacy and the Right of Access: Purposes and Paradoxes of Information Control." 30 Administrative Law Review 45-92 (1978).

_____. "Reasonable Expectations of Privacy: Principles and Policies of Fourth-Amendment-Protected Privacy." 13 New England Law Review 662-738 (1978).

O'Connor, Thomas H. "Right to Privacy in Historical Perspective." 53 Massachusetts Law Quarterly 101-15 (1968).

Parker, Richard B. "A Definition of Privacy." 27 Rutgers Law Review 275-96 (1974).

Perry, Michael J. "Abortion, the Public Morals, and the Police Power: The Ethical Function of Substantive Due Process." 23 U.C.L.A. Law Review 689-756 (1976).

_____. "Substantive Due Process Revisited: Reflections on (and beyond) Recent Cases." 71 Northwestern University Law Review 417-69 (1976).

Plamenatz, John. "Privacy and Laws against Discrimination." 4 Rivista Internazionale di Filosofia del Diritto 443–55 (1974).

Pound, Roscoe. "The Fourteenth Amendment and the Right of Privacy." 13 Case Western Reserve Law Review 34–55 (1961).

Pratt, Walter F. "The Warren and Brandeis Argument for a Right to Privacy." Public Law 161–79 (1975).

Prosser, William L. "Privacy." 48 California Law Review 383–423 (1960).

Rehnquist, William H. "Is an Expanded Right of Privacy Consistent with Fair and Effective Law Enforcement? or, Privacy, You've Come a Long Way, Baby." 23 Kansas Law Review 1–22 (1974).

Ruebhausan, Oscar M., and Orville G. Brim, Jr. "Privacy and Behavioral Research." 65 Columbia Law Review 1184–211 (1965).

Scanlon, Thomas. "Thomson on Privacy." 4 Philosophy and Public Affairs 315–23 (1975).

Shils, Edward. "Privacy: Its Constitutional Vicissitudes." 31 Law and Contemporary Problems 281–306 (1966).

Slough, M. C. "Privacy, Freedom and Responsibility." 16 University of Kansas Law Review 323–47 (1968).

Swanton, Jane. "Protection of Privacy." 48 Australian Law Journal 91–103 (1974).

Symposium. "Symposium: Computers, Data Banks, and Individual Privacy. On the Needs and Values of Data Banks." 53 Minnesota Law Review 211–45 (1968).

Thomson, Judith Jarvis. "The Right to Privacy." 4 Philosophy and Public Affairs 295–314 (1975).

Tribe, Laurence H. "Foreword: Toward a Model of Roles in the Due Process of Life and Law." 87 Harvard Law Review 1–53 (1973).

_____. "Structural Due Process." 10 Harvard Civil Rights-Civil Liberties Law Review 269–321 (1975).

Wade, John W. "Defamation and the Right to Privacy." 15 Vanderbilt Law Review 1093–125 (1962).

Warren, Samuel D., and Louis B. Brandeis. "The Right to Privacy."
4 Harvard Law Review 193-220 (1890).

Weiss, Jonathan A., and Stephen B. Wizner. "Pot, Prayer, Politics
and Privacy: The Right to Cut Your Own Throat in Your Own
Way." 54 Iowa Law Review 709-35 (1969).

Wellington, Harry H. "Common Law Rules and Constitutional Double
Standards: Some Notes on Adjudication." 83 Yale Law Journal
221-311 (1973).

PUBLIC DOCUMENTS

U.S., Congress, House and Senate. Joint Committee Print. Committee on Government Operations and Committee on the Judiciary. Freedom of Information Act and Amendments of 1974
(P.L. 93-502), Source Book: Legislative History, Texts, and
Other Documents, 94th Cong., 1st sess., March 1975.

U.S., Congress, House and Senate. Joint Committee Print. Committee on Government Operations and Subcommittee on Government
Information and Individual Rights. Legislative History of the
Privacy Act of 1974, S. 3418 (Public Law 93-579), Source Book,
94th Cong., 2d sess., September 1976.

U.S., Congress, Senate. Committee on the Judiciary, Subcommittee
on Administrative Practice and Procedure of the Committee of
the Judiciary. Freedom of Information Act Source Book: Legislative Materials, Cases, Articles, 93d Cong., 2d sess., 1974.

U.S., Domestic Council Committee on the Right of Privacy. National
Information Policy. Report to the President of the United States,
1976.

U.S., Library of Congress. Congressional Research Service. The
Administration of the Freedom of Information Act: A Brief
Overview of Executive Branch Annual Reports for 1975, by Har-
old C. Relyea, September 2, 1976.

_____. Basic Information on the Use of the Privacy Act of 1974 and
the Freedom of Information Act, by M. Elizabeth Smith, March
24, 1976.

_____. The Freedom of Information Act as Amended (5 U.S.C.
§ 552). Background, Judicial Construction, and Selected Bibliography by Paul S. Wallace, Jr., March 23, 1974, rev. April
12, 1976.

U.S., The Privacy Protection Study Commission. Personal Privacy
in an Information Society. Report of the Privacy Protection
Study Commission, July 1977.

Index of Supreme Court Cases

Name and Subject Index

About the Author

DAVID M. O'BRIEN received his Ph.D. from the University
of California in 1977 and is an Assistant Professor in the Woodrow
Wilson Department of Government and Foreign Affairs, University
of Virginia. He previously taught at the University of California and
the University of Puget Sound, where he also served as chairman of
the Department of Politics. He was a recipient of a National Endowment for the Humanities Fellowship and has published articles in
several law reviews and other professional journals.